SOMEBODY ELSE'S
DREAM

DAKOTA, THE BUOYS, & "TIMOTHY"

Peace Out!

MAXIM W. FUREK

Maxim W Furek
2022

SUNBURY
PRESS

Mechanicsburg, PA USA

Published by Sunbury Press, Inc.
Mechanicsburg, PA USA

www.sunburypress.com

For information about special discounts for bulk purchases, please contact Sunbury Press Orders Dept. at (855) 338-8359 or orders@sunburypress.com.

To request one of our authors for speaking engagements or book signings, please contact Sunbury Press Publicity Dept. at publicity@sunburypress.com.

FIRST SUNBURY PRESS EDITION: October 2021

Set in Adobe Garamond Pro | Interior design by Crystal Devine | Cover by Danielle Crockett | Edited by Lawrence Knorr.

Publisher's Cataloging-in-Publication Data
Names: Furek, Maxim W., author.
Title: Somebody else's dream : Dakota, The Buoys, & "Timothy" / Maxim W. Furek.
Description: First trade paperback edition. | Mechanicsburg, PA : Sunbury Press, 2021.
Summary : 2021 marks the 50th anniversary of the *Billboard* hit about cannibalism in a Pennsylvania coal mine. "Timothy," known as "the worst song ever recorded," was banned by major radio stations, while launching the careers of playwright Rupert Holmes, The Buoys, and Dakota. Their amazing story represents a cautionary tale of substance abuse, the pitfalls of fame, and the true price of the rock and roll fantasy.
Identifiers: ISBN : 978-1-62006-568-6 (softcover).
Subjects: MUSIC / Genres & Styles / Rock | BIOGRAPHY & AUTOBIOGRAPHY / Music | SELF-HELP / Substance Abuse & Addictions / General.

Product of the United States of America
0 1 1 2 3 5 8 13 21 34 55

Continue the Enlightenment!

DEDICATION

Several years ago, an attempt was made to organize a regional Rock and Roll Hall of Fame. It was a lofty project that unfortunately failed. *Somebody Else's Dream* is my vision of how that group would have looked. This book is dedicated to those musicians and bands who created our regional songbook and shared their music with us. For that, I thank them.

ALSO BY MAXIM W. FUREK

The Jordan Brothers:
A Musical Biography of Rock's Fortunate Sons

The Death Proclamation of Generation X:
A Self-Fulfilling Prophesy of Goth, Grunge and Heroin

Sheppton: The Myth, Miracle, & Music

CONTENTS

INTRODUCTION

"Timothy," the song, was the gold standard and the most successful rock song from our region before Synch, the Badlees, and Breaking Benjamin came upon the scene. *Timothy* was also the name of my tabloid newspaper promoting NEPA musical talent.

I always felt that the impact of "Timothy" had been neglected, and I wanted to reintroduce the story of the Buoys, Dakota, and other regional bands to a younger audience. My book of music history is also a cautionary tale promoting an anti-drug message. "Timothy" happened fifty years ago, a period of faded memories, blurred recollections, and questionable facts. During my research, not everyone was on the same page, spoke the same reality, or shared the same truths. For example, the character of Harold "Hollywood & Vine" Vealer is presented as a composite of several individuals to protect his privacy, and, as far as the story within the story, I leave it to the reader to decide who's on the square and who's zooming who.

My manuscript was completed during the COVID-19 pandemic. I was living on the Florida Gulf Coast, and writing became my therapy. *Somebody Else's Dream* was gleaned from many years of interviews, concerts, and a genuine love for the music created by musicians from Pennsylvania's Great Northeast. Still, there is much more to the story, and hopefully, the next generation of rock journalists will write those chapters.

★ PART I ★

THE PIONEERS

1

JOE NARDONE'S ALL-STARS

R ock and roll's driving, pounding vibrations reverberated against the segregated streets of New Orleans, Memphis, and Chicago. It came in the Midnight Hour, uninvited, and, although criticized as being "devil's music," rock preached its gospel of sex and rebellion. Rock, the new "opium of the masses," was about to transform the world.

During the riptide of the 1950s, the insistent cries of seminal rockers—Chuck Berry, Elvis Presley, and Little Richard—ignited a social upheaval among the teen masses. Rock scripted the songbook for a generation of youth hungry for Maslovian connection and group identity. The music reverberated through plastic earphones, secretly plugged into a seafoam green or bright red Zenith Royal 500 pocket transistor radio, educating American teens in tiny two-minute assaults.

Joe Nardone's All-Stars, considered to be the first rock and roll band to perform in the Wilkes-Barre Valley, surged upon that riptide. First, they played the Catholic Youth Center, Granada Ballroom, and then, like storm troopers, commandeered the San Souci ballroom. The band featured Bill Brown, lead vocalist; Leo "Lefty" Harkins, lead guitar; Glen Johnson, drums; Joe Nardone, vocals and sax; Carl Swinski, keyboards, and then Pete Urchak. (The Four Stars, Joe Nardone's first band, were formed at Coughlin High School. They became the All-Stars and, in 1958, played their first gig at the Wilkes-Barre CYC and were the first rock band to play at Sandy Beach at Harvey's Lake. Nardone left the group in 1973.)

In 1991, Bob Gryziec stepped in on bass; before that, the band "had a specially designed, electronic rig to pull bass out of the electric piano," Nardone told columnist Jerry Kishbaugh. Gryziec contributed driving bass lines, rhythmically aligned with Glen Johnson's beat, adding another dimension to the band. Said Gryziec:

Joe Nardone's All-Stars (L-R) Carl Swinski, Bob Burdenski, Dave Dunsavage, Eddie Sisko, Joe Nardone.

The bass guitar added a lot more bottom because I played a five-string bass, so I had the extra octave on the bottom with the low B. That added quite a bit. It gave it the same feel that Joe had at Souci because he was using piano bass at Souci and or organ bass on some of the records.

MADISON RECORDS

Founded in the late 50s, Joe Nardone's All-Stars recorded for Madison and Red Bird, and in 1960 released "The Wiggle" b/w "Pizza Pie" on Times Square Records. During their brief recording career, the All-Stars brushed shoulders with some of the major players in the industry, including Jerry Leiber and Mike Stoller, and Larry Utall. In 1955, at age 32, Larry Utall decided to quit his job selling shirts and go into the music business. But, attracted by the excitement of Tin Pan Alley, he only wanted to play the piano and write songs.

Utall founded Madison Records in 1958, signing groups such as Nino and the Ebb Tides, Tico and the Triumphs, and the Viscounts. The Viscounts, from New Jersey, had one hit single, the instrumental classic "Harlem Nocturne"

(Madison, 1959), which peaked at #52 on *Billboard* in early 1960. The sax-driven classic was re-released five years later (Amy, 1965) and hit #39 in its second go-round. "Harlem Nocturne" has been re-recorded numerous times by artists including King Curtis, Mink DeVille, and Quincy Jones. Bonnie Bramlette and the Mr. Groove Band's Roots, Blues & Jazz (Zoho Music, 2006) included another definitive cover.

The All-Stars represented one of Madison's popular sax-driven groups. Their first release was "Caravan Rock" (Madison, 1960) b/w "Ten Little Indians." "Caravan Rock" was a frenetically layered rave-up that threw in everything but the kitchen sink. It was written in 1936 by Duke Ellington and Juan Tizol, with lyrics by Irving Mills. Nardone wrote the 'B' side, "Ten Swinging Indians," a Duane Eddy-inspired remake of the children's nursery rhyme. (NOTE: For the record, Nardone's song predated, by almost a decade, the Beatles foray into children's nursery rhymes, that included "All Together Now," "Yellow Submarine," and "Maxwell's Silver Hammer" (Apple, 1969). "Caravan Rock" was innovative in its production and recorded in New York City, Nardone told this writer:

> I made that with two saxes, the alto and the tenor on the same record. There was a drum break in there, so I had a chance to switch saxes during the session. We played "Caravan Rock" on our dates, so when we went into the studio, it was one, two, three, and it worked.

But sensing a hit record with The Viscounts, Madison threw their weight behind "Harlem Nocturne" while "Caravan Rock" died from lack of corporate promotion, said Nardone:

> Madison gave "Caravan Rock" a little promotion, but not enough to make it click. I remember that Larry Utall, President of Madison Records, was actually in the recording session doing the hand clapping to the other side of the record ("Ten Swinging Indians").

Madison lasted until 1961, when Uttal absorbed the label into his newly acquired Bell Records. After launching Bell in 1964, he sold the company to Columbia Pictures for $3.5 million. The corporation agreed to give him "autonomous power to run the company." In the early '70s, Utall commuted between offices in London, New York, and Los Angeles, telling a reporter that radio airplay was crucial to success:

> Without radio, it's still impossible to make a hit. The interrelation between radio and television, radio and films, or all three puts the sales into the record class.

At the time, Bell was home to the Box Tops, Bob Crew, Mitch Ryder, Del Shannon, and the Toys. As Bell president, Uttal signed entertainers Melissa Manchester and four-year-old Ricky Segall. He launched the career of David Cassidy, then a 23-year-old teenybopper idol and star of TV's *The Partridge Family*. Utall had the Midas touch, and according to writer Barbara Lewis, "increased the business more than five times," signing The Fifth Dimension, Dawn, and Mountain.

In two years, Bell Records scored eleven gold singles and nine gold albums. Other Amy-Mola-Bell winners were The Boxtops' #1 "The Letter" (Mala, 1967), "Little Girl" by the Syndicate of Sound #8 (Bell, 1966), "I'm Your Puppet" by James and Bobby Purify #6 (Bell,1966), and "Angel in the Morning," by Merrilee Rush & the Turnabouts #7 (Bell, 1968.) Utall abruptly left Bell Records in 1974 and began his label, Private Stock Records, signing singer Benny Mardones. After Utall's departure, Bell celebrated its final #1 hit in January 1975 with Barry Manilow's "Mandy" (Bell, 1975). Years later, Joe Nardone, as the promoter, brought Manilow, at the beginning of his career, to Wilkes College and then was invited to a Manhattan "high-end party." There he met with Clive Davis, founder of Arista Records, and Barry Manilow, and, as Nardone put it, "it was one hell of an experience."

RED BIRD RECORDS

The All Stars' regional hit was "Shake A Hand" (Red Bird, 1966) b/w "Ride Your Pony," recorded in New Jersey. First released by Faye Adams, "Shake A Hand" (Herald, 1953) topped the *Billboard* R&B chart for ten weeks and reached #22 on the US pop chart, selling one million copies. Legendary R&B songwriters Jerry Leiber and Mike Stoller owned Red Bird. They penned such monster hits as "Hound Dog," #1 (RCA, 1956), "Jailhouse Rock" #1 (RCA, 1957), and "Stand by Me" #4 (Atco, 1961). In addition, Red Bird boasted hit-making "girl groups," such as The Dixie Cups #1 "Chapel of Love" (Red Bird, 1964), The Shangri-Las' #1 "Leader of the Pack" (Red Bird, 1964), and the Jelly Beans #9 "I Wanna Love Him So Bad" (Red Bird, 1964).

The All-Star's "Shake A Hand" went to #3 on the WARM charts and was that station's "Pick Hit of the Week." Nardone's record is a rare collectors' item listed on some sites with a value of up to $50. "Shake A Hand" did well in certain parts of the east coast. The song was a solid regional favorite. He told this writer:

> Red Bird did some promotion, and it made some noise in south New Jersey
> just outside of Philadelphia and a little bit in Allentown. In the Wilkes Barre-
> Scranton market, it did exceptionally well and is one the most requested songs

for us to play when we play our annual reunion at the Irem Temple Country Club Pavilion.

SANS SOUCI PARK

The All Stars became the house band at Hanover Township's Sans Souci Park during the summer and the Stardust Ballroom in Wilkes-Barre in the winter months. They backed up artists like Neil Diamond, Dion, and Freddy "Boom Boom" Cannon when they came to town. Brooklynite Neil Diamond played there five times, from 1962 to 1967. San Souci hosted Frankie Valli and the Four Seasons, Mitch Ryder (who brought a fifteen-piece band), and Sam the Sham and the Pharaohs, who drew around 2,000 teenagers, the biggest crowd ever. They kicked off their set with "Wooly Bully" #2 (MGM, 1964) rather than saving it for their encore. In 1968 Sans Souci showcased Nardone's All-Stars plus The Eddy Day Group, and on December 26, presented bubblegum sensation, the 1910 Fruit Gum Company, with their monster hits "Simon Says" #4 (Buddah, 1968) and "1,2,3, Red Light" #5 (Buddah, 1968). San Souci was a special venue. It cost fifty cents for admission to the dance and $1 to see the recording artists. Souci offered a better location than smaller clubs with dead-sounding stages or echoey high school gyms. It complimented, perhaps personalized, Nardone's sound. Bob Gryziec observed that Nardone's All-Stars took full advantage of San Souci's unique design and natural acoustics:

> Souci lent itself to Joe's particular kind of sound because, first of all, many bands didn't play that loud. Souci had a half-moon-shaped bandshell, and it projected the sound off the stage. It always sounded good down there; even with that bass coming through the piano, it still sounded whole. They used the bottom of the bass keys on the piano for most of the stuff that they did.

Just as the Beatles' thrived at the Cavern Club, the All-Stars excelled at San Souci. They hammered out their trade-marked, sax-laden rock style with a slick, professional delivery. Bob Gryziec:

> Joe had the 'Souci Sound' down there. Joe had his own sound, he had an echo chamber on the vocals, and no matter where he played around here, even Irem Temple, he never sounded the same as he did at Souci. He always sounded good at Souci.

The San Souci Park operated from 1880 to 1970, featuring four roller coasters; the Ariel Railway, Bear Cat, Kiddie Roller Coaster, and the Wild Mouse. The actual ballroom was a wooden structure built on stilts that often moved

Joe Nardone's All Stars (L-R) Lefty Harkins, Bill Brown, Joe Nardone, Ray Nutaitus, Jim Shaffer.

from the pulsating rock vibrations. Finally, after seventy years, the fifty-three-acre park with a seven-car diesel train called the San Souci Limited, a modern miniature golf course, a funhouse, and picnic groves, closed its doors. Today, the Hanover Area Junior-Senior High School stands where the park once was

DOO-WOP

Soon Nardone began promoting concerts but lost much-treasured memorabilia after the devastating 1972 Agnes flood, including two saxophones, a Kohn tenor sax, and an alto. His home in South Wilkes Barre had water over the roof. He said, "Over the years, I was able to find some memories, but all the good stuff was destroyed."

Nardone's rock concerts have included superstars Chicago, Joe Cocker, Grand Funk, the Grateful Dead, Jethro Tull, and Barry Manilow. Still, after attending an out-of-town Doo-wop concert featuring Jay and the Americans and Kenny Vance, Nardone decided to bring Doo-wop acts to the area. So "Joe Nardone's Doo-wop Volume One" kicked off on October 2009 with the Skyliners, The Duprees, The Chiffons, Kenny Vance, and the Planotones and

Scranton's Paramounts. The concert was MC'd by "The Duke of Doo-wop, Bobby V, who paid Nardone a sincere compliment:

> I can tell you this, having spoken with many of the artists. The artists well respect him as a promoter. He knows his music. He spends the right money for a great sound system. When he does his shows, he produces them well. He gets great artists. He's thorough, honest, and part of the show. Joe's a great promoter, and there aren't too many of those guys left anymore.

Nardone struck gold again when he brought in *Doo Wop Vol. 6*, another graduating class of early rock pioneers. Acts like Jimmy Clanton, Jay Siegel's Tokens, The Spaniels, the Passions, Willie Winfield and Kenny Vance, and the Planotones performed on May 18, 2013, for the sold-out FM Kirby Center for the Arts.

On November 15, 2015, he brought another Best of Doo-wop Concert Series to the FM Kirby. They included The Coasters, The Platters, The Chantels, and Gene Chandler, famous for "Duke of Earl" (Vee-Jay, 1962), considered one of the top ten doo-wop songs of all time. Nardone told *Times Leader* writer Gene Axton:

> I never get any group that doesn't have at least one member from the original group, but as time goes on, many groups can't perform anymore because they're too old or members pass on. This is where we're at in the era of Doo-wop.

In his article, "Delightful doo-wop," *Citizen's Voice* contributor and record authority Richard Chisak described the essence of this fascinating sub-genre of rock. He offered:

> Doo-wop's primary characteristic is its intriguing three, four, or five-part harmonies of background and rhythm lines (shoop-shoop, doo-wop, doo-wop, sh-boom sh-boom, etc.) while a lead singer belts out the main melody line of a song.

Chisak listed the Marcel's "Blue Moon," #1 (Colpix, 1961), the Cords "Sh-Boom," #9 (Cat Records, 1954), and Dion and the Belmont's "I Wonder Why" #22 (Laurie, 1958) as examples of doo-wop "street corner singing." With releases by early Motown groups, Frankie Valli and the Four Seasons, the Beach Boys, and the Shirelles, the tradition continues.

Ron Harris, the host of *The Doo-Wop Shop* on Toledo, Ohio radio station WRQN-FM, cited "Earth Angel," "Sixteen Candles," "Come Go with Me," and "In the Still of the Night" as perfect examples of the doo-wop style. "Since I

Don't Have You," by Pittsburgh's Skyliners, #12 (Calico,1958), remains a time-less classic, revived by artists including Guns N' Roses, Art Garfunkel, Don McLean, and Eddie Holman.

Many of the prolific doo-wop groups named themselves after birds, cars, or precious stones. The so-called "bird groups" abounded during this era as The Cardinals, Robins, and Flamingos took flight with smooth harmonies. In contrast, "car groups" were exemplified by the Cadillacs, El Dorados, and Diamonds.

Bobby Vanderheyden (aka Bobby V) has produced "The Doo-Wop Sock Hop" on The River 105 and 103.5 for the last 15 years and presented with The Pennsylvania Association of Broadcasters Radio Hall of Fame award in 2018. This is because of the unique genre, authority Bobby V explained:

> Doo-wop, in my view, is almost the beginning of rock and roll. In its purest form, it's acapella singing without instrumentation. It came from the streets of New York and Philly, primarily. It started as all-black music, and then eventually, we had integrated groups. Johnny Maestro and the Crests were perhaps the first integrated group. The Crest's "Sixteen Candles" was a #2 hit (Coed, 1959.) After that, Doo-wop became a place where anybody could have a hit record. All you had to do was harmonize, and you could get a hit.

PIONEER AND MENTOR

"Music Authority" Joe Nardone was a pioneer and mentor, doo-wop revivalist, and so much more. Many artists from the '50s and '60s were exploited and shut out from lucrative royalties from record sales and airplay. Nardone wanted to give these groups their due and a well-deserved paycheck. He told writer Kristen Gaydos, "Most of the doo-wop groups didn't get any royalties. These groups are still on the road making a living." But with venues such as Nardone's Doo-wop concerts, these often-forgotten groups are now receiving the attention and financial compensation they rightfully deserve. Bobby V and Joey Shaver have been the hosts of Joe Nardone's popular Doo Wop concerts. Bobby V reflected:

> I'm such a lucky guy. I've had such a remarkable career and met some terrific people. I know it sounds corny and contrite, but I still get a thrill out of introducing these artists I used to listen to when I was growing up in high school.

Nardone represents the musical heartbeat of Northeastern Pennsylvania, bringing extraordinary talent into the area and sharing his philosophy. For example, in one of his half-page Gallery of Sound ads, he proffered:

CONFIRMED! MUSIC IS THE GREATEST THERAPY FROM DOC-
TORS . . . Music will bring happiness! A brain booster! Music is medicine!
Improves memory! Music pulls your attention away from other thoughts.
Sometimes music is the only thing that can get your mind off of everything
else.

Nardone wrote that inspirational message in 2020, during the horrible
pandemic that, at the time, had claimed more than 150,000 American lives.
Even then, he was an astute, business-minded musician (Nardone graduated
from Wyoming Seminary's School of Business in Kingston) who dealt in the
currency of optimistic positivity. A humble and unassuming Joe Nardone reflected on his career:

> I am not looking for any glory. I've had enough in my career. But, to my
> knowledge, no band came through the early days of rock n roll in Northeastern
> Pennsylvania that can still run a 'dance' and still sell it out as we do every year
> at The Irem Temple Pavilion. I'm very proud of that, and I hope you under-
> stand what I'm trying to say. I do not want to sound like a big deal. I'm just
> happy that I can still blow the horn and sing the tunes, the same tunes we did
> in the '60s. These are great memories, and I think that is what the folks that
> come to our reunion dance every year are looking for. Memories Matter!

2

EDDIE DAY AND TNT

E d Pashinski, aka Eddie Day, began his musical odyssey in 1963 as lead singer with the Star Fires garage band. The group was named after an Oldsmobile and masterminded by drummer Richard Gumbravich, bass guitarist Roger Griffith, and saxman Bob Gardner. The Star Fires recorded "You Done Me Wrong" b/w "Like Socks and Shoes" (Laurie, 1966).

Writer Dan Styklunas wrote in Timothy that Eddie Day and TNT are among "the few rock bands that have been able to endure throughout the 1960s, '70s, and into the '80s." Styklunas wrote that back in 1981, and Eddie Day is still going strong today. Day has hired and mentored an entire rock orchestra, including such luminaries as Steve Furmanski and Bob Gryziec (The Buoys), John Gonska, and Mike Bobeck (Great Rock Scare, Great Bear), Jim Hakim (Backdoors), and sound engineer Mike Stahl.

In 1965 he formed Eddie Day and the Nightimers, recording "How to Be A Musician" that landed on the compilation LP Last of the Garage Punk Unknowns, Vol. 3, along with "Trust in Me" (BB, 1967) and "Summer's Gone" b/w "For My Girl" (Onyx,1968). Several years before the Buoys stepped into Scepter Records, Day recorded Rupert Holmes' "Our Town" (Decca,1968) and "Don't Want to Lose You" (Wand, 1968).

Several years later, he evolved into Eddie Day and TNT recording "Smiling Phases" (Fayette, 1969) b/w "Trust Me Lord," "Whiter Shade of Pale" (RoxAn, 1971), and "Stand up For Jesus" (RoxAn, 1972). Years later, Dakota's Kelly and Hludzik produced TNT's "Chance You Take" (1986), written by Ray K. and Dewey Styles and Joe Lemongelli aka "Joe Cella." The band later evolved into Twice Shy.

ROXANN RECORDS

RoxAnn Records, a small recording studio located in West Nanticoke, was owned by Mike Stahl and named after his wife, Roxanne Sardoni. RoxAnn

```
┌─────────────────────────────────┐
│                                 │
│      ──── TONITE ────           │
│     Don't Miss The Great        │
│      "EDDY DAY"                 │
│            AND                  │
│    "The Nightimers"             │
│             AT                  │
│    SANDY BEACH                  │
│     HARVEYS LAKE                │
│    8:30 P. M. to 11:30 P. M.    │
│    ─ADMISSION ─                 │
│       75ᶜ                       │
│                                 │
│     DANCING EVERY               │
│      FRIDAY NITE                │
│                                 │
└─────────────────────────────────┘
```

Records specialized in producing and recording advertising jingles for local businesses and provided sound gear for live events. After the gasoline crisis in the early '70s, Stahl closed his business and Claire Brothers Audio in nearly Lititz, Pennsylvania, the largest live sound company in the world, hired him. Stahl became one of the chief sound engineers on the company's road staff, providing high-quality sound for mega artists like Michael Jackson, Queen, Chicago, and Kenny Rogers. The gifted Stahl, exuding success in his every breath, was later hired as general manager for Mountain Productions and then Maryland Sound International (MSI). Promoted to general manager at MSI's West Coast Division, he then became president of ATK Audiotek. His career spanned more than four decades, and Stahl emerged as one of the most critical connectors for the Jerry-Kelly Band and Dakota.

Around 1987, Hludzik and Kelly created DAK Enterprises, a management company to "eliminate any middlemen." DAK included Stahl and the Stone Balloon's Bill Stevenson, resulting in several independently produced albums: *Lost Tracks* (1987), *The Last Standing Man* (1997), *Little Victories* (2000), *Deep 6* (2003), and *Long Road Home* (2015). Bill Kelly praised the talents of Michael Stahl, "He was our best friend, he was our biggest cheerleader, and he was brilliant."

Eddie Day's groups were popular at Hanson's Amusement at Harvey's Lake, and The Starfire Ballroom was named in their honor. Over the years, the Star Fires played with musical celebrities such as Chubby Checker, Frankie Valli and the Four Seasons, and Bobby Goldsboro. The musician took a six-year hiatus from live performances but returned in 1988 for several successful reunion events. Additionally, Pashinski was employed as a music teacher and choral director in the Greater Nanticoke Area School District and is currently a Pennsylvania state representative. As popular as ever, Eddie Day and the Star Fires and Joe Nardone & the All-Stars have created a rock legacy by hosting annual reunion concerts at Dallas' Irem Temple Country Club.

The 1981 version of Eddy Day and TNT (L-R) Eddie Day, Mike Boback, Dewey Vasquez, Joe Limon-gelli, Mark Todd.

3

MEL WYNN AND THE RHYTHM ACES

R egionally, Bob O'Connell and Joe Nardone were the earliest proponents of rock and roll, but O'Connell furthered the Buoy's journey into professional music. O'Connell was with Mel Wynn and the Rhythm Aces (Ron Ashton, Rich Garinger, Jerry Sechleer, Larry Sechleer, Tommy Wynder, and Mel Wynn). They played their first gig at Wilkes-Barre's Catholic Youth Center in 1958.

The Rhythm Aces released six singles and scored a regional hit with "Mohawk Rock" (Roulette, 1959). The band opened for Duane Eddy, Tommy James and the Shondells, and Freddy and the Dreamers during their heyday. However, their biggest concert was opening for Dion and the Belmonts and Freddie Cannon at Pittsburgh's Kennywood Park, drawing over 50,000 fans.

In 1969, the re-vamped Mel Wynn Trend performed at the 1969 "Square Happening II" rock festival, organized by the Lackawanna Arts Council. As an indication of the region's massive talent, the festival included The Amaris, The Buoys, Fat Cat, Glass Prism, The Smithfield, and Thee Avantis (Robey Schnessel, Billy Lombardi, Bill Trevicki, Nick Fata, Teddy Moss). They later released the Beatlesque "I Want to Understand" b/w "Nancy" (Samron, 1979.) The festival, held on the court-house lawn, drew over 5,000 attendees and mounds of litter.

"STOP SIGN"

The Mel Wynn Trend's best song should have been a national hit. "Stop Sign" (Wand, 1969) was an upbeat R&B tune with backing female vocals and horns. O'Connell co-wrote the song with Wynn and Jerry Sechleer.

Julian Gill and Bob Di Lorenzo were the producers, and C. Michael Wright the Audio Engineer. O'Connell recalled:

> I met Michael Wright and Rupert Holmes in New York City while recording at Scepter Records. Mel Wynn and the Rhythm Aces did a record titled 'Stop Sign.' It was covered by an artist called Abs and became a #10 international hit in the United Kingdom and very successful in other countries. They used the original tracks and mashed in contemporary sounds.

O'Connell was correct in his recollection. After three decades, English rapper and singer Richard Abidin Breen, better known as Abz Love, covered the song "Stop Sign" (Sony BMG, 2003) with an electronica, hip hop treatment that included a sampling of the Rhythm Aces' version. Abz Love, a former member of the British boy band Five, updated the lyrics on his hit record, promoted with a sex-upped dance video. The tune went to #10 in the UK and #53 in Australia.

Holmes and Wright had connections in Northeastern Pennsylvania with O'Connell, being one of them. Using his pen name "Julian Gill," Holmes produced several Mel Wynn and The Rhythm Aces projects. "Don't Want to Lose You" (Wand, 1968); produced by Gill and Danny Jordan and arranged by Jerry Sechleer and Bob Connors. Gill also produced "Our Town" (Decca, 1968) for The Eddie Day Group.

Wright scouted the area for new, talented groups. He felt that the Wilkes-Barre-Scranton area was rich in undiscovered rock acts such as, The Cartunes, the Druids, the Elves, Frantic Freddie, Jack, and the Rippers, Ognir and the Night People, Prince Charles, Ralph, and the Royal Tones. O'Connell, who later played keyboards with the group Christopher, suggested that Wright look at The Buoys. O'Connell said:

> I was producing music with Mike. I was familiar with The Buoys and told Mike that he should check them out for a future project. I thought that they were fine musically and recognized the excellence of Bill Kelly.

The Buoys were not Wright's first choice. He originally wanted to produce The Glass Prism, but since they were under contract to RCA Records, he followed up on O'Connell's recommendation to visit the area. Wright drove down to Exeter to observe The Buoys performing at Pete's Place and was immediately hooked by the band's energy and talent.

They recorded the all-important demo tapes at Pete's Place, where they played every Friday and Saturday. The vocals and instruments were recorded on separate tracks, utilizing a primitive two-track recorder, and re-mixed at the Plymouth home of Ron Schacht, Chief engineer for Berwick's WBRX. Schacht recalled that two songs were submitted to Scepter, "These Days," which would be their first release, and "Lift Yourself on An Elevator." He added:

> Scepter was amazed that the tape sounded so good. We took longer with the instruments than with the vocals that were reverberated. The instruments took about four or five hours to get what we wanted. If we had a multi-track, we could have done it a lot faster.

Schacht, who later worked for WBRX, WYZZ, WNAK, and WMJW, was one of the unsung heroes at the beginning of The Buoys' incredible journey but was not the only one.

4

THE BUOYS FROM WBAX

The Buoys were living proof that a local band could break out nationally and land on the coveted *Billboard* charts. They did it with what some have dubbed the "grossest song ever recorded."

From the outset, the journey of The Buoys was one of destiny, their success a combination of action and providence, not a random act, but a deliberate design, of kinetic energies blending and slowly assuming shape.

Thirteen-year-old Bill Kelly was in the proverbial right place at the right time. Looking back on those innocent days, one could see how the Rock and Roll Universe slowly unfolded. It all started in 1964 when Kelly heard music coming from the West Wyoming Hose Company, on Stites Street, only one block from his home.

He stuck his head in to investigate. Inside he saw Fran Brozena, age thirteen, on guitar, his cousin Bob Gryziec, fifteen, on bass guitar, and Johnny Staschak, the youngest and shortest of the group, his legs dangling above a high stool, on drums. After introducing himself, Kelly screamed out a convincing rendition of the Beatles' "All My Loving." (Capitol, 1964.) It was all the audition he required. The Escorts needed a confident lead singer, and Kelly convincingly passed the test.

THE MOFFATS

Red-headed Billy Kelly lived in the Atherton Park section of West Wyoming, known as Toy Town. It was located strategically between the larger cities of Wilkes-Barre and Scranton, which was necessary for a fledgling band looking for possible venues. His father was William Edward Kelly, and his siblings included brothers Mike and Tommy and his sister Teresa. The multi-instrumental Kelly played guitar, flute, and banjo.

Fran Brozena lived one block from Kelly. He played in a band called the Escorts and later taught Kelly proper guitar technique so that Kelly wouldn't "plunk so much." Bob Gryzic was born to play the bass guitar and developed his talents as one of the most proficient musicians in the region. As the Escorts, they dressed in white socks, Beatle boots, white shirts, dickeys, and black pants. Mesmerized by the sounds of the British Invasion, they began to perform the Beatle's songbook, focusing on tight harmonies and instrumentation, and then changed their name to The Moffats.

It was easy to see why. On April 4, 1964, the Beatles occupied the top five US *Billboard* Hot 100 chart positions with "Can't Buy Me, Love," "Twist and Shout," "She Loves You," "I Want to Hold Your Hand," and "Please, Please Me." And that wasn't all. The Beatles were represented by another seven titles on the chart that week: "I Saw Her Standing There" (#31), "From Me to You" (#41), "Do You Want to Know a Secret" (#46), "All My Loving" (#58), "You Can't Do That" (#65), "Roll Over Beethoven" #(68) and "Thank You Girl" (#79). Two more Beatles singles, "There's a Place" and "Love Me Do," would join the others on the April 11, 1964, *Billboard* chart, giving them fourteen singles on the Hot 100.

The Beatles' impact on youth culture was phenomenal. The Fab Four were magical influencers, Pied Pipers, who encouraged teens to pick up cheap electric guitars and learn the basic three chords. They prompted Bob Dylan to go electric. The Moffats were among the bedazzled converts. Bill Kelly saw The Beatles on The Ed Sullivan Show. He, along with several million other American teens, was hooked. Although he attained a degree in philosophy from King's College, Kelly's most significant achievement was signing a record contract at age nineteen and watching "Timothy" climb the charts as a Top Twenty hit. After relocating to Nashville, Kelly told reporter Ken Beck of the Lebanon, Tennessee, Wilson Post:

> My career was laid out by the time I was nineteen. I had my first record deal, and by twenty had a Top-20 hit record, 'Timothy.' The Buoys were the proverbial garage band. We went from playing high school dances to touring with The Young Rascals. We did a lot of covers. Our sound was a kind of

an amateur Crosby, Stills, and Nash. We loved three-part harmony and The Beatles. We always did Beatles, Hollies, and Crosby, Stills, and Nash. The band was good.

Their first gig was a surprise concert staged for the morning assembly at Kelly's school, the old West Wyoming High School. The band included Brozena and Kelly on guitars, Gary Atherholt on sax, and John Staschak on drums. The response was tremendous. The Moffats paid the price of success and had to rehearse additional songs after being booked to play another dance.

STASCAK'S CAFÉ

Bill Bauchman worked at WBAX Radio 1240, organizing weekly dances at the Jackson Township Fire Hall. He was a passionate twenty-year-old, full-time radio personality, working for General Manager Jim Ward, the legendary Mr. Radio of Northeastern Pennsylvania. WBAX was in constant competition with regional powerhouse WARM (The Mighty 590), attempting to "creep up to WARM's ratings" through live concerts, talk shows, and special broadcast events. Says Bauchman:

> I loved everything about top 40 radio. I just ate it up. FM was almost just experimental back then. AM Radio was a big deal. It was an era of really true air personalities and a different era than today. We had a higher standard in the language that we used. The Federal Communications Commission was much more stringent than it has become in the recent past.

Bauchman's association with The Moffatts began after a curious phone call started the wheels turning. "I had received a call off air from a guy who said, 'I'm the owner of Frank's Quality Meats and Produce. My kid is thirteen years old and trying to develop a band. Would you listen to him?' It was Brozena's father, Frank." At that point, Bauchman thought there might be an opportunity with The Moffats but was skeptical.

Drummer Stascak's mother owned Stascak's Café and allowed him to rehearse in a small second-floor meeting room. As it happened, in the early evening hours of a 1960s summer's day, Bauchman drove over to the building, and through opened windows, heard the pounding vibrations inside:

> This was something that has stayed with me for decades. I can remember that like it was yesterday. And I walked upstairs, and I heard this music coming from upstairs. I think these kids can't be thirteen or fourteen years old. I'm smart enough to know that. I've only been on the radio for two years.

With fifteen-year-old Billy Kelly screaming out the lead vocals, the group was raw, unpolished, and primitive. They had no stage attire or lighting. All they had were three-floor microphones and a $50 amplifier, and, in an attempt to be more theatrical, miniature light bases. But they did have something else Bachman observed:

> Quantitatively, these guys are so much further ahead than thirteen or fourteen-year-olds. They were jammin' Beatles, and it was incredible. I went up and listened and introduced myself. They were aware that I was going to come over. I said, 'Truly, you guys have a unique sound.' They were looking for a manager at the time. I said, 'I have not done this before, but I think I can do this. I will manage you guys, and I will get you into some places to play.

NAME CHANGE

As a homage to the Beatles, they had changed their name to the Moffats, but Bauchman insisted that they rebrand themselves to something hipper and more marketable. The band agreed. Bob Gryziac explained the group's connection to the nationwide surfing craze:

> At that time, Bauchman needed a band for BAX promos at the Paramount Theater. The opening theme of his radio show was the Surfaris's "Wipeout" #2 (Dot, 1963). Since surf music was popular at the time, he felt the 'Buoys' would be a fitting name. The surf music of the Beach Boys, Dick Dale and the Del-Tones, and Jan and Dean was huge during this period.

"Bill Bauchman and the Buoys from BAX" eventually changed into simply "The Buoys," and Bauchman's fortuitous remote broadcasts exposed them to a substantial regional market:

> All I did was introduce them, that's all. And I guess they had the benefit of a budding, aspiring, professional air voice to introduce them, and at the end of the evening, we'd promote the next place they were going to be for the regular followers.

The Jackson Township Fire Hall, one of the first places that Bauchman booked, became a regular gig. Because none of the group members

Manager Bill Bauchman

THE BUOYS
IN CONCERT
★ ★ AT ★ ★
NORTH SCRANTON
JUNIOR HIGH SCHOOL
FRIDAY, JANUARY 21st
8 TO 11 P.M.

were old enough to drive, he chauffeured them around. They soon played matinees for reverent teens at the Paramount Theatre; spacious, regal, and castle-like. It was the epitome of accomplishment for the group and the proverbial "big stage." In a sense, they had arrived, having already played all of the high schools, YMCA gymnasiums, and fire halls in the area.

Patty Phillips was approximately sixteen years old when she furtively observed the Buoys at rehearsal on George Avenue in the Parsons section of Wilkes-Barre. Phillips, a 1973 graduate of Bishop Hoban High School, recalled those early days. She said:

> I never saw the Buoys on stage. I was young and didn't drive or work yet. But I remember walking up to George Avenue, the Main Street in the tiny town of Parsons, to hear them rehearse. They rented a storefront on the corner across from the Bank and in the same building as Kaufer's Market. Even though they had the windows covered so that we couldn't see in, we could still hear, and to us kids, it was almost like getting to see them in concert, for free. They were just getting to be well known, and they were here, in our little town, on our Main Street, rehearsing. What a thrill for all of us.

NEW LINEUP
In 1967, the band made two significant changes to their lineup, adding Kingston drummer Chris Hanlon and rhythm guitarist Steve Furmanski from nearby Swoyersville. Both played in a band called The Sound Barrier, and both were sixteen years old. Hanlon was also a fan of the group. He remembered paying only fifty cents to see the young Billy Kelly and the Buoys playing Saturday night dances at the Wilkes-Barre Catholic Youth Center.

Hanlon didn't understand why he got the call to replace drummer John Stascak. "I thought John was a pretty good drummer," said Hanlon. His parents, Dr. and Mrs. Paul Hanlon, let the band play in their large Kingston basement and purchased equipment for them. Hanlon remembered the early years with The Buoys as the best of times:

> When I first got in the band, we played at Pete's Place in Exeter. After that, I remember going to the Golden Eagle Restaurant because it was open all night, and my parents would let me break my curfew.

Furmanski graduated from Kingston's Central Catholic High School and was a classmate of Fran Brozena. Fermanski said, "I used to watch them and follow them, and when Bob Gryziac left, they asked me to join, and that was how it went."

That year, Barbara Ann Wozniak reported in the Pittston Sunday Dispatch on the Halloween Dance sponsored by the Sophomore Class on November 3, 1967:

> Music, the key to a perfect evening, was supplied by The Buoys, who caused plenty of movement at the dance and created a happy, spirited atmosphere. It was evident that everyone who attended had a simply delightful time. The proof will be manifested by the increasing number of students seen at future St. John's Dances.

HOTTEST BAND ON THE ROCK CIRCUIT

The grand scheme seemed to be working, as evidenced by *The Sunday Dispatch's* Jack Smiles:

> The new lineup (that added Chris Hanlon and Steve Furmanski and replaced John Staschak and Bob Gryziac) took off. By 1968, the year Kelly graduated from Wyoming Area, The Buoys were arguably the hottest band on the local rock circuit.

After his graduation, Kelly began to play music professionally. In four years, The Buoys created a tribal ritual embracing screaming fans, sold-out auditoriums, and standing-room-only crowds at just about every school gym, bazaar, bar, and prom in the region. They frequented St. John's on Williams Street in Pittston, the Hearthstone Pub in Dallas, and the West Pittston Armory. Sold-out crowds were the order of the day in places like Dunmore's Bishop O'Hara Auditorium (Couples, $3—Singles, $2), North Scranton's St. Mary's Hall, Archbald's Tomaino's Lounge.

There were other suitable venues, offering The Buoys a wealth of opportunities. Located in the city's heart, the old Paramount and Comerford Theatres, with elegant architecture, spacious auditoriums, and massive stages, were on adjacent sides of the Wilkes-Barre square. WBAX would conduct live Christmas shows at the Comerford, drawing as many as 800 screaming attendees.

Kelly spoke about the early days with Alan K. Stout on his *Music on the Menu* podcast and recollected the initial grind:

> The competition was fierce. You had to step on stage in the valley with your 'A Game' every weekend that you were at a high school dance. You could go to Scranton. You could hit five to six high schools, all of them having dances on a Friday night after a football game, and the place is slammed with people, and the bands were all great. Growing up in that atmosphere was something special for Jerry and me and all the guys.

Another of those guys was professional musician Lou Cossa, a former member of the Boxtops, Ralph, Jerry Kelly Band, and Dakota. Cossa agreed:

> At one time, there were forty-eight bands in the Scranton area alone. All the high schools ran dances, and everybody was in a band. I've been across the country three times, and there's no area like this for bands, especially rock and roll. There are so many in this area. I don't know why. I guess people just love to play around here.

That exceptional talent, referenced by Cossa, was on display during the University of Scranton's concert for "Peace and Other Partially Sane Things." The show was held on Friday, October 30, 1970, and included The Buoys, Ralph, 8th Street Bridge, 13th Floor, Fat Cat, American Asphalt, folk singers Tim McGurl and Jim Dietz, and Button Gwinnett. Scranton-based Button Gwinnett was named after one of the signatories on the Declaration of Independence and included Buddy Mecca, Lou Cossa, Thea Sanseverino, Frank Frankosky, and Christopher Rapp. Steve Furmanski and Bobby DeRiggi joined later, and in 1974, with Jack Martini, Harold Price, David Race, Greg Rozycki, and Dewey Vasquez, they recorded at Electric Lady Studios.

It was a freeze-frame of the Buoys, captured at their finest hour, soaring higher and higher. They excelled at covering Steely Dan, Jackson Brown, the Doobie Brothers, and the Eagles and Poco, with precise vocal harmonies. Kelly's band could pack a college gymnasium in Wilkes-Barre or a nightclub in Scranton. Embracing that magical success, Kelly remarked:

It seemed like one day were playing fire halls and gyms, and the next day we were at a pop festival in front of 200,000 people.

They say it's all in the timing. The revised Buoys, consisting of Brozena, Furmanski, Gryziec, Kelly, and Hanlon, recorded "Timothy," and then Gryziak and Furmanski left. At that moment, the planets magically aligned, and the song ascended the *Billboard* charts. Despite their youth and lack of experience, The Buoys had reached the proverbial "big time." Their smash hit climbed up the charts, magically hovering longer than anyone had dared to imagine.

Carl Siracuse and Jerry Hludzik replaced Furmanski and Gryziec, recording the final *Dinner Music* songs. Multi-instrumentalist Carl Siracuse was from Swoyersville, Pennsylvania, and a Central Catholic High School and Wilkes University graduate. He was the son of Joseph Siracuse. He played with the steel guitar-themed Ram Rods and the Berwick-based El Caminos, who evolved into The Glass Prism, scoring with "The Raven" (RCA, 1969). In 1970, Siracuse quit his job at Central Catholic High School (later renamed Bishop O'Reilly) to join The Buoys, who hit the road supporting "Timothy."

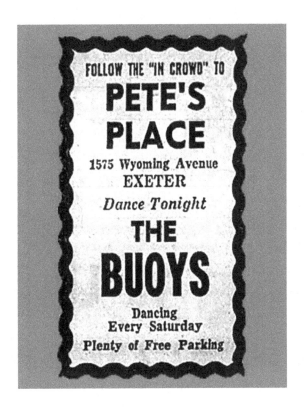

Jerry Hludzik, who played with the Hazleton group Moses, also joined the group. Hludzik was from Japan-Jeddo, in the Freeland-Hazleton area, and son of John Hludzic. Jerry, a graduate of the Mining Mechanical Institute, was an accomplished athlete and played basketball and baseball. He joined the Buoys days before he was to leave for Florida, selling equipment from the steps of Luzerne Area Community College to pay for the trip.

In 1966, Bill Bauchman left the Wyoming Valley as a full-time student at the New York Institute of Technology. He would ride the Martz bus back to Forty Fort every Friday night and work at WBAX 1240 AM to make enough money to stay in school, but of The Buoys' ultimate success, Bauchman said:

> I was thrilled to death for them because I know the odds are so stacked against anybody achieving that level of success. It's purely by the numbers. Consider the odds: There were probably thousands of "garage bands" in the '60s and '70s. And then, all of a sudden, The Buoys do something really dynamite with 'Timothy.'

Fran Brozena, Chris Hanlon, Jerry Hludzik, Bill Kelly, and Carl Siracuse, the latest incarnation of The Buoys, were about to enter the Scepter Records recording studio to complete the controversial *Dinner Music* album.

The early Buoys (L-R) Fran Brozena, Bob Gryziec, Bill Kelly, Chris Hanlon, Steve Furmanski.

★ PART II ★

SCEPTER / WAND RECORDS

5

SCEPTER STUDIOS

I n the mid-1950s, thirty-four-year-old housewife Florence Greenberg exchanged her domesticity for the Manhattan business world. As an officer in the New Jersey League of Women Voters, vice president of the Women's Republican Club, and founder of a camp for blind children, she had developed impressive organizational skills.

After being introduced to the Shirelles, high school classmates of her daughter, Greenberg founded Tiara Records and signed the girl group. She then sold her company to Decca Records for $4,000 and, with that money, founded Scepter Records in 1959 and, two years later, Wand Records. She liked names about royalty, so Tiara, Scepter, and Wand made sense.

Although Scepter's most notable acts were The Shirelles, Dionne Warwick, B.J. Thomas, and Deep Purple, it also launched Maxine Brown, Chuck Jackson, Tami Terrell, and rockers The Guess Who, The Kingsmen, and Joey Dee. In addition, the label released The Isley Brothers' "Twist And Shout" (Wand, 1962), which The Beatles later covered.

Scepter recycled "greatest hits" packages on Citation and Wand Records from older, established performers, introducing "The Best Of" artists such as Deep Purple, the Isley Brothers, Wilson Pickett, Joe Tex, and Flip Wilson. As a further enticement, Citation printed a fake gold record on each album cover.

VELVET UNDERGROUND

Some described the Scepter recording studio as "primitive and decrepit," and many Scepter artists, like Dionne Warwick and B.J. Thomas, recorded their hits at other studios. The only acts that favored Scepter were The Buoys, Great Bear, and the Velvet Underground.

The Velvet Underground & Nico (Verve, 1967) was a minimalist album created by group leader Lou Reed. They recorded the bulk of the songs in

At Scepter Records (L-R) Fran Brozena, C. Michael Wright, Jerry Hludzik, Chris Hanlon, unknown Scepter executive, Carl Siracuse, and Bill Kelly.

mid-April 1966, during a four-day stint at Scepter, but, the following month, "Heroin," "I'm Waiting for the Man," and "Venus in Furs" was re-recorded at TTG Studio in Hollywood. The album was financed by Andy Warhol and Columbia Record's sales executive Norman Dolph and engineered by John Licata.

Roused by the dark realism encompassing beat poetry, jazz, and rock minimalism, The Velvets were among popular music's most influential bands, inspiring generations of artists including David Bowie, the New York Dolls, and Iggy Pop. In a 1982 interview, musician and producer Brian Eno reportedly said the Velvet Underground's first album only sold 30,000 copies during its first five years but that "everyone who bought one of those 30,000 copies started a band."

LUTHER DIXON

Luther Dixon accidentally met Greenberg in an elevator, and she believed that Dixon could help her enter the world of black pop music. Dixon was a former member of The Crests, who charted (at # 4) with "Sixteen Candles" (Coed, 1959). He was a prolific producer, and singer, and songwriter. Elvis, The Beatles, The Jackson 5, B.B. King, Dusty Springfield, and others recorded his songs. Because Greenberg needed someone to work with The Shirelles while she did the promotion, she hired Dixon in 1959 as a producer and arranger and granted him part-ownership of Scepter. As a result, he had complete freedom to sign and produce upcoming artists. According to 'Rockin' All Nite Long' columnist Al Leichter, Dixon agreed to work with the Shirelles if Scepter threw in a few extra bonuses:

> Greenberg made the concessions he wanted, including control of production, serving as the leading writer for the group, funneling songs through his Ludix Publishing Company, and getting a piece of Scepter Records if the group was successful.

And they were. Dixon slathered their trade-marked vocals with heavy orchestration that would define the girl group sound. "Will You Love Me Tomorrow" (Scepter, 1960) went all the way to number one, making them rock's first all-female group to reach that pinnacle. With Dixon as her partner, Greenberg created a vibrant recording dynasty that rivaled the best, bridging rock, pop, and R&B and providing "a priceless legacy within rock history," said reviewer Don Weller:

> With Greenberg promoting and Dixon producing, they created their first wave of hits with the Shirelles. After that, Scepter became a force to be reckoned with, competing on the charts with Phil Spector, Berry Gordy, Bernie Lowe in Philadelphia, Ahmet Ertegun's Atlantic Records, and, of course, the arrival of the Beatles.

Dixon created countless hits for the label, including Chuck Jackson's "I Don't Want to Cry," #5 (Wand, 1961), King Curtis' "Soul Serenade" (Capitol, 1964), Jimmy Reed's "Big Boss Man," (Vee-Jay, 1961). In addition, he wrote the Shirelles' "Mama Said," #4 (Scepter, 1961) and "Boys," another Shirelles' tune, unexpectedly covered on the Beatles debut album, *Please Please Me*.

Greenberg was implicated in a "play for pay" scandal soon after launching her labels. King County Chronicle reporter Lou Terras described Scepter's involvement with payola in a December 1960 column:

> The Federal Trade Commission forbade three record concerns to pay concealed 'payola' to anyone broadcasting their recordings. They are Scepter Music, of 1650 Broadway, N.Y., and Florence Greenberg, an official, the Old Town Record Corp., of 1697 Broadway, N.Y., and Hy Weiss, an official and James Higgins and Robert West, of the B.H. Distributing Co., of Detroit, Mich.

The three concerns were charged in the FTC's complaints with paying radio and television disc jockeys or other personnel of broadcasting stations money or other valuables to have their records played regularly. The FCC charged that disk jockeys concealed lucrative payments, deceiving listeners into believing the records were selected strictly on excellence or popularity. But Scepter/Wand suddenly faced additional turmoil. After his relationship with Greenberg had run its course, Dixon was approached by Capitol Records with the chance to start his own label. With financial backing from media mogul Merv Griffin, Dixon founded Ludix Records. Masco Young's 1962 column, The Grapevine, contained a blurb announcing that Dixon was moving on. It read:

> The news is that Luther Dixon, the Jaguar-driving wealthy song writer-publish-er-recording firm exec, is selling out his interests in Sceptor and Wand records to devote full time to developing his own label.

In 1965, Dixon sold his rights to Sceptor Records for $50,000. By the time The Buoys arrived at Scepter, Dixon had already left for greener, albeit illusionary, pastures, replaced by other writers and arrangers. That same year, Gulf+Western offered Greenberg six million dollars for the Scepter-Wand cata-log, but she told the New York Daily News:

> Why should I sell? The business has been terrific. And I've never had a losing year since I formed Scepter Records in 1956. Each year has always been better than the year that preceded it.

Later, she admitted that was her only mistake. She should have taken the money and run.

THE BUOYS

In 1969, Florence Greenberg had a staff of fifty-four employees when she was introduced to The Buoys. She was the voluptuous, Jersey Jewish housewife who had walked Beale Street in another lifetime, breathing in the essence of black pop. Greenberg was the quintessential networker with an intuitive sense of the business. As an example, she pointed out that a song on the Academy Awards show "can mean a million records to a singer." She cited the case of her top recording stars, Dionne Warwick, who sang the title song "Alfie," and B.J. Thomas, who sang "Raindrops Keep Falling on My Head," from Butch Cassidy and the Sundance Kid. Both made over $1,000,000 in concert dates, she said, "within a year after the show."

C. Michael Wright was the chief engineer, and Rupert Holmes, an upstart songwriter. Her son Stanley, who attained a Ph.D. in music from the University of Rochester, was head of the A&R Department. Although blind, Stanley was an accomplished arranger and remained with the company until it closed in

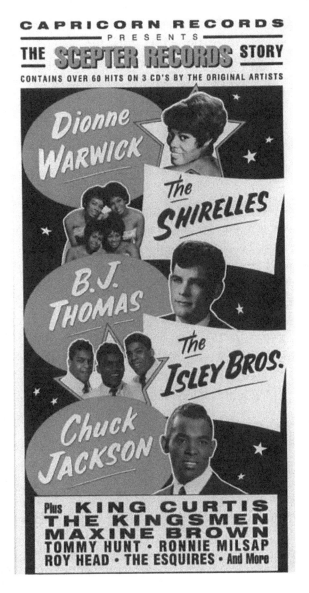

CAPRICORN RECORDS
PRESENTS
THE SCEPTER RECORDS STORY
CONTAINS OVER 60 HITS ON 3 CD'S BY THE ORIGINAL ARTISTS

Dionne WARWICK

The SHIRELLES

B.J. THOMAS

The ISLEY BROS.

Chuck JACKSON

Plus KING CURTIS
THE KINGSMEN
MAXINE BROWN
TOMMY HUNT · RONNIE MILSAP
ROY HEAD · THE ESQUIRES · And More

1976 and then went into social work helping the blind. Her son-in-law, Sam Goff, was vice president of the organization and later a managing partner in Essex Entertainment. In addition, Greenberg had a lucrative working relationship with songwriters Burt Bacharach and Hal David, who penned countless musical gems for Dionne Warwick.

"Mrs. Florence Greenberg is the only woman president of a major record company." This was the headline of a New York *Daily News* article, published on October 5, 1969. A photo with the text "Mrs. Florence Greenberg gives pointers to the young group, The Buoys, in the studio of her Scepter record company," accompanied the story, providing The Buoys with their first Big Apple promotion. The article revealed that she had few luxuries, such as diamonds and fancy clothes. Her biggest spending splurge to date had been a Rolls Royce, which she rarely used. She told reporter Bob Lardine:

> I let the chauffeur go because the car sat in the garage for weeks on end. There was nothing for him to do. I simply can't find time to use the car. I'm going to sell it, as it's nothing but a waste.

HOLMES AND WRIGHT

Aspiring songwriter Rupert Holmes was a struggling twenty-year-old working for Scepter Records. He had been in the record business for almost a year, and his friend, C. Michael Wright, was a junior engineer at Scepter. Together, these opportunists pulled off the proverbial "inside job," locating an extra set of keys that Wright used to unlock the vacant Scepter studio on weekends. This allowed them to experiment with the evolving music technology.

Wright used the same game plan for recording artists The Buoys and Great Bear. He snuck them into Scepter, on the sly, while Greenberg was being chauffeured around in her shiny Rolls Royce enjoying Manhattan's opulence. According to Great Bear guitarist John Gonska:

> C. Michael Wright was good to work with, and, as a kid from Wilkes-Barre, I was thrilled to be recording in New York City. We would go into New York on weekends and sometimes at night, for one or two days at a time, over quite a few months, when the studio was open for C. Michael Wright to play around with us at little or no cost. I was thrilled when we got an advance, and, after management cuts, I got $500. I immediately went out and bought a Marshall half stack.

Wright's mission was to recruit aspiring rock acts to produce. West Pittston's Bob O'Connell, a jazz pianist with Mel Wynn and The Rhythm Aces, had ties with Scepter and prodded engineer Michael Wright to visit Pete's Place in Exeter to see The Buoys. Wright liked what he heard and, in turn, invited The Buoys to drive up to New York to meet Rupert Holmes.

STUDIO 54 DISCO

It took about three hours for The Buoys to drive into Manhattan, where they had a meeting at the Scepter Records recording studio located on 254 West

54th Street. The Buoys of Wilkes-Barre were introduced to the boys of Scepter, and New York City looked to them like the planet Mars.

The Scepter Records studio was the same structure that would later become the infamous Studio 54 Disco, arguably the most well-known discotheque in the world. Studio 54, which operated from 1977 to 1991, helped popularize disco music and a decadent nightclub culture encompassing recreational use of cocaine, amyl nitrate, and Quaaludes, the popular sedative-hypnotic shamefully made notorious by convicted serial rapist Bill Cosby.

Woodstock ideals were replaced by the "Sexual Revolution" after pornographic films such as *Deep Throat* (1972), *Behind the Green Door* (1972), and *Debbie Does Dallas* (1978) went mainstream. Sex clubs like Plato's Retreat and sex-enhancing drugs, including cocaine and methaqualone, were prevalent. Called "ludes," "disco biskets," or "sopers," methaqualone became famous as a recreational club drug in the late 1960s and 1970s. Sales of the drug were terminated due to widespread abuse and addictiveness, and in 1984 the drug was moved to the Drug Enforcement Agency's Schedule I, making it illegal in the United States.

Scepter was one of the initial labels to release twelve-inch singles intended for the emerging 1970s disco market. It included obscure artists like the Armada Orchestra, South Shore Commission, and Ultra High Frequency.

Steve Furmanski's most memorable moment was just sitting in awe, transfixed at actually being in Scepter Studios and breathing in his first professional studio experience:

> Dionne Warwick was there. B.J. Thomas used to come in. They would sit in
> the control room and listen to us once in a while. Scepter had a pretty nice
> sound.

The facilities were only about four years old, as Scepter had moved its offices to the Manhattan location in 1965. The building included warehouse space, a recording studio, and a waiting room. Fran Brozena recalled that Scepter had a grand piano, a Hammond B3 organ, and Sennheiser microphones. Although Furmanski like the sound, technically, the studio was sparse and had no advanced reverb capabilities.

Others were aware of Scepter's technical limitations. In Phil Ramone's *Making Records: The Scenes Behind the Music* (Hyperion, 2007), he explained how the lack of sophisticated recording technology drove some of Scepter's biggest stars to other studios. For example, Ramone stated that all of the Dionne Warwick and BJ Thomas earlier recordings, such as "Do You Know the Way to

San Jose" (Scepter, 1968) and "Raindrops Keep Falling on My Head" (Scepter, 1969), were recorded at A&R Studios, and not at Scepter. The more advanced A&R Records used two separate studios: Studio A-2, located at 799 Seventh Avenue, while Studios R1 and R2 were at 322 West 48th Street.

"TIMOTHY"

Scepter's master plan was nebulous at best. The label would allow The Buoys to release a few singles, but after that, they were basically on their own. There would be no promotion other than mandatory ads in trade magazines such as *Billboard* and *Cashbox*. If the song was not a hit, The Buoys would be kicked to the curb and on the outside looking in. So instead, Holmes suggested they record a song that would get banned and incite controversy in hopes of encouraging another label to sign them. He crafted "Timothy," expecting to get blacklisted with that

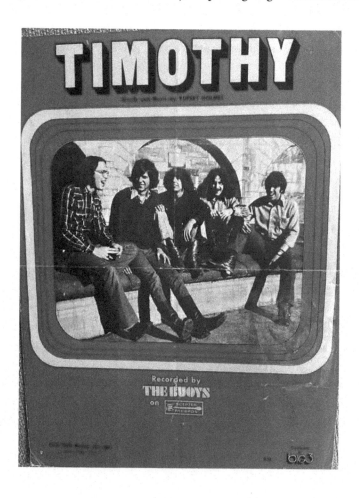

strategy but garner discussion and airplay from other less conservative stations. Their bold plan eventually saw the light of day, but, as Gryziac recollected, because of Scepter's primitive recording equipment, the sound quality was less than perfect on "Timothy" and on the forthcoming *Great Bear* LP:

> My memory is somewhat foggy regarding the inside of the studio, but when we first started recording, I believe they had an Ampex 4 track, which we did 'Timothy' on. When I joined Great Bear, Scepter got a new Ampex sixteen-track machine and had an engineer build a new sixteen-track mixing board for it. Almost all boards had to be built from scratch or use a modified radio station switchboard in those days. The Great Bear record was kind of the guinea pig for the new equipment, so the Great Bear record sounds kind of thin. It could have been the mastering or a combination of both.

Gryziac said that Scepter "didn't have any decent reverb tanks" and that the intro to "Timothy" was "totally flat sounding." Billy Angelo Stella, the owner of The Drummer's Workshop, addressed "Timothy's" overall sound:

> The recording of "Timothy' wasn't a "full" sound. It lacked separation, and the various parts seemed to roll into each other. You could hear Hanlon's high hat and snare, and you couldn't miss the guitar solo and Kelly's sharp vocals, but the other parts were buried underneath the sonic avalanche. On top of that were the strings and the horns.

Scepter had a poor reputation as far as recording quality. Still, The Great Rock Scare's bass player, Fran Festa, (who played with, among others, Child, Gibbs and Cullen, Public Enemy, and The Glass Prism) appreciated the production of the song, hearing it through the ears of an experienced musician:

> Regarding the recording quality, by the standards of audiophiles, or compared to Abbey Road, 'Timothy" may sound a bit rough, but it was more than adequate for that time and any time. It captured an energy that could easily have been ruined if it were overproduced and glossy. It would have lost its darkness and mystery. It almost sounds as claustrophobic as the subject matter, if that's possible. To me, that sound is just right! The average fan may miss these nuances, but musicians like me probably 'get it.'

Michael Kuzmin, the creator of the "'60s PA Teen Bands" Facebook page, noted that the Beach Boys' Brian Wilson listened to songs destined for airplay through a car radio to sense its overall sound. He knew that many music fans first became familiar with a song through primitive car speakers. He said:

I've no problems with the overall production of 'Timothy.' The B-side, 'It Feels Good,' is a quality song in its own right, perhaps being a decent guitar break away from being an A-side on its own merits. Overall, I think the members of the Buoys on the record should be pretty proud of their #20 ranking on national charts. As a collector of obscure '60s records, I realize there were loads of quality 45s out there deserving airplay that never stood a chance for various reasons. The Buoys beat the odds.

"I Feel Good" was not included on their LP. Kelly said that they hated it and refused to play it live. However, because DJ and A&R man Jim Drucker was friends with Rupert Holmes' manager, Stan Herman (owner of Two Plus Two Music), Drucker was able to secure "Timothy's" flip-side with "I Feel Good" on Drucker Publishing.

BABY, IT'S YOU

The music industry is like a revolving door, as innovative personnel come and go. Luther Dixon sold his rights to Sceptor and founded his own label. C. Michael Wright left Scepter to work for the new Group C, a Multi-media recording complex and a joint venture between Consolidated American Investment Corporation and England's Trident Recording Studio Ltd. The new studio included a twenty-four-track recorder, a sixteen-track recorder, and two separate mixing rooms, perfect for Wright's pop sensibilities. The equipment was worth an estimated $1.4 million and more advanced than what Scepter offered.

Florence Greenberg retired from the business in 1976, selling all her labels to Springboard International, regurgitating the lucrative Scepter catalog into the oldies marketplace. She died on November 2, 1995, of heart failure at Hackensack University Medical Center. Unfortunately, she was eighty-two and did not live long enough to savor the impact of her recording empire.

In 1996 The Shirelles were inducted into the Rock and Roll Hall of Fame with Gladys Knight and the Pips. They were presented the award by Merry Clayton, Marianne Faithfull, and Darlene Love, the unrecognized singer on so many Phil Spector classics.

Controversy soon followed like a rabid mongrel when things came full circle on November 9, 1998. The garage band, The Kingsmen, had their day in court and were awarded ownership of their Wand recordings, including "Louie, Louie." The group alleged that they were not paid royalties on the tapes since the 1960s. It was complicated. Gusto Records had purchased the Scepter/Wand label catalog, which had been acquired by Springboard International earlier in 1974.

Former Scepter producer and songwriter Luther Dixon died on October 22, 2009, in Jacksonville, Florida, his hometown. Shortly before his death, he was nominated for the Songwriters Hall of Fame. A further tribute came in March 2012, when the play *Baby It's You* premiered on Broadway to rave reviews. The national tour told the story of Florence Greenberg and the rise of Scepter Records. It played on Broadway for one-hundred and forty-eight performances, opening at the Broadhurst Theatre on April 27, 2011, and closing on September 4, 2011. There was more! Because Carol King planned to do her own musical, she refused to allow the Broadway play to use her song, "Will You Still Love Me Tomorrow?", the Shirelles' biggest hit.

Additionally, in 2011, the use of their "likenesses without permission" led Chuck Jackson, Dionne Warwick, and former Shirelles' singer Beverly Lee, as well as the estates of Doris Coley and Addie Harris, to sue Warner Bros. and the Broadway play *Baby Its You,* stating that the group, having "been cheated out of their royalties when they were young and popular, are now victimized again."

After all those decades, that was how it ended for Tiara, Scepter, and Wand. But the burning question left unanswered was, "Why did Rupert Holmes claim that his song was about cannibalism of a fellow miner while Florence Greenberg argued it was only about a mule."

6

RUPERT HOLMES

David Goldstein was born in Northwich, Cheshire, UK, to an American GI father and a British mother. When he was six, his family relocated to Nanuet, a suburb of New York City.

His father, Leonard Eliot, a U.S. Army bandleader and high school music teacher, started him on the clarinet at age eight, and music became his passion. After high school, Goldstein studied theory and composition at the Manhattan School of Music but, after three years, dropped out. Instead, he found work in New York City's Tin Pan Alley as a session musician and producer. Young and hungry, he amassed a multitude of styles learned in this vibrant musical epicenter. "At the dawn of the '70s, he cut his teeth in the junk factory of prefabricated pop," wrote biographer Stephen Thomas Erlewine:

> As a clever, versatile singer/songwriter who split the difference between Brill Building pop bubblegum kitsch, McCartney-esque pomp, and Broadway.

His portfolio swelled with promise during these early days. He arranged the Charlie Pride song folio, wrote lead sheets for The Five Blind Boys of Alabama, wrote the marching band arrangement for "Jingle Bell Rock" and the high school arrangement of Santana's "Oye Como Va." In addition, he wrote Short & Sassy shampoo commercials for Dorothy Hamill, the 1976 Olympic champion and skating celebrity.

DAVID JULIAN GILL
Goldstein changed his name and, as David Julian Gill, cranked out several catchy pop hits. He wrote the Tommy James sound-alike "Dance For Me" (Roulette, 1967) for the Court Jesters and replaced lead singer Ron Dante of the "non-group" Cuff Links. He arranged, co-wrote, and sang the bubble-gummy "Jennifer Tomkins" #36 (Musicor, 1970) for the Street People and arranged for

the Platters and Drifters, classic groups attempting to revisit past days of greatness. The Drifters recorded "Black Silk" (Atlantic, 1970) b/w "You Got to Pay
Your Dues," two of his compositions.

Julian Gill produced several projects for Northeastern Pennsylvania bands,
including "Our Town" (Decca, 1968) for The Eddie Day Group, and "Don't
Want to Lose You" (Wand, 1968), and the splendid "Stop Sign" (Wand, 1969)
for the Mel Wynn Trend (formerly the Rhythm Aces).

"TIMOTHY"

The best was yet to come. On April 17, 1969, he married Elizabeth Wood
Dreifuss, later memorialized by The Buoys in "Liza's Last Ride" (Polydor,1973).

Now using the name "Rupert Holmes," he wrote his tribute to coalmine
cannibalism. Many believed "Timothy" shadowed the tragic Sheppton mine
disaster, a dreadful piece of Coal Region mythology. In both cases, three individuals crawled into a mine, but only two came out. Allegations of cannibalism
during the 1963 Sheppton disaster had been around for a long time. Rupert
Holmes did not invent them; he merely resurrected them. He claimed that he
knew nothing about Sheppton and that his song was purely an experiment in
musical fantasy, intended to stoke the flames of controversy. Nonetheless, like a
praying mantis, the song inched its way up the *Billboard* charts, fueled by hard-
driving rock and cryptic lyrics. Holmes addressed the success of his composition:

> It did better than we intended it to do. It was supposed to just start the contro-
> versy; instead, it actually was a hit. I was a twenty-year-old kid hungry, not for
> human flesh, but hungry to do something successful in the music business.

PINA COLADA SONG

Holmes experienced his most considerable success after "Timothy." His first
album, *Widescreen* (Epic, 1974), caught the attention of Barbra Streisand, who
hired him to co-produce and arrange her *Lazy Afternoon* LP (Columbia, 1975)
and included four of his songs. In describing *Widescreen*, *Philadelphia Inquirer*
entertainment writer Jack Lloyd observed:

> Rupert Holmes is a dreamer. He has exotic visions, elaborate widescreen
> fantasies starring Rupert Holmes as the genius who comes to the rescue of pop
> music in the mid-'70s, lifting this somewhat stagnant art form to incredible
> heights of creative energy.

Those creative energies were re-discovered after Holmes received long-
awaited national recognition. Both "Escape (The Pina Colada Song)" #1

(Infinity, 1979) and "Him" #6 (Infinity, 1980) made his breakout LP, *Partners in Crime*, a singles-driven commercial success. His lyrics often reveal personal flaws and vulnerabilities, speaking of social commentary and interpersonal relationships. As disclosed to this writer:

> It's very difficult for me to write songs with happy endings. But the problem is that we will do things like falling in love with the wrong people, hanging in there five months too long when we knew from the first day it wasn't going to work out no matter how many self-help books we read.

Barry Manilow, Dionne Warwick, B.J. Thomas, Manhattan Transfer, and Mac Davis recorded his material. Additionally, he produced albums for London-based artists, The Strawbs, Sailor, Sparks, and John Miles.

BLOOMSBURG FAIR

On Friday, September 26, Holmes played two sets at the 1980 Bloomsburg Fair. The Rupert Holmes Band consisted of Phil Guidos, keyboards; Dean Bailey, lead guitars; John Caruso, bass; Bennie Graham, drums; and Chrissy Faith, back-up vocals. Holmes was featured on the Yamaha keyboard for the composition "Near Sighted." Other pieces performed by the group included "Let's Get Crazy Tonight," "Who, What, When, Why," "Him," "Answering Machine," "BlackJack," "Studio Musician," "Everything," and, of course, "Escape."

The Bloomsburg Fair traditionally hires country acts. In 1980, they brought in the Mills Brothers, Barbara Mandrell, T.G. Sheppard, the Statler Brothers, Lynn Anderson, and Ray Stevens. The only other rock act was the well-attended Dr. Hook concert. Despite his success, Holmes was not familiar to rock fans, and regional newspapers that advertised the upcoming show did not mention his association with the Buoys or "Timothy." Jerry Hludzic attempted to have Holmes and Dakota on the same bill but had no luck with the Bloomsburg Fair officials, probably unaware of the group's massive following. All in all, this was poor judgment and poor promotion by the Fair committee. The show was held on a cold Friday night with a combined crowd of twenty-three hundred for both shows. The total seating capacity for the two shows was around sixteen thousand.

DROOD

Although Holmes' magic touch would continue, his pop hit with The Jets "You Got It All" #3 (MCA, 1987) had a bitter-sweet taste. Before its release, his ten-year-old daughter, Wendy, died suddenly of an undiagnosed brain tumor, which devastated him for years.

Rupert Holmes appearing at the 1980 Bloomsburg Fair. (Maxim Furek photo.)

Like a chameleon, he found renewed success as a playwright on the Great White Way. He turned Charles Dickens' unfinished novel, "The Mystery of Edwin Drood" (1986), into the musical Drood, winning numerous Tony Awards. He wrote *Say, Goodbye Gracie* (2002), a one-person play starring Frank Gorshen and the musical-mystery-comedy Curtains (2007). Holmes also adapted John Grisham's *A Time to Kill* (2013) for the stage.

Metamorphosing into other personas, Holmes kept making it difficult to label him. He had already been saddled with "bubblegum pop," "one-hit wonder," and "Pina Colada man." But Holmes was more than those identities. Winston Churchill, while describing Russia, could have easily been describing Rupert Holmes when he spoke of "a riddle, wrapped in a mystery, inside an enigma."

7

CASEY KASEM

Nationally, the two-minute and forty-nine-second record "Timothy" was introduced to America by the silky-voiced disk jockey Casey Kasem. His 206 words, elemental to the song's success, set the stage for one of the most fascinating songs in the history of pop culture. "Timothy" appeared on Kasem's American Top 40 Countdown as the highest-debuting record for the week of April 11, 1971. That same month President Richard Nixon ended the blockade against the People's Republic of China, 200,000 anti-Vietnam War protesters marched, Concert Promoter Bill Graham closed down Fillmore East and Fillmore West, the US Supreme Court upheld the use of busing to achieve racial desegregation, and killer Charles Manson was sentenced to life for the Sharon Tate murders. Casey Kasem addressed the song "Timothy" and said:

> This next song is about the most difficult life and death decision that any man ever had to make. It tells the story about three men trapped in a mine disaster, starving to death, and faced with an impossible choice. When rescue comes, two are alive and not starving, but there's no trace of the third man.
>
> Now, this is fiction, created by the songwriter. But a similar incident in American history in 1845 was very real. A band of pioneers known as the Donner Party were heading west over the Sierra Nevada Mountains on their way to

the Promised Land of California. Their food supplies had run out when they were stranded by a heavy snowstorm. Immediately the weaker members of the party began dying of malnutrition, and the others were faced with this choice.

Certain death by starvation or life by eating those who had died. Many chose cannibalism and were eventually rescued. But the ordeal haunted the survivors for the rest of their lives. It was a case of damned if you do—dead if you don't.

Based on a similar theme is the song at number 32 this week. It's by a four-man group called The Buoys. Here's the story of "Timothy"!

8

"TIMOTHY" LYRICS

Trapped in a mine that had caved in, and everyone knows the only ones left, was Joe and me and Tim.

When they broke through to pull us free, the only ones left to tell the tale, was Joe . . . and me.

CHORUS: Timothy, Timothy, where on earth did you go? Timothy, Timothy, God, why don't I know.

Hungry as hell, no food to eat, and Joe said that he would sell his soul for just . . . a piece . . . of meat.

Water enough to drink for two, and Joe said to me, I'll take a swig, and then . . . there's some . . . for you.

CHORUS: Timothy, Timothy, Joe was looking at you. Timothy, Timothy, God, what did we do?

I must have blacked out just about then cause the very next thing that I could see was the light of the day again.

My stomach was full as it could be, and nobody ever got around to finding . . . Timothy.

CHORUS: Timothy, Timothy, where on earth did you go? Timothy, Timothy, God, why don't I know?

Timothy . . .   . yea . . . . Timothy!

9

THE "TIMOTHY" SESSIONS

Fran Brozena, a high school senior at the time, thought that "Timothy" was recorded earlier than the rest of the *Dinner Music* album, possibly between January and June of 1969. An obscure sixteen-mm film captured The Buoys performing their hit song, today forgotten and collecting dust on somebody's living room bookshelf.

Returning from Manhattan, they introduced the song during their live concerts and received standing ovations. This was a sign of what was to be, as Kelly recalled the frenzy:

> Our fans enjoyed the song, and we played it for quite a while before its release, and it was always well received. One of the exciting things was how everyone thought they knew what 'Timothy' was, a mule, a dog, a coal miner, etc. They were all wrong, but the controversy was great.

It seemed that the mantra of the day was "the more, the merrier" as scores of Northeastern Pennsylvania fans flocked to Scepter's crowded studio, by special invitation only. During the recording sessions, an entourage of roadies, girlfriends, and friends of the band assembled there. Brozena recalled "Steve," a mysterious stranger:

> I do remember one exciting individual that attended the Timothy sessions. I believe he was possibly an English major at Wilkes College at the time. Personally, I recall him making the comment that 'Wow, so many people are out there involved in the protest movement and singing songs about peace and love, and you guys are going to release a song about cannibalism.'

Recording music is often an amalgamation of disparate styles and ideas. During the "Timothy" sessions, several musicians were at the ready. Keyboard chores, for example, were handled by an assortment of musicians, Fran Brozena,

The Buoys (L-R). Bill Kelly, Jerry Hludzik, Chris Hanlon, Fran Brozena, Carl Siracuse. (Photo courtesy of Bill Kelly Music Productions.)

Rupert Holmes, and Bob O'Connell, from the Rhythm Aces. They assisted Wright with suggestions for songs and arrangements. O'Connell played a role in the song's recording:

> Yes, I was part of the production of 'Timothy.' I was there when Rupert taught the song to the guys, adjusted the tempo of the tune upwards, and sang background parts on the recording. In addition, I helped set the EQ levels on the instruments and voices to get 'that' sound.

O'Connell left the project to pursue other ventures, concentrating on "original ideas for songs and tracks," which, he said, "never really came to fruition." He worked with other bands, including Christopher.

In between the recordings, band members joked around with Wright and Holmes. Chris Hanlon remembered that Holmes was "quite the character" and adept at movie trivia, quickly guessing the names of popular film actors like Jodie Foster, Anjelica Huston, and Al Pacino. From New York's East Side, Wright and his wife Diane were "nice people" and "easy to get along with."

Michael Wright was listed as one of the Top Producers of 1971, ranked at number 88 with three chart listings. Wright later worked for SIR in New York City and is believed to have been the (uncredited) mixer for the *Frampton Comes Alive* LP (A&M, 1976).

Even though all of the group members provided input into the creative process, Kelly was struck by Holmes' singular inventiveness:

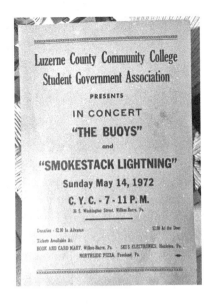

> Rupert was doodling on the piano and played and sang 'Timothy' for us one day during a break in recording at Scepter. We laughed our heads off and agreed to record the song, really just for the fun of it. We thought it was a great joke. We all laughed and decided to record it just to see what it might sound like.
>
> When it was done, I don't think anyone thought it was some great smash hit. In fact, it sat on the shelf for nearly a year before Michael Wright, our producer and engineer, brought in Howard Reeves to do strings and horns on it. Then it came to life!

Brozena remembered that Holmes introduced the song by playing it on a grand piano as a slowed-down funeral elegy:

> He played us his initial version of 'Timothy,' and I believe it was done in the key of E minor and was very slow, almost like a funeral dirge. He wanted a Creedence Clearwater Revival to feel to the tune, something like the up-tempo 'Proud Mary.'

A lot was going on during the sessions, with at least eight musicians laying down lines, grooves, and spontaneous improvisations. However, it never approached anarchy but functioned within a framework that somehow held together. Lead singer Kelly used a 1967 Gretsch Country Gentleman guitar played through a double-stack Marshall, jacked up to ten for the recording session. Kelly remembered the event:

> Ha. Everything was on ten in those days. I had difficulty with that track. I used light gauge strings in those days, and I had to hit a very hard upstroke with my

pick to get just the right 'pop.' Just as I would have a great take going, I would break a string! We'd have to stop, put on a new string and try to stretch it so it wouldn't slip while playing. Of course, it would slip anyway and go out of tune and ruin the take. This went on for several strings and many more takes before we got the idea to have Rupert listen to my guitar as I played in headsets and re-tune the string AS I WAS PLAYING IT! That's how we got the final performance.

"Timothy" was recorded by Brozena, Furmanski, Gryziec, Hanlon, and Kelly. It was released, made a little noise, and then died. At that point, Gryziec left (amicably) to play with Child. Marty Straub stepped in to play bass for a short time and then left. Pete Roman, an excellent finger-style picker on both six and twelve-string guitar, and bassist Bob Zitney, local folkies from King's College, came aboard, but because of ego differences, they split up. Brozena, Hanlon, and Kelly stood alone as Furmanski, Roman and Zitney left for greener pastures. It was time for Plan B: Siracuse was recruited from the El Caminos, and Hludzik, who was always selling microphones in front of LCCC, to finance a trip to Florida, came over.

Tom Fox entered the picture around this time. Wright wanted to keep The Buoys out of trouble and suggested that Fox, then age twenty-three, take over as manager because he was older and more mature. Fox assumed the role of road manager for about one year and then became manager and booking agent. Fox, along with Siracuse and Hludzik, joined The Buoys around the same time.

DINNER MUSIC

Although recording at Scepter allowed them to refine their studio skills, there were pressures to complete *Dinner Music* observed Brozena:

> We had been kind of thrust into making an album quickly. I think it was a real rushed album. It was rushed from a writing perspective because we were thrust into it. Whatever you got, let's put them on. But we had only four or five songs. We wanted to write and wanted to be writers, but we didn't have many songs to choose from. So 'Timothy' took a long time to make. We recorded it in drips and drabs. And then the band had broken up.

Siracuse noted that the *Dinner Music* sessions allowed for individual embellishments that supported the various songs. As a result, essential elements blended into a musical yin-yang that created the whole, without "conflict or controversy," said Siracuse:

Between Fran and me, it depended on whether one of us was playing guitar or had worked out a keyboard part. Sometimes we both played keyboards, and sometimes one of us just wanted to play a specific instrument or had worked out a song on a particular instrument. If Fran wrote a song on guitar or the piano, I would pick up a different instrument.

CUSTOM GATEFOLD COVER

The *Dinner Music* LP featured a custom gatefold cover, a lyric sheet, and three group photos shot at New York locations, Timothy and the Steer Palace. Scepter photographer Ronald Naschak shot the five band members standing before the New York City building entrance under an awning that says "Timothy" alongside a spray-painted "Give Up Your Guns." The album was dedicated to Tom Fox and Rupert Holmes, "Two very special People."

Scepter's marketing efforts were confusing, at best. Jim Owston, Dean of Online and Individualized Learning at Mountain State University in Beckley, West Virginia, described the ambiguity of the album cover:

> The Buoys' LP is kind of confusing as to its title. The band was standing under an awning on the album's cover that had 'Timothy' written on it. To the left of the band, 'Give up your Guns' was mock spray-painted on the wall. OK, which is it, 'Timothy' or 'Give up your Guns?'
>
> If that wasn't confusing enough, the back cover had 'Dinner Music' printed in large script with a band photo inside a restaurant. OK, that's three names—but wait, we haven't seen the label yet. Title number four is 'The Buoys by The Buoys.' Well, I hope you've had your fill of our smorgasbord of album titles. I must go as the maître de is calling: 'Donner party of five; Donner party of five.'

THE REVIEWS

Dinner Music has been described as psychedelic rock, progressive rock, and "pseudo-sophisticated pop/rock with arty pretensions." Scranton *Tribune* writer Lance Evans detected a contrast in production values between *Dinner Music* and Jerry Kelly's *Somebody's Else's Dream*, recorded almost ten years later. He said:

> At the time of its completion, *Dinner Music* was highly representative of professional standards at that time, featuring Kelly's tenor wailing to full advantage. But, when played immediately after hearing *Somebody's Else's Dream*, the songs on *Dinner Music* take on a kind of tinny, less-than-full quality.

The Buoys were attracting lots of attention. For example, Terry Hazlett's "Disc Talk" in the Canonsburg, Pennsylvania's *Daily Notes* observed:

> The Buoys, who took over a year before making 'Timothy' a number one song in the area, have returned with 'Bloodknot.' It's very boring the first time through, but after a few listens, it grows on you. Could be very, very big.

The Buoys boldly ventured into experimental folk-rock and psychedelia. An album review in the Carlisle *Sentinel* gave *Dinner Music* four stars (out of five) and praised the group for having "much inventiveness and a musical depth which most groups don't obtain until they are established for years." The cuts "Give Up Your Guns," "Castles," and "Sunny Days" were singled out as among the best on the LP. The unknown reviewer observed:

> The group's writing is really out of the ordinary and marks the group for an exceptional future in music.

Writing in the Honolulu *Advertiser*, reporter Wayne Harada was lavish in his praise for *Dinner Music:*

> The Buoys, a quintet known for the bizarre title tune (strange, because of a hint of cannibalism), should rocket to the top of the charts with this debut LP. 'Give Up Your Guns' also is chart-active, and because the group creates its own music, for the most part, long life is inevitable.

Not everyone was that kind. Some critics pummeled the album and watched gleefully as everyone piled on. The following text from Fred Beldin's *All Music Guide* blended the bitter with the sweet:

> The centerpiece of the LP is, of course, 'Timothy,' the tasteless Top 40 hit that earned the Buoys temporary stardom and launched the career of songsmith Rupert Holmes. It's a classic death pop number, the sprightly tale of three miners trapped by a cave-in who turn to cannibalism for survival during their ordeal. Despite the gruesome theme, 'Timothy' has a hooky chorus and a production rich with brass and strings, so it's likely that many of the song's fans never listened much deeper than the melodious tune.

All Music's Bruce Elder review of the LP was unwaveringly critical as he refused to allow the group the luxury of stretching out into other musical realms and refused to acknowledge the LP's experimental creativity:

> This is the kind of material that made many '60s people loathe the 1970s— highly produced midtempo pop/rock, with flutes, horns, and other attributes

that didn't have a lot to do with rock & roll. Apart from 'Timothy,' which at least has a sort of beat, the material here is pretty lame pseudo-sophisticated pop/rock with arty pretensions.

The flowery compositions ("Sunny Days/Memories," "The Prince of Thieves," etc.) come complete with prominent string sections and flutes, and the occasional guitar run and prominent drum roll, just to remind people that this is a rock band they're listening to.

"Timothy" jump-frogged up the charts despite relentless criticism from individuals such as *Rolling Stone*'s Paul Gambaccini, who reviewed their single on June 10, 1971:

> At the time, the pedestrian instrumental line obscured the lyrics. After several months, programmers and listeners alike discovered that the song was about cannibalism: three friends are trapped in a mine, two emerging upon rescue sans Timothy. Everyone who understands the words gets a charge out of the grossness, so the record has been a hit wherever and whenever played.

But, like an alien life form, "Timothy" demonstrated the ability to take hold, replicate, and sustain itself. It landed on *Billboard*'s Top 40 on April 17, where it stayed for eight weeks before peaking at #17 on May 1, 1971. It also charted in *Cashbox* and reached #8 in *Record World*.

"Timothy's" ascent was slow and insistent, persevering for an astonishing 17 weeks. The Pittston *Dispatch*'s David Yonki, in his *Teen Record Review*, observed the record soaring up the charts, as he anticipated better days ahead for the record:

> The underground newspaper, Crawdaddy, ran a half-page ad plugging the record, which should increase sales among the beautiful and flower people out on the West Coast.

NOT REPRESENTATIVE

Banana Joe Montione, host of Flashback Top 40 Radio with Banana Joe, felt that *Dinner Music* had more to offer than the hit single:

> They had a tremendous first album full of melodic, musically sound compositions, with 'Timothy,' this offbeat story of survival in a mining accident. The powerful lead vocals by The Great Bill Kelly created a unique sound played on many stations and sold enough to be a hit. Too bad some of the excellent songs from that first album didn't get the attention that 'Timothy' received. In a way,

'Timothy' was not representative of their overall polished and very commercial-sounding album.

"Timothy," released locally to capitalize on the fanbase, did well but then sputtered. The single garnered little national attention and was put on hold for eight months. The song was initially released in February 1970 and quickly sold ten thousand copies. It was re-released in September due to "the tremendous sales and airplay it received in many markets," especially Denver and Syracuse, and according to Hazleton's *Standard-Speaker*:

> Although it didn't make the *Billboard* charts until January 2, 1971, it had already been receiving scattered airplay in select test markets such as Syracuse, New York.

"Timothy" resonated through the all-important radio waves. According to Ron Wray, historian at Syracuse Music, it became the greatest chart-selling single of all-time on Dinosaur Radio, formerly WOLF. It charted for a record twenty-two weeks on the WOLF Music Charts, seventeen weeks in the Top Ten and four weeks at #1 (July 8-28, 1970) and again (August 12-25, 1970), "a record that may never be broken as a single release."

It was a very good year. *Billboard* listed "Timothy" at #87 on the Top Pop 100 Singles of the Year.

★ PART III ★

TIMOTHY ANALYZED

10

"TIMOTHY" PROBED

Attention from the trades was imperative in generating interest for the 45, while the coveted "with a bullet" designation was the icing on the cake. *Cash Box* acknowledged the song's momentum:

> The single "Timothy," by the Buoys, celebrated its 16th month in release by climbing to the No. 16 slot on the Best Seller list. Originally released on Scepter in December 1969, the outing this week hit 16 with a bullet on the *Cash Box* charts, action reflecting new sales in Detroit and Cleveland, and continued radio support from Cleveland, Boston, Miami, Chicago, Cincinnati, Detroit, and Philadelphia.

"Timothy" inched up the charts around the same time as the Jackson Five's "I'll Be There" (Tamla, 1970), Crosby, Stills & Nash's "Our House" (Atlantic, 1970), and R. Dean Taylor's "Indiana Wants Me" (Rare Earth, 1970). Those were a strange mix of diverse styles that shared radio airplay. "Timothy," the most unconventional of the bunch, received its fair share of attention. Not all, however, was good.

Some liked the finished product; others didn't. Nonetheless, the added effects, while borrowing heavily from the orchestral pop of Nelson Riddle, Burt Bacharach, and Phil Spector, gave the straight-ahead rock song additional punch, setting it apart from other rock productions of the era. That counterpoint added to the song's uniqueness: a blend of rock against strings and horns, a grotesque song sung with an inspired sensibility. Jerry Beebe's "'Timothy' Probed," in the Port Angeles, Washington, *Evening News Record Review*, liked what he heard:

> It's a well-recorded disc with a background arrangement orchestrated and conducted by Howard Reeves. Violins seem to scream out as the orchestra adds a sublime and eerie touch to this bizarre tale. The group's vocal quality is good, with few adjustments. Echoes are used in adding a haunting quality found in

Publisher Maxim Furek interviewing Hall and Oates for Timothy: Northeast-
ern Pennsylvania's First Music Publication, with columns by Richard Chizak,
George Graham, Dave Karchner, LA Tarone, and the usual list of suspects.
(David Beathier Schloyer photo.)

very few songs. After listening to the lyrics of the song for the first time, you
are left with a rather peculiar feeling.

That feeling was as subtle as an atomic bomb, as other ardent fans enthusiastically applauded the song. Music critic Richard Chisak was among them:

> 'Timothy' was simply a great pop record—a catchy, well-crafted pop tune
> with a good hook, ably performed by a great teen band. Plus, it sounded great
> on the radio. The cannibalism hype may have initially gotten the attention of
> radio programmers, but as they say, 'a record's gotta have it in the grooves if
> people are going to buy it.'

Or, as Motown's Berry Gordy mused, "It's what's in the grooves that counts."
So Rhythm Aces' keyboardist Bob O'Connell listened to those grooves through
the ears of a seasoned musician, determining the essence of this rock classic:

> I found the concept of 'Timothy' brilliant. I didn't ponder the allegations of cannibalism. Instead, I was more tuned into the musicality of the record, like tempo, rhythms, melody, and harmony.

Still, O'Connell, like many others, wasn't pleased with what some thought was an "overproduction" of the song:

> I did feel that the orchestrated parts were over the top and a bit distracting, but my main areas of concern were rhythm tracks and harmonies.

Although banned by numerous radio stations, "Timothy" refused to die a proper death. WRNJ Music Director Rich Appel noted the sustainability of the song that simply did not go away:

> That it did so well, for so many stations that did play it, I think proves how strong it is. While not a song you'd hear a lot on classic hits-based radio today, it's fun to hear on special weekends, countdowns, or as an 'oh wow.' Its staying power is due, I feel, to its great hooks, the horns, and a singable chorus, meaning I bet few listeners even now have any idea what the song's about.

Radio personality Shadoe Steele, the long-time host of KRZ's *Saturday Night Live at the Oldies* and one of the highest-rated and longest-running oldies show in the nation, knew what the song was about. Thus, he broke down "Timothy's" basic formula for success:

> Recipe for a hit record: 3:05 running time + catchy hook + local historical element if available and oh, yeah, throw in a pinch of controversy = *Billboard* Top-40 smash!"

Former Great Bear and Great Rock Scare guitarist, John Gonska, aka Sonny California, while working for Scepter, had the advantage of first hearing the song through a massive mountain of speakers:

> I remember hearing 'Timothy' before it was released on big, loud studio monitors and thought, 'Wow. This is really good. I think they might have a shot with this.

And the shot landed squarely. The song resonated commercially but also impacted other unexpected areas. One-time WBAX Music Director, David

Allen Karchner, believed that the song tapped into something more critical than the *Billboard* charts. He observed:

> 'Timothy' naturally cooled with the broad market but remained part of Northeast Pennsylvania's regional rotation long afterward. We didn't have a lot of national representation, vis-à-vis charting songs, so there was, and possibly still is, a bit of regional pride that still lingers for 'Timothy.'

Tommy James and the Shondells' bass player, Mike Vale, struck gold with hits such as "Hanky Panky" #1 (Roulette, 1966), "Crimson and Clover" #1 (Roulette, 1969), and "Crystal Blue Persuasion" #2 (Roulette, 1969), which he co-wrote. Vale, who launched the Crystal Blue Band's (Mike Vale, Mike Wilps, Eddie Gray, Ron Rosman) 50th Anniversary Tour, asserted:

> 'Timothy's' baseline was progressive for the time but a little too 'rambling' for my taste. It had a tendency to captivate the song rather than compliment it.

Fran Festa shared more than a casual relationship with the group. After The Buoys split up, he played with Chris Hanlon in Out Of the Blue and with Steve Furmanski in Grand Tour. Festa had a different take on Gryziec's bass run, viewing it with the student's adoration of a Zen master:

> Being a bassist, he is one of my heroes, one of the most badass players we've ever seen in these parts. In 'Timothy,' in particular, wow. It's an unusual song, right? So, it's worthy of an unusual bass part, which he delivered on. He could have played it safe and did all roots and fifths, and it may still have worked. We'll never know! But I love the fact that he drives the song, and dances around without getting in the way. It's a busy part but still serves the song. My current band, The Wanabees, still plays this song nearly every week, and out of sheer respect, I play his parts as faithfully as possible. It still goes over great, and we always point out to audiences who the Buoys were and the song's rightful place in both local and national history.

For some, the song was personal. The Glass Prism's Lester T. Verano said that C. Michael Wright initially wanted his group to record the song. So it was a bit surreal when he heard "Timothy" for the first time, perhaps envisioning what that might have been like to have recorded it for Scepter:

> When I finally heard the song and Bill's interpretation, I was so impressed. I thought, he was perfect for the song and his soulful expressions, especially near the end, were just the best. No one could have done it better. At that time,

Billy had a voice like no other. He was a standout. I'm glad they were successful and had a nice career.

Like many area drummers, Chris Hanlon purchased cymbals and sticks from Angelo Stella, the famed instructor. His son, Billy Angelo, performed with the Buddy Rich Band and toured with The Orlons, who had national hits with "Wah-Watusi" #2 (Cameo, 1962), "Don't Hang Up" #4 (Cameo, 1962), and "South Street" #3 (Cameo,1963). Stella has been featured in *Modern Drummer* and *DRUM! Magazine*. Stella, the owner of The Drummer's Workshop, observed that Chris Hanlon was a "solid" drummer, and not flashy like Buddy Rich or Neil Peart:

> He lays drum parts right in the pocket. Never 'overplays.' When I listen to him playing on The Buoys album, in my opinion, he is right on the money. In other words, he is performing the song, not for himself, but for the music, for the band. He plays music. His timing and technique are spot on. Lots of drummers put all these types of drum fills here and there to get noticed, but I have to say Chris is playing with the band. His drumming is perfect, especially on 'Timothy' and a beautiful part of the song.

After Hanlon's drumming and all of the other parts of "Timothy" had been recorded, Wright asked Howard Reeves to sweeten it up with overdubbed horns, strings, and precision orchestration. The result was similar to Elton John's "Madman Across the Water" (UNI, 1971), with piercing violin shrieks and an extended full orchestra fade out. Reeves, who played piano with B.J. Thomas's touring band and conducted Johnny Carson's Tonight Show Band, played an essential role in the completion of "Timothy," said Kelly:

> Reeves did indeed write the arrangements for the horns and strings on 'Timothy.' Rupert was never really happy with them. I believe he was not involved in it, so that may be why. However, I thought they brought the song to life. It sat on the shelf for about a year before they were added. Then WOW! Hitsville!

It didn't end there. Rupert Holmes re-recorded a slowed-down version of "Timothy," perhaps as he initially heard the song in his head. It was included in the five-disc *Rupert Holmes – Cast of Characters: The Rupert Holmes Songbook* CD box set (Hip-O/Universal, 2005). For those who felt that the original was overproduced, a monaural version with the strings separated is included in *The Scepter Box Set.*

11

"TIMOTHY" BANNED

T hings began to get speed-freak crazy after the 1969 Woodstock celebration. Manson, Altamont, and Vietnam smothered Aquarian love
with protest, violence, and an escalating body count on the nightly news.
It was during one of our nation's most tumultuous periods, an era of censorship and repression, that America first heard "Timothy."

"STREET FIGHTING MAN"

Chicago Mayor Richard Daley banned The Rolling Stone's "Street Fighting
Man" (London, 1968), fearing it would incite more trouble during the 1968
Democratic National Convention. Unfortunately, there was already plenty of
trouble in Chicago. The "Battle of Michigan Avenue" pitted twelve thousand
police officers and another fifteen thousand state and federal officers against
thousands of anti-war protestors in a televised bloodbath.

Years later, the tendrils of censorship writhed in a slow, snakelike motion.
The American Armed Forces Radio Network, "where the hits keep on coming," was ordered to stop playing "The Battle Hymn of Lt. Calley" (Plantation,
1971). The song became a best-seller after Lt. William Laws Calley Jr. was convicted of murdering at least twenty-two unarmed South Vietnamese civilians at
the My Lai Massacre in March 1968.

The song lamented the fate of a young soldier who served his country, only
to find that "They've made me out a villain" and "They've stamped me with a
brand." In just four days, the single sold over one million copies, was certified
gold by the RIAA, and sold nearly two million copies. Although convicted as
a war criminal, Calley was released to house arrest under orders by President
Richard Nixon. His conviction was met with widespread public outrage due to
the commonplace embedding of Viet Cong in the civilian populations. Calley
became a kind of scapegoat as the solitary officer involved in My Lai.

SCEPTER 7''		SERIES 12000		RELEASE DATE JAN. 29,1970	PREFIX AND SELECTION NO. SCE 12275
PRESSING LOCATIONS		LABEL COLOR & INK BLK. INK ON SCEPTER BACKGROUND			DATE: ORIGINAL JAN. 12,1970
EAST	MID-WEST	WEST	On Stereo version set the word "STEREO"		DATE: REVISION ✓
PITMAN TERRE HAUTE	MONARCH	On DJ version set the words "PROMOTION COPY" "NOT FOR SALE"			

NOT SET	SIDE A MATRIX NO. 61315		TIME	PUBLISHER
	** TIMOTHY ** (RUPERT HOLMES)		2:45	PLUS TWO MUSIC (ASCAP)
	ARTIST: THE BUOYS PRODUCED BY MICHAEL WRIGHT ORCHESTRATED & CONDUCTED BY HOWARD REEVES RECORDED AT SCEPTER RECORDING STUDIOS, N.Y.C.			

NOT SET	SIDE B MATRIX NO. 61316		TIME	PUBLISHER
	IT FEELS GOOD (WAYNE BRANHAM)		2:51	DRUCKER MUSIC PUB. (BMI)
	ARTIST: THE BUOYS PRODUCED BY MICHAEL WRIGHT ORCHESTRATED & CONDUCTED BY HOWARD REEVES RECORDED AT SCEPTER RECORDING STUDIOS, N.Y.C.			

A stench hung in the air. Government agencies insisted upon additional radio content restrictions. The Federal Communications Commission told the nation's broadcasters on March 6, 1971, to not "air song lyrics tending to promote or glorify the use of illegal drugs." The notice raised the threat of license withdrawal for violating the order, specifically citing lyrics promoting "the use of illegal drugs such as marijuana, LSD, 'speed,' etc." Echoing that mindset, Mongo Jerry's "Have a Whiff on Me" (Roud, 1971) was banned by the BBC due to pro-drug lyrics. The song was a cover of a Lead Belly folk song with references to cocaine use.

"BRING THE BOYS HOME"

That same year, Saigon's US Command banned Freda Payne's "Bring the Boys Home ("Bring 'em Back Alive") #12 (Invictus, 1971) from the American Forces Radio Network, claiming it would give "aid and comfort to the enemy." The song urged that "Everybody ought to lay your weapons down." The word "boys" reflected that the average age of American soldiers in Viet Nam was only nineteen.

Payne's song resonated with blacks as African Americans suffered disproportionately high casualty rates. In 1965, for example, they comprised fourteen percent of combat deaths, whereas they only comprised approximately eleven

Jerry Hludzik. (Photo courtesy of Bill Kelly Music Productions.)

percent of the US population. Moreover, of the twenty-seven million draft-age men between 1964 and 1973, Blacks often made up a disproportionate twenty-five percent or more of combat units while constituting only twelve percent of the military.

SPECIAL PROMOTIONAL SINGLES

Censorship was everywhere, with the path leading to the top of the charts impeded by increased scrutiny and regulation. Because the song was banned for "inappropriate content," "Timothy's" climb proved difficult. It languished for over two years before reaching the *Billboard* chart in late 1970. All-important airplay did not come in a majestic, thunderous roar but in scattered and sporadic spurts. As reported by the Allentown *Morning Call:*

'Timothy's' lyrics were changed three times to please producers. Even so, WABC New York still banned the song, which is allegedly about cannibalism, from its charts, while other stations "bleeped" out a naughty word here and there.

To appease the stations refusing to play the song, Scepter released two special promotional singles with the original version on the A-sides and two differently edited versions on the B-sides.

Scepter (SDR-12275) was a white-labeled promo 45. The A-side was unedited, while the B-side indicated "REVISED LYRIC" under the song title. Kelly's "My stomach was full as it could be" was changed to "Both of us fine as we could be."

Scepter (SDJ-12275) was a white-labeled promo 45. The A-side was unedited, while the B-side indicated "EDITED, BLEEPED OUT" under the song title. Kelly's "My stomach was full as it could be" was left unchanged, but the word "hell" in the second verse is distorted with a quick bleep.

Timothy revised lyrics.

At least four powerhouse stations, including Chicago's WLS, refused to give the song a proper spin. In addition, former WARM disc jockey Jim Drucker, owner of "Timothy's" flip side, "It Feels Good," on his Drucker Publishing Company label, had a personal interest in the ban and resultant controversy:

> WABC's Rick Sklar, the number one Program Director in the United States, refused to play 'Timothy' because of 'inappropriate content.' The RKO chain of radio stations, Boston's WRKO, New York City's WOR, and Philadelphia RKO stations were also forbidden to play the record.

Another influential powerhouse was the Drake-Chenault chain of stations. As an example of their clout, DC may have purposively doomed Tina Turner's majestic "River Deep, Mountain High" #88 (Phillies, 1966), as detailed in her book *I, Tina*. Owner Bill Drake, who lived in Los Angeles, was angry because somebody shipped a copy of the song to Johnny Hayes at KRLA, the most crucial station in Los Angeles, and not to Drake's station KHJ. Drake and many others refused to get behind the song because of a blatant dislike for Phil Spector. It became a perfect opportunity to turn the tables on the "Wall of Sound" producer, even though "River Deep, Mountain High," with Tina's flamethrower vocals, is considered a true musical masterpiece. *Rolling Stone* had ranked it No. 33 on its list of the 500 Greatest Songs of All Time and recognized by The Rock and Roll Hall of Fame on its list of the 500 Songs That Shaped Rock and Roll.

WABC

Scepter needed radio airplay if "Timothy" was going to break out, and WABC, the #1 Radio Station in the World, was the mother lode of New York's major-market stations. WABC's 50,000-clear-channel signal was heard across the Hudson River and halfway across the country from its broadcasting tower in Lodi, New Jersey. The other major NYC players were the all-talk format WMCA, the MOR-oriented WNEW, and 66 WNBC-AM. WABC Musicradio 77 was the only game in town.

Jim Drucker argued that if other radio corporations had promoted the song and placed it on regular rotation, it would have climbed another eight notches into the coveted Top Ten. Drucker clarified:

> If WABC alone had aired "Timothy," it would have sold in excess of one-half million records! Also, if the RKO Chain had played 'Timothy,' we would have had a two million-seller easily. I know, because I personally called all of my brother's music directors at major markets.

The Buoys were well aware of the burning debate raging around their hit song, as Brozena recalled:

> Many radio stations did ban the song. The one that comes to my mind is WABC in New York City. It's ironic that New York City was then, and is now, regarded as a hotbed of liberalism! I remember other stations that would not play the record. I know there were quite a few.

THE TIMOTHY CONTEST

Florence Greenberg claimed she had no idea that the song was about cannibalism and launched a "Timothy was a Mule" contest. Most savvy radio listeners refused to buy into that sanitized explanation, assuming that Scepter was playing them for fools. Rupert Holmes agreed:

> Scepter Records started a rumor that Timothy was a mule to try to get the taint of cannibalism out of the picture and try to make it a Top Ten record. Someone called me and said, 'Was Timothy a mule? You wrote it.' And I said, 'No, what can I tell you? They ate him.'

Scepter stoked the fire of teen frenzy with their incipient "Who was Timothy? A mule? A canary? A man?" contest. Realizing they could exploit the controversy, they placed ads in *Billboard* and *Cashbox* magazines promoting a "Timothy Contest" and resurfaced the record issuing a record sleeve of a donkey.

Music historian Cary Pall viewed the partial hysteria as a catalyst for a strange regional mythology and noted:

> Frankly, 'Timothy's' one of my favorite songs of the late '60s-early '70s pop era. At the time, I was surprised at all the anecdotes about the storyline. The word at the time from Scepter was that 'Timothy,' while appearing to refer to a third miner, was, in fact, a reference to the miners' donkey. Since this wasn't made apparent in the lyrics, the cannibalism theme was born. Kind of like a Northeastern Pennsylvania spin on the 'Paul Is Dead' myth.

"Timothy" lurked inside the teen psyche, embedded in its gray matter. WPGA's Rock Crumless referenced an earlier musical puzzle. Bobbie Gentry's "Ode to Billie Joe" #1 (Capitol, 1967) posed the question about what really happened, said Crumless:

> What exactly did Billie Joe McAllister and his girlfriend throw off the Tallahatchie Bridge? Was it a ring, a locket, flowers, a draft card, a bottle of LSD pills, or an aborted baby? And why did Billie Joe later commit suicide by jumping into the dark waters of the Tallahatchie River?

Yes, it was only a song, but a song that provoked controversy and sundry theories about its meaning—much like the song "Timothy."

With the "Tim is Dead" campaign, the enduring hullabaloo afforded a successful marketing strategy, applauded by The Buoys lead singer Bill Kelly:

> I remember that plenty of stations banned the song while others requested a different version to get them to play it. One version bleeped the word 'hell,' and another had me singing a new line near the end. It was very silly, but it certainly helped sales. You can't tell a teenager they can't listen to something! That only adds fuel to the fire. And it did. The public hungered for more.

It was a puzzle within a puzzle. While Scepter played games with "Who Was Timothy," the radio listening public was asking, "Did they really eat him?" Stations that refused to play the song probably triggered a demand for the product, opening up a strategy for Scepter to exploit. Former KRZ Saturday Night Live at the Oldies host Shadoe Steele explained:

If you wanted to get a song played on coveted AM Top-40 radio in 1971, just tell those listeners calling your request line that the station refuses to play it. That positively ensures your phones won't stop ringing until you add 'Timothy' to the station's hourly playlist rotation!

Michael Kuzmin, a researcher of obscure Pennsylvania garage bands, argued that there is no blatant reference to cannibalism in the lyrics, just suggestiveness:

> Listening to The Buoys' hit record before writing this, I was more surprised no one made an issue of the words 'God' or 'hell' in the lyrics. I never noticed that on the radio in 1971. But I guess most people catch onto a song through its music rather than words. It is incredible how hard it sometimes is to understand all of the words in a tune despite good production, even hit records. But we still run those songs through our heads even if we use some incorrect lyrics.

Rupert Holmes believed that before "Timothy" was banned, fickle program directors played the song because it had a nice Creedence Clearwater rhythm:

> It was catchy enough, but then they'd hear what the song was about and say, 'We can't be playing this; it's about cannibalism!' and they'd pull the song off the air. The kids would call in and say, 'Why'd you pull the song off the air,' and they'd say, 'Because it's disgusting, you shouldn't be listening to stuff like that.' Well, all you have to do is tell a teenage kid that he shouldn't be listening to something because it's disgusting and vile and loathsome, and he'll demand it.

B. Derek Shaw observed that the early 1970s' music scene was filled with all types of experimentation. "Timothy" was unusual because it was musically up-tempo and lyrically solemn and popular because it was well produced and orchestrated:

> Yes, the song was banned in many markets because of the theme and because of the lyrics. 'Hell' and 'damn' in 1971 were still very offensive words, at least in the minds of the FCC. Radio stations felt they had to self-police to avoid the wrath of the FCC. Interestingly, six months earlier that year, All in the Family debuted on CBS, paving the way for more lax censorship of words and thoughts.

The song was not banned everywhere, and where you lived in the early 1970s provided an important lesson in geography, as explained by Holmes:

Whenever people talk about 'Timothy,' I always say, 'Where did you come from?' Because that always lets me know. If they were from Florida, it was big there. If they were from Pennsylvania, very big. Texas, they know it. But if you're from New York, you've never heard of it.

"Timothy" may have been even more popular than Holmes realized. It received heavy airplay on New York state radio stations such as Utica, Rome, Syracuse, and especially Buffalo, where it had frequent airplay at WKBW.

Although banned by major U.S. stations, the song gained popularity, ascending the *Billboard* and *Cashbox* charts. WRNJ radio talk show host Rich Appel saw things with a keen professional eye:

> Possibly, the only major city in the US where both top 40 stations did play it was Detroit, where it got to #4 on CKLW and #3 on WKNR. It was first in Pittsburgh on KQV, #8 on WCFL in Chicago, and I believe it was first or close in Buffalo's WKBW and Syracuse's WHEN.

A ton of political and pragmatic algorithms went into slotting a record into the "regular rotation" stack. Former WBAX Music Director David Allen Karchner saw that first-hand:

> 'Timothy's' success lies in the writing skills of Rupert. A lesser composer might have been more direct and less subtle. Instead, the 'tasteful' lyrics were the keys to the *Billboard* charts. As to programming for airplay, back in those days, there were far fewer syndicated stations. As Music Director for WBAX, I based playlists on listener response, format considerations, local record sales, and *Billboard* charting.

Karchner said that smaller stations had more flexibility and fewer restrictions on their program selections. And on that note, music critic Richard Chisak disagreed that the song was being denied airplay, especially in his backyard:

> I don't think any local pop stations banned the record. WARM probably was the most conservative of all the local Top 40 stations, and they were playing it, so I'm pretty sure all the others were too.

In the 1970s, the success of any record was predicated on the amount of airplay it received from powerful AM stations. AM wielded an uncanny Rasputin-like influence upon legions of teenage Baby Boomers, a group of seventy-seven million youths fixated on transistor radios, 45-RPM records, and popular teen idols. Across the nation, AM radio was all about spinning "hot wax," generating hype, airplay, and controversy. Airplay meant record sales, concerts, and interviews. It meant money, money, and more money, and the fact that "Timothy" was actively promoted at WARMLAND was conceivably one of The Buoys' most potent weapons. Regular rotation with WARM's Sensational Seven (including "Little" Joey Shaver, Harry West, and Tommy Woods) and continued airplay at WARM-sponsored record hops helped fuel excitement for the record.

One such event at Rocky Glen Park drew over twenty-five thousand people to see their favorite WARM personalities spinning hot wax. WARM was a test market, a grand and dynamic experiment that had its finger on the pulse of Teenage America, with the ability to make or break a record, as *Times-Leader* writer Bill O'Boyle explained:

> WARM had sixty percent to seventy percent of the radio listening audience tuned in every day in its heyday. The powerful 5,000-watt station reached beyond Wilkes-Barre, Scranton, and Hazleton—its signal pierced the air all the way to Manhattan, Philadelphia, and Binghamton.

Although "Timothy" found itself trapped within the censorship insanity, banned by some stations and enthusiastically played by others, so, too, was the "pornographic" song "Louie Louie."

12

"LOUIE, LOUIE"

T he songs "Timothy" and "Louie Louie," part of the Scepter/Wand catalog, did their share to stoke individual controversies. In their comprehensive *The Scepter/Wand Story*, researchers Mike Callahan and David Edwards cited "Timothy's" radio censorship and the resulting uproar:

> In the firestorm of protest and radio banning that followed, Holmes offered that Timothy was a mule, so it wasn't what it seemed, but the stigma was there. The rumored sexual lyrics of 'Louie Louie' were one thing, but cannibalism quite another.

Callahan and Edwards were totally wrong about Holmes. The songwriter knew what his song was about and never referred to "Timothy" as an animal. "They ate him," Holmes said. Plain and simple. Timothy was a human being. Still, Scepter/Wand knew the magnitude of the controversy. Teenage angst and corporate record sales were as interconnected as high school kids and chewing gum. "Timothy" and "Louie Louie" pitted conservative voices against free thinkers touting First Amendment rights.

CRAZY TRAIN

Florence Greenberg purchased the rights to "Louie, Louie" (Jerden, 1963) from Jerry Dennon, who had produced the tape recording for his small Seattle-based label. The primitive song was one of the earliest examples of raw, primal garage rock. Unfortunately, Jack Ely's lead vocals were garbled and incomprehensible, suggesting "dirty lyrics" if one were listening for them.

The Scepter Records Story (Capricorn, 1992), a three-disc retrospective, contained hits by the Shirelles, the Isley Brothers, and the Buoys. Included in the box set was a 30-page booklet, in which Greenburg reflected on "Louie, Louie," her biggest hit:

> People thought it had dirty lyrics, which was the biggest lie in the world. Those rumors started when some kid played it on a record player at 78 rpm instead of 45 rpm. And it seemed like the words of the song changed into obscenities. I got hundreds of letters saying. 'How dare you put this out!'

"Louie, Louie" became the focal point in the debate over obscenity and censorship. Radio stations across the country banned it, and, going a step further, Matthew Welsh, the Governor of Indiana, declared the song "pornographic." Though admitting the song's lyrics were unintelligible, Welsh said the disc "made his ears tingle" and encouraged radio stations in his state to ban the song.

The FBI initiated a thirty-one-month investigation of the song, concluding that they could not interpret the accurate lyrics. Still, the Kingsmen's drummer, Lynn Easton, later confessed to yelling "fuck" during the song's recording after dropping a drumstick. Blurring the lines further, the band attempted to cover up any possible sexual content by slurring the lyrics during live performances.

After sophomoric college students altered the lyrics, changing them into vulgar and sexually charged stanzas, the song became a cult sensation. On the strength of this secretive underground following, "Louie, Louie" rocketed up the national charts landing at the #2 spot on *Billboard* on December 14, 1963, remaining on the charts for 18 outrageous weeks.

The song, written by Richard Berry, was an innocent love song with a driving rock beat, but you couldn't tell that to the fans or critics. "Louie" rode the crazy train of controversy, burning down the house in the heated debate surrounding free speech. "Louie" became the most controversial and best-selling record in the Scepter/Wand catalog. In 2007, *Rolling Stone* declared it the "#4 most influential recording of all time."

13

FILTHY FIFTEEN

I t did not end with "Timothy" and "Louie, Louie," as radio censorship played on, repeating the same old soundtrack of repression and intervention. It didn't matter if the topic was sex, drugs, or cannibalism. Lou Christie's "Rhapsody in the Rain" (MGM, 1966) and the Byrds' "Eight Miles High" (Columbia, 1966) both faced radio censorship for allegedly dealing too explicitly with sex and drugs, respectively.

The Stalinist iron fist continued into the 1980s. Although Frank Zappa was recognized as a highly accomplished musician, his most outstanding achievement was to advocate for free speech in popular music. He intelligently and skillfully debated prominent conservative voices such as John Lofton, columnist for the Washington Times, and Tipper Gore.

Mary Elizabeth "Tipper" Gore was the second lady of the United States (1993 to 2001) and former wife of Al Gore, the 45th vice president of the United States. Listening to a copy of Prince's *Purple Rain* (Warner Bros, 1984) with her eleven-year-old daughter, Gore was offended with the track "Darling Nikki," which included a line about a "sex fiend masturbating with a magazine."

Because of that song, Gore co-founded the Parents Music Resource Center (PMRC), advocating for advisory labels on album covers featuring profane language. The PMRC took an uncompromising look at the heavy metal, punk and hip-hop genres and identified fifteen songs—the so-called "Filthy Fifteen"—as obscene.

The barbarians charged at the gates, clutching their list of dirty songs: Prince's "Darling Nikki" (1984), Sheena Easton's "Sugar Walls" (1984), Judas Priest's "Eat Me Alive" (1984), Vanity's "Strap On Robbie Baby" (1984), Motley Crue's "Bastard" (1983), AC/DC's "Let Me Put My Love Into You" (1980), and Twisted Sister's "We're Not Gonna Take It" (1984).

The remaining songs were Madonna's "Dress You Up" (1984), WASP's "Animal (F—k Like A Beast)" (1984), Def Leppard's "High 'n' Dry" (1981), Mercyful Fate's "Into The Coven" (1983), Black Sabbath's "Trashed" (1983), Mary Jane Girl's "In My House" (1985), Venom's "Possessed" (1985), and Cyndi Lauper's "She Bop" (1983).

The Senate's Committee on Commerce, Science and Transportation became involved in the controversy and held a hearing on September 19, 1985. After the PMRC presented its case about the warning labels, Frank Zappa, Twisted Sister's Dee Snider, and John Denver testified. Zappa said, "If it looks like censorship and it smells like censorship, it is censorship, no matter whose wife is talking about it," referring to Al Gore's wife. Snider argued that it was a direct infringement of civil liberties, and John Denver equated the censorship to Nazi book burnings in the 1940s.

Gore's campaign might have scored points with community PTAs, but those warning stickers placed on records were akin to using gasoline to smother a fire. Motley Crue's Vince Neil said years later: "Once you put that sticker on, that parental-warning sticker, that album took off. Those kids wanted it even more."

During his statement to the Senate's Committee, Zappa sidestepped pop music advocacy, articulating a more comprehensive message:

> Children in the vulnerable age bracket have a natural love for music. If, as a parent, you believe they should be exposed to something more uplifting than 'Sugar Walls,' support Music Appreciation programs in schools. Music Appreciation costs very little compared to sports expenditures. Your children have a right to know that something besides pop music exists.

As a result of the PMRC campaign, albums were required to include warning labels. By August 1985, nineteen record companies agreed to place "Parental Guidance: Explicit Lyrics" labels on specific albums. The PMRC even devised its own "porn rock" rating system, with an "X" for profane or sexually explicit lyrics, "O" for occult references, "D/A" for lyrics about drugs and alcohol, and "V" for violent content.

Ostensibly, if Tipper Gore had conjured her "Filthy Fifteen" years earlier, "Timothy" and "Louie, Louie" would have received their own parental warning labels.

14

THE WORST SONG EVER

Rock music has never shied away from sex, drugs, and the forty miles of bad road leading to self-annihilation. Since its primal beginnings, rock has screamed and moaned teenage angst, at times straying increasingly deeper into the dark morass of Freudian complexities.

Once forbidden topics, including incest, can be found between the grooves of the 45 RPM. Aerosmith's "Janie's Got a Gun (Geffen, 1989), The Doors' "The End" (Elektra, 1967), and Megadeth's "Family Tree" (Capitol, 1994), as well as Joni Mitchell's "Cherokee Louise" (Geffen, 1991), Pearl Jam's "Alive" (Epic, 1991), Prince's "Sister" (Warner Brothers, 1980), Scorpion's "Daddy's Girl" (Mercury, 1993) and Steely Dan's "Cousin Dupree" (Giant, 1999) are samplings of forbidden familial secrets.

Other songs present despondent ideas wrapped within a gauze of lightness and joy, the realm of the mainstream pop tune. Tom Reynolds compiled "the fifty-two most depressing songs you've ever heard" in *I Hate Myself and Want to Die*. Among these are songs of car accidents such as Ray Peterson's "Tell Laura I Love Her (RCA, 1960), Mark Dinning's "Teen Angel" (MGM, 1959), and J. Frank Wilson and the Cavaliers "Last Kiss" (Josie, 1964), and also songs about drugs, such as Billy Joel's "Captain Jack" (Columbia, 1973), Nine Inch Nails' "Hurt" (Interscope, 1995), (later covered by Johnny Cash) and Marianne Faithfull's "Sister Morphine" (Decca, 1969).

Within the secular universe of rock, there is a cluster of the vilest of songs, representing not just a violation of established norms but a dramatic crossing of the line. "Timothy," considered perhaps the worst in this morbid cluster, does not stand alone.

A macabre collection of recordings, known only to vinyl zealots, have embraced cannibalism as a musical theme. These offerings include The Cadets' re-working of "Stranded in the Jungle" (Modern, 1956), which consists of the line, "I smelled something cooking, and I looked to see, that's when I found out they were cooking me." Chicago's Four Sounds sang their obscure "Mama Ubangi-Bangi" (Ran-Dee,1962), which cautioned, "Look out if she says you look good enough to eat." "I Want My Baby Back," by Jimmy Cross (Holly, 1965), deals with a boy who digs up the grave of his decomposed girlfriend. Screamin' Jay Hawkins' "Feast of the Mau Mau" (Philips,1967), Roky Erickson's "I Walked with a Zombie" (CBS, 1980), and Total Coelo's "I Eat Cannibals" (Razor & Tie, 1982) all presented similar variations on a theme.

"TIMOTHY" AND "DOA."

Was "Timothy" the worst rock song ever recorded, and can The Buoys claim that dubious award? Maybe not. In Dave Barry's *Book of Bad Songs* (1997), the author listed "Timothy" at #5, right after Bobby Goldsboro's "Honey" (United Artists, 1968) and just before Billy Ray Cyrus's "Achy Breaky Heart" (PolyGram, 1992). Barry noted that "Timothy" was a song intentionally written for shock value as a publicity stunt. Sarcastically and to the point, he observed that "Timothy" was "a song about—really—three trapped miners, two of whom wind up EATING the third."

However, WHLM Music Historian Cary Pall has argued that "Timothy" doesn't come close to copping the hypothetical prize:

> In my opinion, it's not even close. "DOA" (Capitol, 1971) by Bloodrock (a song about an airplane crash victim and his girlfriend dying on the way to the hospital) graphically described the last moments before death. I find a seven-minute ode to "Cocaine" (RSO, 1980) by Eric Clapton much more

BLOODROCK
PLUS: THE BUOYS
IN CONCERT
8:00 P.M. DECEMBER 3 FRIDAY NIGHT
ST. JOSEPH'S GYM (5th and Laurel Sts.)
Tickets $4.00 in advance from: SKI'S ELECTRONICS, MORATTO & LeSANTE'S MUSIC SHOP, BEEF 'N' BREW, HIGHACRES
All Tickets at the door $5.00 — No Reserved Seats

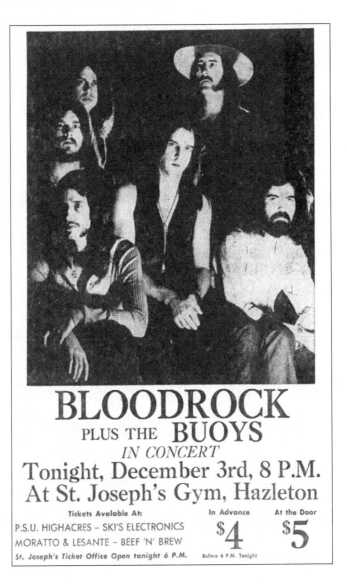

BLOODROCK
PLUS THE BUOYS
IN CONCERT
Tonight, December 3rd, 8 P.M.
At St. Joseph's Gym, Hazleton

Tickets Available At: In Advance   At the Door
P.S.U. HIGHACRES – SKI'S ELECTRONICS
MORATTO & LESANTE – BEEF 'N' BREW $4 $5
St. Joseph's Ticket Office Open tonight 6 P.M.   Before 6 P.M. Tonight

offensive. Alice Cooper, in the same era as The Buoys, had many disturbing songs in their repertoire. Check out "Ballad of Dwight Fry" (*Love it To Death* LP; Warner, 1971) sometime. Sung from the viewpoint of Mr. Fry, a person with a mental health condition being tortured by his captors, the picture it paints is just plain scary.

Even though "DOA," like "Timothy," was banned by many US radio stations, the single still reached #36 on *Billboard*, indicating that bloody plane crashes and flesh-eating were acceptable themes among college intelligentsia. As proof, two of the leading proponents of "deathrock," The Buoys and Bloodrock, described as a "pounding six-man band," played a double-bill at Penn State's St. Joseph Auditorium. James Tarone, the Hazleton representative of Celebration Music, attempted to defend the December 3, 1971, double-bill:

> The local concert is of the type that is currently popular on college campuses throughout the nation. The shows have proved so successful that many colleges hold one every month.

But why? What is the appeal of such downbeat themes of despair and loss? Clinical psychologist Paul Costa noted that most popular song lyrics revolve around generally positive, emotionally evocative aspects of the human experience, and he questions how "Timothy," with such implied horrifically morbid content, became popular with the younger generation:

> Ultimately, the question of why humans would intentionally seek out popular music entertainment with morbid themes is seemingly an anthropological paradox. We already know that humans consistently report enjoying hearing positive news instead of negative news. Yet, conclusive research indicates that people will always maintain longer sustained attention when exposed to negative news in contrast to positive news. The interpretation of this apparent paradox is both anthropological and sociobiological in nature: It alerts our primitive survival instincts to a possible danger.

That danger, Costa believes, lies in our quest for sordid entertainment, such as "Timothy" and "DOA." It has been going on for at least two or three thousand years and may satisfy some psychological need for us as a species. He lists four possible reasons why we expose ourselves to otherwise repulsive or negatively themed media:

> 1.) To commiserate with the characters due to shared experiences. 2.) To learn effective versus ineffective ways of handling adverse circumstances vicariously and thus safely, consuming such fare in vitro instead of in vivo. 3.) To form socio-cultural bonds with the subculture of other consumers. 4.) To engage in a form of social comparison in which we basically feel grateful that we are not the victim.

Costa concludes that these songs represent another step in expanding popular media past the boundaries of social acceptability. Still, psychological theory or not, it remains perplexing as to why one would purposively choose such unpleasant fare for entertainment purposes.

WAR-TORN WORLD

"Timothy" provided a convenient distraction from the Vietnam War that spanned two decades and traumatized the nation. Boomers dwelt in a shell-shocked, war-torn world that had hardened their hearts. Seasoned music critic Richard Chisak, who actively followed the career of The Buoys and attended the 1980 Radio City Music Hall Queen-Dakota concert, believed that Baby Boomers (1946-1964) weren't a naïve or easily shocked generation:

> The idea of a song obliquely referring to cannibalism really wasn't that shocking to my friends or me, especially in 1970. Remember, we'd already had a naked Beatle on an album cover, and we'd been through Woodstock and Kent State. Battlefield scenes from Vietnam were on the evening news every evening. I think authorities were more concerned with anti-war lyrics or lyrics about drugs creeping into pop songs. As if only lyrics about cannibalism were all they had to worry about.

Berwick sports historian Fred Takacs agreed with Chisak's assessment. In the late spring of 1971, Takacs was commuting to the Penn State Hazleton campus, riding along in his friend's 1963 Plymouth Valiant. Because of the high altitude, they were able to pick up WABC-AM, home to DJs Harry Harrison and Dan Ingram, Takacs recalled:

> One day 'Timothy' came on, and we recognized the song because The Buoys had played at a Berwick YMCA dance. It was a good song and cool that a local group hit the Top 40 Charts, finishing at #87 on the *Billboard* Top 100 for the year. As I recall, there was no controversy about the lyrics. Our real concern focused on the daily carnage of American troops thousands of miles away in Vietnam.

Scott Campbell, a columnist for The Arizona *Republic*, also connected the song to the times, concluding:

> Many Top 40 songs are interesting sociological documents. Leaving the syrupy teenage sentiment of yesteryear far behind, today's songwriters dig deep to come up with provocative, hard-hitting lyrics, which get right to the heart of society's most pressing problems. Most original offering in some time is a Top 10 ditty called 'Timothy,' in which two companions trapped in a caved-in

mine fight off starvation by devouring their third companion. It sure beats 'Puppy Love.'

BUBBLEGUM CANNIBAL POP

"Puppy Love" and "Timothy" were worlds apart. Yet, some reviewers errone-ously labeled The Buoys "bubble gum," and others used the term "bubblegum cannibal pop," a distasteful concept that The Buoys could not stomach. But words are cheap and opinions many.

Near-sighted columnists, ignorant of the group's potential, charged that the group was only a flash-in-the-pan "bubblegum" band. This was based on sev-eral misperceptions. First, Scepter's unfocused promotional attempts presented amateur photos of the Buoys. Second, they lacked the hard-edged, cool-looking persona of "authentic" front-line rockers, looking more like truant school kids.

Yet, the first song they recorded was an apparent attempt to capitalize on the trendy "bubble gum" craze. Steve Furmanski recalled that Scepter was look-ing for a band to do a bubble gum song and that the obnoxious "bubble gum" tag "came from "Smackin' Good Lovin,'" a blues song that they gave an Archie's bubble gum treatment:

> At that time, bubble gum music was popular, and to get a record on the charts, Scepter wanted us to do it. I didn't want to do it. I was outvoted on that one. So, we did it anyway, and I guess that's how we got that reputation.

Despite the stereotyping of the band, the song turned out to be a sound recording. It was co-produced by C. Michael Wright and Bob O' Connell. Bob Gryziac laid down the bass parts on "Smackin' Good Lovin" and agreed:

> We didn't pick it. Michael Wright picked it. That's why it was only a demo. We never picked it. In the original version, some blues band was doing it, and it was a soul thing that they wanted us to do 'bubblegum.' They wanted us to interpret it as a bubblegum song. Someone, one of the powers that be, or Michael, or one of the guys, thought it would be a hit if it were a bubblegum side. It really isn't bad.

"Smackin' Good Lovin'" was The Buoys' first recorded song for Scepter and was met with collective enthusiasm. The entire group jumped at the opportu-nity to record in a major studio, recollected Brozena:

> We threw everything in there but the kitchen sink, doot-doots, and bop-bops. The demo originally had a great R&B feel, very soulful. We did some ugly things to it.

The result was an acceptable first-time studio venture for the Wilkes-Barre group. Gryziac added:

> The demo version we heard of it sounded like Stevie Winwood with the Spencer Davis Group. But Scepter wanted it done as a bubblegum tune. It was supposed to be a single, but they chose 'These Days' instead.

Andy Bergey rejected the premise that the song fit the bubblegum classification. And Bergey should know. As the *Classic Bubblegum Music*'s Editor and Historian, he rejected the Buoy's bubblegum tag:

> 'Timothy' is a clever song that fits neatly into the Novelty genre. If it has been classified as a Bubblegum song, it shouldn't have. It doesn't appeal to that pre-teen crowd; it has a subject matter that is clearly not fit for gum, and, ultimately, it doesn't "sound" gummy. I've always compared it to story-songs like 'Werewolf' by Five Man Electrical Band and 'Swamp Witch' by Jim Stafford—all gimmicky but not gum.

Music authority B. Derek Shaw doesn't buy into The Buoys "bubblegum" persona, contending that it is historically incorrect:

> Actually, bubblegum music's heyday was five years prior, with mainly studio bands like The Ohio Express, The Lemon Pipers, The 1910 Fruitgum Company, The Archies, The Monkees, and even Tommy Roe. This type of music appealed to the pre-teen audience who had limited cash for an LP but could afford a 45 single. 'Timothy' is more straight-ahead rock and roll.

Name-calling abounded. While "Timothy" was called "the worst song ever recorded" and The Buoys labeled "one-hit wonders," the taunt that cut the deepest was when they were called "bubble gum."

PART IV

THE OUTLIERS 1

15

THE WHAZOOS AND GREAT BEAR

Hermann Hesse's Siddhartha, a 1922 novel about self-discovery, could have been written about the nomadic Bob Gryziec. As one of the founding members of The Buoys, he left them in 1965 to join The Whazoos, rejoined The Buoys in 1969, playing on "Timothy," and left once again.

★ ★ ★

The Whazoos (L-R): Top, Paul Metzger; Bottom, Bob Gryziec; Left, Mike Boback; Right, Joe Scovish.

Len Brader managed the Whazoos (Mike Boback, keyboards; Paul Metzger, drums; Joe Scovish, guitar; Bob Gryziec, bass guitar, and Barry Rogers, guitar) who, for years, performed at East Coast colleges, bazaars, and summer dances. They worked all of the venues of the day, including Moosic's Rocky Glen Park and a host of other dance spots, and played a double bill with The Buoys at Sans Souci Park on July 19, 1969, and other headliners. First, the Whazoos opened for The McCoy's, Drifters, and Blues Magoos. Then, they warmed up for Easton, Pennsylvania's Cyrkle, who scored the #2 hit "Red Rubber Ball" (Columbia, 1966).

"INSIDE OF ME"

The Whazoos were part of an amazing musical experiment, following in the wake of 1967's *Sgt Pepper's, Disraeli Gears, Are You Experienced*, The Doors, Moby Grape, and The Velvet Underground and Nico, as well as numerous other brilliant examples. They thrived in an era encouraging innovation and forages into uncharted territory, all part of a wild cultural essence that gave birth to one of the most creative periods in popular music. For example, Boback played a Rock-Si-Chord, an electronic keyboard that sounded like the harpsichord, associated with renaissance and baroque music. The Rock-Si-Chord was invented in 1967 by Rocky Mount Instruments of Macungie, Pennsylvania. It was designed specifically for rock music because a standard acoustic harpsichord would be overpowered and drowned out by the other instruments. Boback got the idea from a Philadelphia band, the Mandrake Memorial, which also used the device.

"Inside of Me" #12 (National, 1968) was a psychedelic rave-up with fuzzy distortion and reverb suggesting the musical domain of "Pictures of Matchstick Men" (Cadet Con., 1968). But, again, Boback wrote and sang the tune. The flip side was a cover of Sir Douglas Quintet's "The Rains Came" (Tribe, 1966), with Metzger's lead vocals.

Joe Scovish used a Jordan Fuzz-Tone plugged into his Gibson SG to produce a distorted sound on the recording. The only other device marketed was the Gibson Maestro Fuzz-Tone used by Keith Richards in the Rolling Stones "Satisfaction" (London, 1965). The Jordan version was smaller, had more

LAST BIG WEEK OF DANCING
Newton Lake Park
— TONITE —
THE WAZOOS
SATURDAY: Rhythm Blues Inc.
SUNDAY: Mel Wynn
LABOR DAY: Blue Horizons
DANCING 8:30 to 12
Newton Lake Park

sustain, and was conveniently plugged into the guitar. The larger Maestro used a floor pedal. Jordan was a relatively unknown California company that manufactured amplifiers. The Association, who recorded "Along Comes Mary" #7 (Valiant, 1966), was one of the first groups to use Jordan amps.

Whazoos' member Barry Rogers added his Les Paul guitar and vocals to the recording session. He said:

> I played on both tracks and sang all the high parts on the B Side, Sir Douglas Quintet's 'The Rains Came.' Paul sang lead on that. I was hired as a lead singer, but I had just joined the band right before that. Former Whazoo Rick Belza also played keyboards on the B side.
>
> Joe (Scovish) and I did many double leads, which were popular in those days. Joe had an old plug-in fuzz he used in that song, like a Maestro or something similar.

VIRTUE RECORDING STUDIO
The songs were cut at Frank Virtue's Studio, noted for a great library of Philly soul tunes. Classic R&B hits recorded at the studio included Barbara Mason's "Yes I'm Ready" #4 (Arctic, 1965), Cliff Nobles and Company's "The Horse" #2 (Phil-LA of Soul, 1968), and Eddie Holman's "Hey There Lonely Girl" #2 (ABC, 1970).

The gun-toting Frank Virtue was the founding member of The Virtues, who scored an instrumental hit called "Guitar Boogie Shuffle" #5 (Hunt, 1959). His Virtue Recording Studios, located at 1618 N. Broad Street, was founded in 1963 and became one of the top studios in Philadelphia. The flat fee of $300 to $500 included recording two songs, plus a 45 pressed on either the artist's own label or the Virtue house label. Boback remembered that Virtue Recording was a "nice studio—not fancy." It had good separation, a decent piano, a drum kit, and a Hammond organ.

The recording studio was a happening place with lots of action. Frank Virtue, an avid gun collector, had constructed a sound-proof shooting range inside the studio, and an unlikely cluster of gun enthusiasts and musicians often congregated alongside each other.

During their recording session, Metzer was ushered out of the room to play cowbell on another session. Interestingly, the same thing happened when they were at Scepter recording the Great Bear LP. Only this time, Boback was asked to play tom-tom on a track for Wadsworth Mansion's "Sweet Mary" #7 (Sussex, 1970). It was a percussion track with cowbell, tambourine, tom-tom, and a chance in a lifetime for Boback to contribute to a Top Ten hit.

PROCOL HARUM

One of The Whazoos' most memorable events was opening for the progressive English rock group Procol Harum; Gary Brooker, Matthew Fisher, David Knights, Robin Trower, B.J. Wilson, and lyricist Keith Reid.

Procol Harum's biggest hit was "Whiter Shade of Pale" #5 (Deram, 1967). It sold over ten million copies, was the Summer of Love's biggest hit, and one of the best compositions to come out of the decade. "Whiter Shade" was John Lennon's favorite song. Obsessed over Reid's haunting lyrics, he played it incessantly. It was the only song that Paul McCartney said he wished that he had written. In 2018, the Rock and Roll Hall of Fame inducted the song into the brand-new Singles category.

Located on Betty Street in Archbald, Tipper's A-Go-Go was just north of Scranton. It was known for its revolving stage and zealous fans. During this early tour promoting their monster single, Procol Harum traveled in a rented van (and not a larger box truck) with minimum equipment. Tipper's A-Go-Go had to provide the acoustic piano, and Procol Harum borrowed the Whazoos' PA system, Boback recalled.

While Gary Brooker played piano and did the cryptic lead vocals, Matthew Fisher's Hammond B3 organ hinted at the sounds of a majestic religious ceremony. Regrettably, the Procol Harum performance was a mixed bag of audience response. Not everyone was interested in progressive rock and instead preferred gratuitous three-chord dance music. Still, for Whazoos' guitarist Barry Rogers, it was a night of music and fellowship:

> What I remember is what great musicians the Procol Harum were. Gary Brooker was the friendliest. I spent some time with their sound guys that night. One of them told me that Robin wanted to buy my '52 Les Paul that I used that night. I didn't sell that, but the sound guy did ask to buy my new Moby Grape *Grape Jam* album that I bought on the way up. I did sell that (with no profit). We loved them, but the crowd didn't like them. They did 'Whiter Shade of Pale' and 'Homburg' and then mostly loud bluesy stuff. Top Forty was king in those days, and that's only what some people wanted to hear.

Sunday Dispatch writer Jack Smiles, in his article "How I Rocked My Life Away," reminisced about that evening:

> There was a place in Archbald called Tipper's A-Go-Go. There I saw the Lemon Pipers (Green Tangerine) #1 (Buddah, 1968) and Procol Harum (A Whiter Shade of Pale). My friends and I actually met the Procol Harum guys. We talked to them for a while, but with the British accents, the only words I could understand were the four-letter ones, and there were lots of them.

Smiles also documented that The Whazoos did a killer version of The Swingin' Medallions' "Double Shot (Of My Baby's Love)" #17 (Smash, 1966), in which the lead singer lay on the floor and spun around like Curley of the Three Stooges.

SCEPTER CONTRACT

Because Gryziec was still under contract with Scepter, leaving the Buoys and joining the Whazoos presented a potential problem. Said Gryziac:

> The Whazoos asked me to play with them, but I was still under contract with Scepter. I had never got a release. So, I said to them, 'You're going to have to clear that with Scepter.' They were going to sign with Scepter, so it was a weird thing. I was still signed with The Buoys. I had never gotten a release from The Buoys. The Whazoos called me to play with them. They called Michael Wright and talked with the people at Scepter, and they said, 'that's all right.'

Absence makes the heart grow fonder. The following year, in 1969, Gryziec rejoined The Buoys, recorded "Timothy," but didn't stick around to celebrate the song's eventual success. Instead, he left the Buoys in August of 1969 to play with Child, a Brooklyn-based heavy-rock group who had just released an album on Musicor Records. Unfortunately, Gryziec only played with the five-piece Child for about four months, falling victim to failed expectations. Child's promised Florida tour never materialized, relegating the band to New York City gigs like the Action House.

Enough was enough. Gryziec left Child, disheartened, but in the spring of 1970 rejoined The Whazoos, who were just signing with Scepter Records. Gryzic, the oft-traveled bass player, signed with Scepter for the second time. He was eventually replaced by Jerry Hludzic, who recorded the remaining *Dinner Music* LP. Gryziec made the transition with no second thoughts and no regrets. He said:

> I didn't regret leaving initially because I was immediately re-signed to Scepter
> with Great Bear after I returned to Wilkes-Barre.

On June 20, 2015, The Whazoos organized a Tribute Reunion Concert as a fundraiser for Carol Scovish and tribute to her husband Joe after his sudden passing. The Bartolia Winery, Falls, Pennsylvania, hosted the event, which was organized by original Whazoo member Rick Belza.

GREAT BEAR

The Whazoos were rechristened "Great Bear" after the name of the spring water company servicing New York City. Located in Elmsford, New York, the company promo blared out, "We Deliver! Enjoy Great Bear Natural Spring water delivered to your home or office like hundreds of other happy customers."

The hard-rocking group replaced lead guitarists and presented the new line-up of Mike Boback, keyboards; Paul Metzger, drums; Bob Gryziec, bass; and John Gonska on lead guitar. Gonska, aka Sonny California, got his name while playing with Chubby Checker, who christened him "Rex Montana." Later they called him "Rex California," and, upon returning from California, somebody tagged him "Sonny California." Metzer summed up the band's persona in a Great Bear Press Release:

> Our music comes because our heads are all in about the same place. This is the
> first group I've ever been in that we could sit down on stage, jam, and sound
> great together. It seems the only arguments we get into are about which route
> to take when we're going to a gig.

A single eponymous album titled *Great Bear* (Scepter, 1971) was recorded in total anonymity for Scepter. Produced and engineered by C. Michael Wright,

Great Bear Circa 1968 (L-R) Mike Boback, John Gonska, Bob Gryziec, Paul Metzger.

the LP was recorded on weekends over several months. To save money, they frugally (just like The Buoys did previously) stayed at Wright's East Side apartment with him and his wife, Diane.

Metzger invited his neighbor, J. Michael Reagan, to New York City while recording the LP. Reagan managed The Techniques, an all-girl band from Plymouth, founded by Carol Yuscavage. Says Reagan:

> Michael Wright, Scepter's sound engineer, and I became friends, and I'd stay with him on weekends. He had a great pad with cork walls for perfect acoustics.

During his visits to Scepter, Reagan met Dionne Warwick and BJ Thomas and hung out with Rupert Holmes. He moved to Boulder, Colorado, in 1973 and relocated to California in 1984.

All of the songs on Great Bear were written by Michael Boback except Mac Rebennack's "Headin' Closer to Home"; G. Spreen, Joseph Longeria, and M. James's "I'm Gonna Build A Mountain"; and Chuck Berry's "Almost Grown." The progressive rock LP selections were Side One's "I Took It Too Long," "Headin' Closer to Home," "All of Her Best," "Poor Rich Man," "I'm Gonna Build A Mountain," and "Hand Me to the Lord." Side Two included "Almost Grown," "Cinderella," "Going Away," "The Singer Left Before His Song," "Summation," and "The Last Page Came Too Soon."

HOB RECORDS

Boback performed all the leads except for "The Last Page Came Too Soon," which drummer Paul Metzger "squeezed out at 2:00 A.M.," suffering from lack of sleep and an ocular migraine.

Metzger had a history with Scepter Records, specifically with their Hob (House of Beauty) gospel label. Hob Records included gospel sensations Mighty Clouds of Joy, the Blind Boys of Alabama, and Rev. James Cleveland. On November 11, 2013, Metzger posted on the Bordel Do Rock blog site:

> I was fortunate to be hired by C. Michael Wright, our producer and engineer, to do studio drum tracks for many artists, including gospel great Albertina Walker. Dionne Warwick's dad, Speedy, produced her.

Although her gospel career began in the 1950s, Albertina Walker's most significant success came decades later after she recorded the reunion album, *Paved the Way with The Caravans. Billboard* called the album "one of the most memorable releases of 2006." The LP entered the charts in the top ten and remained in the top forty for sixteen weeks, later nominated for a Grammy, Dove, Soul Train Music Award, and two Stellar Awards.

ALBUM RELEASE PARTY

Great Bear was treated to their unique award when Scepter hosted an album release party. It took place at Wilkes-Barre's Paramount Theater in the fall of 1970, with WNBC shock jock Don Imus (1940-2019) as Master of Ceremonies and featuring The Murge and the Gemini Light Show. The event brought out a horde of fans and great expectations. Said John Gonska:

> Scepter records promoted us at a few shows. We had a record release party at the old Sterling Hotel, and one show was at the Comerford Theater in Wilkes-Barre. We did one show at an auditorium in New York City. I remember that

one because we all had to rejoin the Musician's Union. I'm not sure if it was the NYC Union. We also did a show somewhere near Boston with The Buoys.

Boback felt that "I Took It Too Long," a faster number, and "Poor Rich Man," a slower tune, had great commercial hooks and could have been released as singles, but Scepter wanted more of an album-oriented radio (AOR) sound from Great Bear. College stations were all playing AOR and the deeper, more experimental cuts. Scepter wanted Great Bear to be different than The Buoys and didn't seem concerned about singles.

Not everyone liked the album tracks. Gryziec thought that the recording wasn't up to professional standards due to recent, untested technology:

> It was kind of thin-sounding because Scepter had just installed a new sound-board, and it had not been tweaked yet.

Metzger agreed. He wasn't happy about the overall production of the LP and wasn't afraid of naming names:

> C. Michael Wright was a rookie, but he must have known someone on the inside to get his job so quickly. At his age, nobody walks into a major studio and takes off at the top. Maybe he started as an intern if they had them back then. I don't know.
>
> Technically, he had a hard time getting the board to sound right. If he had the board set correctly, I believe a lot of his production would have turned out much better. We weren't really happy about the mix on our album, but still, the album is a collector's item, and two of them recently sold for eighty-seven dollars. Honestly, I don't think Scepter put that much investment money into the album.

Great Bear played Sgt Peppers near the Atlanta airport and gigged with the Buoys in Fall River, Massachusetts, to promote the LP. New York Daily News' Charles McHarry wrote, "Two of the fastest rising rock groups in the country are Scepter's The Buoys and the Great Bear. Their projected income for 1971 is $1 million." Unfortunately, McHarry's perception proved to be a prelude to a nightmare. Great Bear's saga played out like a movie about the Titanic, as they felt the ship taking on water. Said Gonska:

> If I remember correctly, the *Great Bear* album was released and then was stopped. Shortly afterward, they made us send all the albums we had, maybe fifty between us, and boxes of promo materials back to them. I think we were

just a tax write-off. I don't think Scepter knew what to do with rock acts like us or The Buoys. Their foremost artists were B.J. Thomas, Dionne Warwick, and some gospel artists.

Paul Metzger believed that both the *Great Bear* album and the once-thriving Scepter Records were doomed with a mix of bad finances and bad timing:

> I think Scepter probably was going under and out of business at that point. So our album didn't have a chance. The only thing they did was to send us down to Atlanta on a southern tour. We played at Sgt Peppers. That was a lot of fun, and we met a lot of great people.

The music played on, long into the night. Mike Boback joined four other local musicians at the Station Complex when they backed up legendary performer Bo Diddley. They included John Gonska (Sonny California), Joey Miraglia, Dave Steve, and The Great Rock Scare's Bill Space, who recalled:

> When Bo Diddley came here in the mid-1980s, he came alone. He didn't bring a band. But he told the promoter he wanted one, so it became our job. We rehearsed that afternoon for about twenty minutes when he said, 'Oh, you guys will be fine.' He also said we would be on for at least two hours!

Just about twenty years later, on September 13, 1990, The Class Reunion was held at Murray's Inn in Wilkes-Barre with a group reformation. They included founding member Paul Metzger, Mike Hagan, bass (formerly with Zootz

Toyz (Circa 1979) was another of Bob Gryziec's many bands. (L-R): Gryziec, Craig Bevan, Dennis Blanchard, and Dave Burkhardt. Toyz later regrouped as Craig Bevan and the Tourists with former lead singer Burkhardt as manager. (Maxim Furek Photo.)

and Hot Pepper), Ernie Coassolo, keyboards (Take Four, the Dimensions), and Rick Simmers (Grand Tour, The Reflections).

Destiny rushed toward them like the Canadian Pacific as both Great Bear and The Buoys faced an unfortunate common denominator. Scepter and Polydor Records respectively denied them proper album releases and support. One can only imagine what might have happened if things had played out differently for these acts and how far their stars might have ascended.

The Whazoos (L-R): Bob Gryziec, Barry Rogers, Mike Boback, Joe Scovish, and Paul Metzger.

16

HYBRID ICE

May was a huge month for The Buoys. As "Timothy" peaked on *Billboard*, the band trekked out to the Coal Region, performing at Sunbury's Shikellamy High School. Afterward, they played several twin-bills with The Hybrid Ice Co. at Danville's Capitol Theater. The dates were May 27th and June 18th.

The concert capitalized on the Buoys' regional popularity and hit record. Bass guitarist Jeff Willoughby recalled that the business-minded Hybrid Ice organized the show and hired the Buoys for five-hundred dollars:

> Hybrid Ice put their entrepreneurship into gear, taking advantage of the popularity of the Buoys' hits 'Timothy' and 'Give Up Your Guns.' Posters were designed and screened by the Danville High School Art Department, tickets were presold, and radio advertising was secured. Then the band set themselves up as the opening act.

Danville's Hybrid Ice was formed in 1969. The band is most recognized for Rusty Foulke's song "Magdelene," which became a regional radio hit, released on the 1982 album *Hybrid Ice*. "Magdelene" was later covered by Boston on their platinum LP *Walk On* (MCA, 1994). WVIA's George Graham reviewed Hybrid Ice in the *Metro-Tempo Magazine:*

> Hybrid Ice was co-produced by John Palumbo (of progressive rock band Crack the Sky). He contributed his experience with a half-dozen major-label albums to give the band's album a sound that in no way seems 'local.' Despite Palumbo's presence, Toye Foulke handled much of the production and mixing himself, doing a superb job. He also composed all but one of the album's songs.

Graham described the band's sound as a cross between the art-rock of Yes and the more basic sounds of Styx or Kansas, "but with a level of class that

RICK KLINGER - ROBERT SCOTT - GALEN TOYE FOLKE

JEFF WILLOUGHBY - CHRIS ALBURGER

HYBRID ICE

Hybrid Ice: (L-R) Rick Klinger, Robert Scott, Galen Toye Foulke, Jeff Willough-by, Chris Alburger. (RD. Townsend photo.)

exceeds" both big-name bands. He called "Castle Walls" and "Magdalene" "rock masterpieces."

PROMISING ROCK BANDS

Hybrid Ice performed throughout the region. On October 24, 1971, at the Lykens Ballroom Concert, they shared the stage with Mongrel, Granite, Gathering, and Delight Records recording artists, The Other Side.

The Susquehanna Valley, south of Wilkes-Barre-Scranton, was a hotbed of promising rock bands, including the Elves, The Islanders, Steam Machine, Sundae Train, and The Avanti's. In addition, Schuylkill County was home to Angie and the Citations, D Kool and the Kasuals, The Other Side, The Jordan

Brothers, Ma Rutt's, Kings and Queens, The Shan-Tones, and Sterling Koch. At the same time, Columbia County hosted Haji, The Orphans, Pendulum, The Playboys, Inc, and Sothic Cycle.

OPENING ACT FOR TOTO

Hybrid Ice boasted of being "a self-contained touring unit with a sound system capable of handling the largest of club venues or small concert halls" and a lighting package exceeding 60,000 watts. Since their inception, the Ice amassed a cult-like following on the east coast and the southern United States. Working with Atlanta's Century Artists, they played venues from Virginia to Florida

With a mix of heavy metal and keyboard-based rock, they opened for Toto (August 1982) and The Beach Boys (September 1983) in front of 8,000 screaming fans at Williamsport's historic Bowman Field. Then, they played Spring break at Daytona Beach and opened for Hall and Oates, Todd Rundgren, and Steppenwolf with tight renderings of "On We Go," "Rock 'n' Roll Forever," and "Raise a Little Hell."

The Icemen skillfully mastered the art of self-promotion. In 1984, with two sold-out shows, Hybrid Ice claimed to be the first Pennsylvania-based rock band to play at the Bloomsburg Fair. They opened for the Greg Kihn Band, who had hits with "Jeopardy" #2 (Beserkley,1983) and "The Breakup Song (They Don't Write 'Em)" # 15 (Beserkley, 1981). Foulke knew keyboard player Gary Phillips, one of the band members. At the age of seventeen, Foulke submitted demo tapes to Beserkley Records, where Phillips worked.

Calling themselves "The Most Famous Unknown Band in the World," they kept on reinventing themselves. They became the backing band for Jimi Jamison of Survivor, John Cafferty of the Beaver Brown Band, Derek St. Holmes of the Ted Nugent band, and Kevin Chalfant of the Journey Experience. Hybrid Ice also played the "Legends of Rock" Cruise from 2015 through 2017.

Following in the footsteps of The Buoys, they played the celebrated Stone Balloon, and their remastered debut album was re-released on compact disk on the European label, Escape Records (2000), the same label that released Dakota's *The Last Standing Man* (1997) and *Mr. Lucky* (1996).

BRAD DELP

A little-known yet fascinating story is how Bill Kelly almost became Boston's lead singer. After Rusty Foulke's song "Magdelene" won the American Song Festival's "honorable mention," Epic Records asked Tom Scholtz, founder of Boston, to record it. Said Foulke:

Tom asked me to help 'Bostonize' the song, and from my travels up there, I got to know all of the band members. I toured with Fran Cosmo's band for eight years, but I met Brad Delp, first, at Bucknell University.

Brad Delp vocals were heard on Boston's #5, "More Than a Feeling" (Epic, 1976), #4, "Don't Look Back" (Epic, 1978), and #1, "Amanda" (Epic, 1986).

After Delp left, Scholtz needed a replacement and asked Foulke, "Who's the best singer you ever heard in your life besides Brad Delp?" Foulke replied:

> I said Bill Kelly, and Scholtz said, 'OK,' let's see if we can get him up here. So, I called Bill down in Nashville. Rather than saying, 'Hello Bill, this is Rusty,' I said, 'OK Bill, It's your twenty-first birthday. Where are you? And he goes 'Rusty!' He knew me right away.

Kelly celebrated his twenty-first birthday on June 18, 1971, and was paid five hundred dollars to boot to perform at the second Buoys-Hybrid Ice concert. Kelly was born on June 18, sharing the same birthday with Sir Paul McCartney, but, as Foulke added:

> Tom Scholtz flew Bill up to Boston, gave him an audition, and even had his lawyers there. Bill came in second, apparently, to Fran Cosmo, which I think is ridiculous. Bill's way better than Fran. Bill came very close to singing for Boston. I mean, really close.

Kelly didn't get the job, and more heartbreak followed after Delp committed suicide in 2007. He was only fifty-five years old, having been a rock celebrity for over thirty years.

★ PART V ★

WEST COAST
ROAD TRIP

17

SMOKE ON THE WATER: FRANK ZAPPA

Riding high, "Timothy" peaked on May 1, 1971, and, later that month, The Buoys played a free afternoon concert at the Cleveland Convention Center, sharing the stage with Sha Na Na and Delaney, Bonnie, and Friends. Sha Na Na, popular with their retro-'50s act, were frequent visitors to Cleveland and, from 1977 to 1981, the gold lame' or leather-jacketed group hosted their TV show, featuring frontman Jon "Bowser" Bauman.

DELANEY BRAMLETT

One of the first luminaries they met was Delaney Bramlett, an accomplished professional musician, had worked as a session musician and member of the Shindogs, the house band for the ABC-TV series *Shindig* (1964-1966). Bramlett, with long hair and a full beard, evoked the persona of a Southern Baptist minister. Delaney, Bonnie, and Friends were the first white act to be signed to Stax Records. Like bluesman John Mayall, Bramlett was a vital connection who brought Eric Clapton, George Harrison, and Derek and the Dominos together. In addition, he worked with musicians, including Duane and Gregg Allman, Rita Coolidge, Gram Parsons, and Leon Russell.

According to Kelly, a bad snowstorm canceled the concert. So the Buoys went back to the Holiday Inn and hung out with Bramlett while being entertained by two strolling minstrels on acoustic guitar and violin:

> These two guys would stand at our table, and Delaney would request some Italian song. And they would play it. He'd just sit there, and his head would bounce back and forth like he was just digging the fire out of the song. He'd do a little snort, and he would pull out a fifty and stuff it in the guy's pocket. And then he'd make another request. 'Play Sorrento. Play Sorrento.' And they'd play

Sorrento for him. And this went on for hours and hours, and we would watch him snort cocaine and do this for hours. I remember it pretty vividly because it was outrageous.

Kelly and Bramlett developed a close friendship, and Kelly was amazed at the albums Delaney & Bonnie and Friends recorded, such as Country Life (Stax, 1969) and Accept No Substitutes (Electra, 1969). However, Bramlett pushed back on the complement, telling Kelly that he needed to be grateful for "Timothy's" success, and according to Kelly:

> Delaney told me, 'Man, you are so fortunate to have a hit single. I'd give anything to have one.' He emphasized that we had a single going up the charts, and we were going to sell a million copies. 'You need to be grateful,' he said.

"NEVER ENDING SONG OF LOVE"

While paying The Buoys such a compliment, Bramlett failed to mention that his "Never Ending Song of Love" (Atco, 1971) got as high as #13 on *Billboard*, four places higher than "Timothy."

Delaney Bramlett was an influential musician. According to his biography, he taught George Harrison how to play slide guitar and write gospel songs, leading to "My Sweet Lord" (Apple, 1971), the biggest selling single of 1971. Eric Clapton also admitted, "Delaney taught me everything I know about singing."

But Bramlett caused a bit of a dust-up for The Buoys, dramatically wrapped around a bit of mistaken identity. There were several different versions of the Cleveland incident, memories clouded by the passage of time, by ebbing tides and shifting sands. Some thought that Eric Clapton was there and "borrowed" Hludzik's amp and played it while gigging with Delaney, Bonnie, and Friends.

The Cleveland booking proved to be a weird one. Lost in the fog of time and with diminished memories, Kelly recalled that a snowstorm canceled the free concert, but Brozena said, "the show did go on." Fox said that Eric Clapton tried to rip off Hludzik's amp, but Brozena claimed that Delaney Bramlett borrowed it and then wanted to buy it.

As Tom Fox recalled the story, "Eric Clapton blew out his amp, and a stage person began to drag Hludzik's amp towards him so that Clapton could play it." The ever-alert Fox jumped up on stage, yelling at the roadie to stop. He was livid, but the roadie informed him that "Eric Clapton wants to borrow the amp." Fox thought that it was Clapton, but Brozena recollected that it was Delaney Bramlett who ended up using Brozena's Marshal:

Clapton was not there. I had already left the afternoon venue and was unaware of what had happened. Delaney's traveling secretary called my hotel room and told me about the amp. She said that Delaney was interested in purchasing it.

Delaney told Brozena he had not heard a slide sound like that since he used George Harrison's when they played at the Isle of Wight Festival. Dubbed the British Woodstock, the 1970 five-day festival drew an estimated 600,000 spectators. It featured over 50 acts, including The Doors, The Who, Supertramp, Chicago, Sly, and the Family Stone, and, in one of his last live performances, Jimi Hendrix. With Bramlett's business proposition, Fran Brozena came close to providing an exciting footnote in rock and roll history:

> I met with Delaney in the hotel lounge, but we could not reach a deal for reasons beyond our control. I ended up hanging out with him late in the evening. He introduced me to Frank Zappa after Zappa had completed an evening gig with Humble Pie.

ERIC CLAPTON

Alcohol. Marijuana. Cocaine. Drugs were a part of the '70s scene, symbolic of rebellion, individualism, and the culture of the times. Some used, others did not, and the drugs were always there. Eric Clapton was part of that scene, and by 1971 he was severely addicted. Writer Jake Wyatt observed that after Cream broke up in 1968, Clapton struggled with his demons:

> He was an alcoholic and addicted to heroin by the time he began playing solo in 1970. Unfortunately, it wasn't long for his addictions to affect his career. Clapton passed out onstage during George Harrison's Concert for Bangladesh in 1972.

Clapton was the proverbial rolling stone. After his stint with Blind Faith, he played guitar for Delaney, Bonnie, and Friends. After that, he formed Derek and the Dominos, with former members of Delaney's band, keyboardist Bobby Whitlock, bassist Carl Radle, and drummer Jim Gordon. Unfortunately, the band released only one studio album, *Layla and Other Assorted Love Songs,* with Dave Mason, George Harrison, and Duane Allman.

In 1974, three years before she and George Harrison divorced, former model Patti Boyd helped Clapton kick his three-year heroin addiction. In his autobiography *Clapton,* he wrote that he spent roughly $16,000 a week on heroin. Rather than seeking drug addiction treatment, he was often confined to his home. But once he managed to get clean from heroin, he spent the next twenty years drunk and abusing cocaine. Finally, in 1982, he entered treatment at Hazelden and wrote about the experience in his autobiography:

> In the lowest moments of my life, the only reason I didn't commit suicide was that I knew I wouldn't be able to drink anymore if I was dead. It was the only thing I thought was worth living for, and the idea that people were about to try and remove me from alcohol was so terrible that I drank and drank and drank, and they had to practically carry me into the clinic.

Even after he conquered his heroin addiction, Clapton still had his battles. He once had to perform a concert lying on his back, as he was too drunk to stand up and play. He said to *NRP Music* in 2007:

> It didn't seem that outlandish to me, and in fact, probably was all I was capable of. It was either that or just laying down somewhere else. The fact that I was laying down on stage means at least I showed up.

FRANK ZAPPA

And then there was The Buoys' informal meeting with iconoclastic Frank Zappa, the cosmic surfer who journeyed into realms non-existent to others. Frank Zappa & The Mothers of Invention's *Sgt. Pepper* parody album, *We're Only In It for the Money* (Verve, 1968), released earlier, gained notoriety for its attacks against left-and-right wing politics, as well as the hippy subculture. After being introduced to Zappa, Kelly, a philosophy major, sensed that he was in the presence of a kindred spirit, one capable of expanding every conversation into unknown academic realms, like ancient seafarers searching for the New World. All was right with the world. They were breathing in the rarified air and living on rock 'n roll time. And they would talk about this tour for years.

Young and restless, The Buoys were just starting. Tom Fox said that one of Zappa's musicians produced a glass vial and offered it to the group. "It looked like a powered substance, but nobody knew what it was," recalled Fox of the invitation to sample a line of coke. Just a little toot, man. A little snort.

They declined. So did Zappa, who marched to a different beat. He limited his drug use to coffee, cigarettes, and alcohol. With the vast array of drugs, including marijuana, heroin, methamphetamine, and cocaine, he was militantly anti-drug and recorded countless anti-drug commercials. Zappa espoused this point during an interview by *Buzz*'s Dave Turner and Lisa Weisberg:

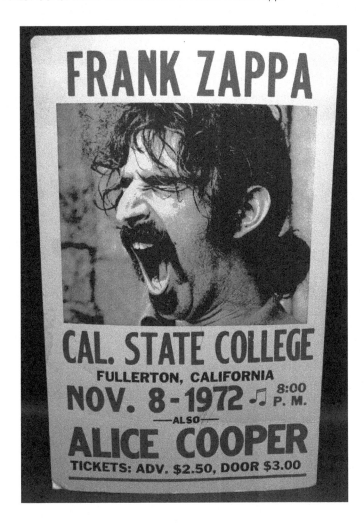

The Libertarians kind of have the right idea on this that you own your own body, and the government should get out of your face. But you also do not have the right to harm other people or to impinge on their rights or space. So, let's apply that to drugs. If you want to get wrecked, and you can afford it, and you have a place to do it where the results of your behavior can't harm another person, I don't see any reason why you shouldn't be allowed to do it.

Frank Zappa made an impression on everyone. They watched him perform on stage and, after the show, were able to hang out with him and his band. He was larger than life, filled with unorthodox ideas and opinions, even for the times. Kelly reflected on his stage presence and charisma:

Zappa had a way of owning the stage. He was like Freddie Mercury. You could stick Freddie on a four-x-four stage, and he'd still own it. You could put him in the middle of an arena, and he'd still own it. All he had to do was step out into the spotlight, and he owned it. Same thing for Zappa. He was so unique and so different. He was not a pompous character, but he was full of himself at the same time. He was a genius.

In addition to his anti-drug views, Zappa was a legendary rock musician, composer, and a force of nature. He liked Cleveland and played the Public Auditorium in 1971, 1974, 1976, and the Cleveland Music Hall in 1988. The Rock and Roll Hall of Fame site inspired his 1986 song "Let's Move to Cleveland."

After the Buoys' scheduled free concert, underground radio station WNCR 99.5 Stereo presented the Mothers of Invention, Humble Pie with Peter Frampton, and Free, featuring Paul Rogers. Head Over Heels also performed. The concert took place at Cleveland Public Auditorium, also called Public Hall. The date was May 30, 1971.

The concert was a transitional phase for some of the musicians. A plugged-in and excited Peter Frampton went solo at the end of the year while Paul Rogers fronted Bad Company, formed from the ashes of Free and Mott The Hoople. The supergroup sang basic blues-rock, charting with "Can't Get Enough" #5 (Island, 1974), "Feel Like Making Love" #10 (Swan Song, 1975), and "Rock 'n' Roll Fantasy" #13 (Swan Song 1979).

Zappa's band was another reincarnation of his original group, a revolving door that, at the time, was comprised of British drummer Aynsley Dunbar, jazz keyboardist George Duke, bass player Ian Underwood, and rhythm guitarist Jeff Simmons. The band also included three Turtles, bass player Jim Pons and singers Mark Volman and Howard Kaylan, who, due to persistent legal problems, adopted the stage name "The Phlorescent Leech and Eddie," or "Flo & Eddie."

Zappa was one of the most controversial American artists of the 20th century. He was the musical James Dean, a non-conforming rebel who explored just about every aspect of music; pop, rock, blues, jazz, and doo-wop. He mixed pop with art, used shifting time signatures and studio effects, sing-song choruses, highbrow and lowbrow techniques, and experimentation with commercialism, all with a twist of satire mocking teenage romance, staples of the Top 40. In 1989, Zappa tried to explain his eclectic musical repertoire:

Since I didn't have any kind of formal training, it didn't make any difference to me if I was listening to Lightnin' Slim or a vocal group called the Jewel, or Webern, or Varese, or Stravinsky. To me, it was all good music.

Zappa and the Mothers were immortalized in Deep Purple's song "Smoke on the Water," # 4 (Warner Bros, 1973), about a fire at the Casino de Montreux in Switzerland where The Mothers of Invention were playing. Things got out of hand when some half-crazed fan fired a flare gun toward the rattan-covered ceiling, igniting a fire that burned down the casino. Zappa and his band barely escaped and could have been burned to death.

Frank Zappa was the most influential musician that The Buoys would ever meet. His career was one of innovation and confrontation. Zappa's musical experimentations and scathing social commentaries reflected an exceptional musician and spokesperson. Although Zappa was inducted into the Rock and Roll Hall of Fame in 1995 and presented the 1997 Grammy Lifetime Achievement Award, he deserved much more.

18

WEST COAST ROAD TRIP

After breathing in the sparkling morning dew of celebration, The Buoys embarked on a West Coast road trip culminating in the Pacific Northwest. It was their "breakout year," and the rock quintet launched an ambitious outing to support their *Billboard* success.

The western swing was organized by Harold Vealer, aka "Hollywood and Vine," a former Disc Jockey and long-time associate of C. Michael Wright. He had worked in New York, Chicago, and Los Angeles and had connections with all of the old school personalities, who would play his records and book his bands. This little-known tour, taking them through numerous states, was their most incredible adventure, and although it was only a two-week period, the experiences they made would stay with them for a lifetime.

The Sunset Strip was a million miles from Wilkes-Barre, and as the cavalcade rolled westward, they felt the warm Pacific breeze and the taste of salt in the air. California was the Promised Land of pink houses, palm trees, and endless summers. This was the home of the Beach Boys, the California Sun, and MCA and Capitol Records. It was where you went to be discovered. So, with music swirling in their heads, they arrived at the Whisky a Go-Go, the iconic rock venue in West Hollywood that launched the careers of Buffalo Springfield, The Byrds, and Johnny Rivers, as well as KISS, Motley Crue, and the Stooges.

Located at 8901 Sunset Boulevard, on West Hollywood's Sunset Strip, the Whisky opened in 1964 and was the first venue inducted into the Rock and Roll Hall of Fame. The Whisky hosted many historic performances, including those by The Doors (1966), Cream (1967), Led Zeppelin (1969), and Guns N' Roses (1986). In addition, the Buoys headlined at the Whisky on August 23rd and 24th.

The Whisky was a dream state, where bands went to be auditioned, vetted, and coronated if the stars were in alignment. It was frequented by record executives, A&R men, and promoters searching for the "next big thing." Thus, it offered a perfect venue for The Buoys. With an intimate club capacity of only five hundred, the audience could appreciate their precision three-part harmonies and Kelly's soaring vocals.

Members of Led Zeppelin were in the audience, and Tom Fox observed Robert Plant taking in Kelly's vocals and the bands' stage show. Siracuse said:

> I have very little memory of the Whisky. Not much of a crowd. I sat and talked with a band named Rachel and with a member of Led Zeppelin. There was some connection between the two, but I don't remember what. I remember Buoys' posters, photos and album covers, and the display windows along the street.

The Buoys were joined onstage for an impromptu jamming session with members of Steppenwolf, and from there, traveled up the road to play the Under the Ice House in Glendale, California, before heading north.

It took over fourteen hours to drive through the redwoods of northern California to arrive, exhausted, at Salem's massive Oregon State Fair, where everyone talked about the heavy rains and the grasshopper infestation devastating farm crops across Oregon and Idaho. One of the fair's most prominent attractions that year was King Estephe, a twenty-eight-year-old, 2,045-pound Charolais beef cattle unofficially declared King of the Beef Show.

The Buoys performed on the massive stage on Friday, September 3rd. Over thirty-two thousand people attended the fair on that day, and for those looking to see the Buoys, an admission ticket cost only $2.50. Despite steady, driving rain, the tenor wailings of Kelly and the Buoys, with opening act Brown Sugar, resounded throughout the midway, a prelude to what would be their largest audience ever.

THE PACIFIC NORTHWEST

The Pacific Northwest boasted a rich bounty of musical acts venerated at The Experience Music Project, a somewhat smaller version of Cleveland's Rock and Roll Hall of Fame. EMP became Seattle's tribute to its musical heritage. It reflected the region's unique and tightly defined, musical contributions including Jimi Hendrix and Heart and Paul Revere and the Raiders, the Fleetwoods, Kingsmen, Sonics, Ventures, Wailers, and grunge acts Nirvana, Pearl Jam, Soundgarden, and Queensryche. The area, surrounded by rain-soaked verdant mountain ranges, was unique, and so was their concept of hosting the first and only "legal rock festival."

Woodstock attracted over 400,000 attendees, setting the bar in both numbers and talent. It would be hard to top that Aquarian gathering, but the Pacific Northwest was willing to give it a shot with the four-day Satsop River Fair and Tin Cup Races.

"Timothy" was famous in the Seattle area. It received extensive airplay on KOL-FM 94.1, Seattle's first progressive album radio station, and Portland's KINK, "The underground link." KQIV 106.7, allegedly the "world's first quadraphonic FM station," was another essential station for them. Reporter Joe Middleton, writing for the Wyoming Valley *Observer*, inked a testimonial to the song's success in the Emerald City:

> In the December 3 issue of *The Observer*, this writer printed an erroneous statement of sales of the record. I stated that 'Timothy' sold 6,000 copies in one week in Seattle, Washington. The truth of the matter is the record sold 6,000 copies in one day.

Those impressive sales and overwhelming radio airplay boosted the popularity of The Buoys in the Pacific Northwest, resulting in an invitation to perform at an oddly named festival called the Satsop River Fair and Tin Cup Races.

19

FESTIVAL ARMAGEDDON

Baton-wielding riot-squads, police dogs, and tear gas canisters crushed Sunrise '71, which proceeded The Sapsot River Fair and Tin Cup Races. Here, there was no love, peace, or brotherhood to be found.

Sunrise '71 had been scheduled for June 1971, about three months before Satsop. Promoters signed nine national bands: Joy of Cooking, Dan Hicks and his Hot Licks, Black Oak Arkansas, Mississippi Fred McDowell, John Baldry, John Fahey, Flamin' Groovies, Stone Ground, and Little Feat. Then, unexpectedly, county officials ruled that the promoters did not obtain permit requests at least sixty days before the proposed festival date. Although the promoters canceled the concert, over 700 young people gathered at the site, were met with overwhelming police response, according to The Spokane *Chronicle:*

Constructing Satsop. (John Caldbick photo.)

Sheriff Ralph Hall had commanded the more than 200 city police officers, deputy sheriffs, and state troopers, who moved into the Marlin area last week to prevent a rock festival.

Riot-police ordered youths out of Long Lake in Grant County. Another thousand gathered at Deep Lake in Sun Lakes State Park were evicted after a roadblock was set up. About fourteen youths were arrested on drunkenness or drug possession charges as the American Civil Liberties Union threatened to file a multi-million-dollar class action suit against Grant County over police "harassment and intimidation."

Memories lingered over the dark history of the Sky River Rock Festival and Lighter Than Air, held in 1969 over Labor Day, near Tenino, Washington, and the Buffalo Party Convention and Pig Roast held in 1970 in Eatonville, Washington. As described by a Centralia Chronicle editorial, anarchy prevailed at both events:

> Both fetes were marked by heavy drug use, exhibitions of crude nudity, and in the Buffalo Party affair, there was one death. Law enforcement agencies have repeatedly argued there is no control of anything that goes on in a mob of thousands of milling, drug-sodden participants short of a military action that could create tragic violence.

"FIRST LEGAL FESTIVAL IN WASHINGTON"

The Satsop River Fair and Tin Cup Races were held September 3 through the 6th on a farm in Satsop, Washington, in the foothills of the Olympic Mountains. With Mount Olympus rising 7,980 feet above, Satsop was handcuffed from the start. Because of past, sometimes violent festivals, the Washington legislature passed a 1971 compromise act titled "Regulation of Outdoor Music Festivals," approving the use of force:

> This invocation of the police power is prompted by and based upon prior experience with outdoor music festivals where the enforcement of the existing laws and regulations on dangerous and narcotic drugs, indecent exposure, intoxicating liquor, and sanitation has been rendered most difficult by the flagrant violations thereof by a large number of festival patrons.

After Satsop organizers sued Grays Harbor County to secure a permit, valuable time was squandered. Finally, just two weeks before the festival started, King County Superior Court Judge Charles Z. Smith ordered the county to

Satsop soggy festival campers. (John Caldbick photo.)

issue the festival permit, conditioned on the promoters posting a $30,000 bond and proof of $50,000 in property insurance.

Satsop was going to be different. The organizers wanted to get this right. Described as "the first legal festival in Washington State," Satsop was taking no chances. There was a sixteen-year age limit. Vehicles were banned from the site. A thirty-nine-man security force, some on horseback, patrolled the fringes of the crowd.

The design and construction of the festival was a huge undertaking, according to The Seattle Times:

> More than 800 workers erected a massive stage with a state-of-the-art, 500-watt sound system (which soon failed), built ninety-five concession stands, made space for two helipads—one for entertainers, one for medical evacuations, planted a forest of utility poles to carry power from a huge diesel generator to the stage and outdoor lighting, ran water lines, helped place 104 Sanikans, and created a fenced-off area as a campground and parking area for motorcycle-club members.

Volunteer groups completed most of the construction, including a sixty-foot-long stage, in the pouring rain. Salem, Oregon's Capital Journal described the enormity of Washington's first legally sanctioned rock festival:

> The cost of security, construction, and entertainment for the festival has already run up to $250,000 of which $100,000 has gone to big-name bands, promoters said.

An advance ticket for the entire four days costs only $24. The organizers used a catchy "Get it on and boogie on Labor Day!" slogan. They started to arrive days before the festival began. Tent cities reminiscent of 19th-century gold-rush towns were erected throughout the location. Youthful onlookers lounged beside their canvass structures or sprawled on the grass near the 15-foot-high stage. Hundreds of campfires smoked and burned. The motorcycle club Iron Lords had a concession stand selling corn on the cob and hamburgers. The Nisqually Tribe operated a booth selling pies and salmon.

THE SATSOP RIVER FAIR AND TIN CUP RACES

One of four property owners who leased their land (for $10,000) to the concert promoters, Leann Paul said, "If Woodstock was the beginning of the story, Satsop was the end." Nevertheless, more than 150,000 concertgoers breathed in the four-day essence of an eclectic blend of rock, soul, jazz, and blues.

Among the signed rock royalty were Eric Burdon, Flash Cadillac, Captain Beefheart, Albert Collins, Spencer Davis Group, Delaney and Bonnie and Friends, Derek & The Dominos (with Eric Clapton), Earth Wind and Fire, the Everly Brothers, John Hammond, Leo Kottke, Charles Lloyd, Steve Miller, Billy Preston, Ike, and Tina Turner Revue, Quicksilver Messenger Service, Jimmy Weatherspoon, Wishbone Ash, War, the Youngbloods, and The Buoys.

150,000

After playing the Organ State Fair on Friday, the Buoys drove over to Sapsot for what turned out to be two opening performances on Saturday and Sunday. The festival started with a near police shootout and an ambulance escort, recalled Siracuse:

> We finally got a call that we should head to the festival grounds. When we got to the gate, there was a standoff between the police and a motorcycle gang. Guns were in hand. They wouldn't let us in. Finally, an ambulance came up behind us and asked where we were headed, why we were there, and who we were. We told them, 'We're The Buoys.'

The ambulance director immediately contacted security head, Ed Geering, who told them they were scheduled to go on stage, recollected Siracuse:

> After relaying the info to the police, we were told to keep our heads down
> and follow them through as they used the loudspeaker system on the vehicle,
> saying, 'Opening act behind us, let them through.' Once through the entrance,
> we could breathe again.

The Satsop Magic Bus. (John Caldbick photo.)

The Buoys should have received a medal for bravery after a near-riot in the middle of thousands of packed concertgoers. Instead, friction developed between festival-goers and an outside group of about 100 motorcycle riders. After negotiations, the bikers agreed to stay within a barbed-wire enclosure with their bikes and not ride through the crowds.

It rained for three days, and as they got on stage, a drizzle persisted. Then, it stopped. The stage crew and roadies began to remove the plastic covering the gear. The Buoys did a quick sound check to listen to the monitors, and miraculously, they were introduced as the sun broke through the clouds. It was showtime. The Buoys knew precisely how to elicit the best response from an audience. They had their act down like a precision Swiss watch, and it unfolded as planned, said, Siracuse:

> As we were introduced, the sun broke through the clouds. Bill said 'hello' and said, 'Now we know what Crosby, Stills, and Nash meant when they told the

people at Woodstock that they were scared shitless.' We immediately went into 'Suite: Judy Blue Eyes.'

They opened the festival for two days in a row, the first band to play each day. Their set was between a half-hour and forty-five minutes. Chris Hanlon was the crowd-pleaser, flipping his drum sticks and, like a rubber band man, leaning backward in his seat, almost tipping over. The crowd responded immediately, packed shoulder to shoulder from the front of the stage to the back, recalled Siracuse:

> I remember ending as usual with Kelly introducing "here's a medley of our hits" as we started 'Timothy.' The recognition by the crowd was instantaneous. Being on a tight schedule due to the weather delay, we had been told that there would be no encore. However, the stage manager had an immediate change of heart and told us to 'Get back out there." He also invited us back for a second show to start the next day's music.

Their gain was another's loss. The story floating around was that the stage manager was threatened with being fired for allowing them to do the encore but said he didn't care. So he was let go by the promoters, even as The Buoys performed that following day. After more than fifty years since that Washington state festival, Chris Hanlon considered those slightly clouded memories:

> It was like Woodstock. There was a stream in the back, and there were lots of people. I remember seeing people jumping on top of a watermelon truck and stealing watermelons and saw the driver peel away, possibly injuring some of the crowd. They brought the bands in by ambulance. They couldn't afford to pay for the helicopters.

The worst part was just before they went on stage to face their largest audience ever. Like a placekicker attempting a field goal in sudden-death overtime, it was make-or-break time. Their anxiety was evident, the sweat beads making icy trails down their necks, as thousands upon thousands of rock enthusiasts expected to be entertained with music and showmanship. Bill Kelly remembered the concert as their largest event:

> First of all, yes, Satsop, in terms of numbers, was the biggest gig I, or the Buoys or Dakota, ever played, and it was incredible. That many people were a bit scary but exciting as well.

Fran Brozena rode Satsop's magic swirlin' ship, taking in its unexpected immenseness:

The infamous watermelon truck. (John Caldbick photo.)

I don't remember being scared, but it was just amazing to look out on what seemed to be a sea of humanity. And yes, Satsop was the largest festival in terms of the number of people we ever played in front of.

Satsop's population was about 1500x larger than Japan-Jeddo, the smallest borough in Luzerne County and Jerry Hludzik's homestead. Hludzik viewed the festival from a different lens:

Looking back years later, it was pretty cool to play a festival of this magnitude in 1971. There were people as far as the eye could see. I just wanted to suck it all in! I thought to myself, 'this was the big time!' Some bands stood out more than others. I was impressed with John Hammond, Delaney and Bonnie & Friends, and Wishbone Ash. I stayed because I wanted to take it all in. I didn't want to miss a thing.

Hludzik was impressed with twenty-nine-year-old John Hammond, one of the greatest traditional blues players and British rockers Wishbone Ash. However, the nineteen-year-old Hludzik, like the others, had no idea how this was going to turn out:

> Suffice it to say, one could make out faces just a little distance back. We set up to start with some acoustic songs as usual at the time. Yes, we were scared but energized. Realize we had no idea how we would be received. Would the crowd be disappointed after such a long, wet, uncomfortable wait? Or happy to hear any music at all!!

They didn't know exactly how many people were sitting there, listening to them perform. They could only estimate Siracuse said:

> We looked out in awe at the size of the crowd. I've heard various accounts of the size of the crowd. They ranged from a high of 150,000 to 100,000 spectators, as estimated by The Seattle Times. Even if these estimates were wrong by fifty percent, this was still a significant concert both in size and scope, the lineup of artists being stellar.

The Buoys wanted to take advantage of their road trip with radio interviews and additional gigs. After each performance, they found extra work at a bowling alley and a local bar. The Seattle area was home to Ann and Nancy Wilson and their future supergroup Heart. Siracuse remembered a curious circumstance:

> Our manager, Tom Fox, promoted a Heart concert in Scranton years later. He was told by one of the Wilson sisters that they attended the Buoys' teen event after telling their parents that they were at a friend's house.

"Timothy" was all over the Seattle airwaves and was immensely popular with record sales and radio. Ann Wilson would have been twenty-one years old and a huge fan of the group.

PARADISE LOST

With the scent of marijuana and driving rock pulsations, Satsop unfolded upon a water-logged, muddied seven-acre site. Northwest rain is a constant variable in the Pacific, and Satsop, with mud and rain galore, would not be the exception. Unfortunately, the heavy rains short-circuited the festival's public address system and cut off musical performances for some time early Sunday, Siracuse said:

> Rain delayed the start of the festival. The festival people were watching the weather closely and saw an opening in the weather window. Remember

that the weather was coming in from the west (the Pacific), so accuracy was difficult.

The concert was plagued by bad weather, a shooting, and a bus accident that injured about 20 people when their bus plunged over a thirty-foot embankment. Two persons were treated for broken ankles after a truck carrying watermelons drove into the crowd. In addition, hundreds of cars were towed away after parking illegally along the road leading to the site, leaving some festival-goers stranded.

STUMBLERS

Drugs were rampant. In the 1970s, heroin and cocaine had emerged upon the drug scene, and it wasn't hard to uncover the source of Satsop's problems, said researcher John Caldbick:

> Much but not all of the bad behavior at Satsop could be attributed to the combination of drugs and alcohol, mainly the cheaper varieties of wine, with gallons of Cribari being favorites. Pot smokers caused little if any trouble, and even those who overindulged on psychedelics—LSD, mescaline, MDA, psilocybin mushrooms, and a pharmacopeia of other reality-warping things— usually got by with a little help from their friends or the folks at the Open Door Clinic.

Washington state had passed guidelines about "Outdoor Music Festivals." The legislation Section RCW 70.108.090, titled "Drugs prohibited," stated:

> No person, persons, partnership, corporation, association, society, fraternal or social organization to whom a music festival permit has been granted shall, during the time an outdoor music festival is in operation, knowingly permit or allow any person to bring upon the premises of said music festival, any narcotic or dangerous drug as defined by chapters *69.33 or 69.40 RCW, or knowingly permit or allow narcotic or dangerous drug to be consumed on the premises. No person shall take or carry onto said premises any narcotic or dangerous drug.

Satsop festival organizers threatened to crack down on any attempts to sell drugs such as LSD or heroin, although marijuana would be tolerated. Still, one drug, in particular, caused more problems than all the others.

Seconal, a relative newcomer to the festival scene, was a powerful barbiturate. It was packaged as small red capsules, called "reds," and openly sold on the festival grounds. Manufactured by Eli Lilly & Company, the drug's effects were potentiated when combined with alcohol. April Dembosky, the health reporter for The California Report and KQED News, addressed the danger of this archaic yet dangerous substance:

> Originally developed in the 1930s as a sleeping pill, it fell out of favor when people died from taking too much or taking it in combination with alcohol. But when intended as a lethal medication to hasten the death of someone suffering from a terminal disease, Seconal is the drug of choice.

The pills, also referred to as "stumblers," hampered the user's ability to walk. Users high on Seconal and wine ambulated about in a near zombie-like state, stumbling onto ditches, campfires, and other obstacles, before being transported to the Open Door Clinic. Drug abuse and bad trips had been anticipated. Counselors were ready to talk people down. The safety of thousands of concert-goers was paramount, according to the Longview Daily News:

A medical facility operated by Seattle's Open Door Clinic received supplies from civil defense officials. Clinic staffers said that most injuries being treated were cuts and burns from campfires, with a few drug overdose cases.

> Times had changed since Woodstock's message of music, love, and peace. But, unfortunately, the drugs had changed as well. Many of the festivals after Woodstock, most notably Altamont, were plagued with alcohol, harder drugs, and violence. Satsop dreamt of the former yet tasted of the latter.

FINANCIAL HORROR SHOW

After the Buoys performed on Saturday, the second day of the festival, Satsop ran out of money. A mutinous revolt was brewing. Threatening to leave, unless they were paid, were a forty-person security staff, clean-up crews, electricians, ticket takers, as well as helicopter pilots who flew in performers and flew out medical emergencies. The individual who owned the sound system warned that he would pack up his equipment and leave by 9:00 P.M. Saturday if he were not paid in full. HistoryLink.org's John Caldbick wrote about Satsop's financial horror show:

> A little more than half the major advertised bands and performers would eventually appear and play; others were at a motel in Olympia, about 35 miles distant, but came no closer. The festival descended into confusion and financial disarray, as notably groups including Ike & Tina Turner, Derek & The Dominos (with Eric Clapton), Quicksilver Messenger Service, War, Earth Wind and

Fire, Leo Kottke, the Everly Brothers, and Captain Beefheart, either demanded payment in advance or found other reasons not to show up.

War was one of the groups that refused to perform and one of the hottest acts at the festival. Although Eric Burdon and War had only one hit, "Spill the Wine" #3 (MGM, 1970), *Billboard* ranked it the number 20 song of 1970. But after splitting from Burdon, who stormed off stage during a European tour, War recorded their fourth album, *All Day Music* (United Artists, 1971), which included the hit singles "All Day Music" (United Artists, 1971) and "Slippin' into Darkness" #16 (United Artists, 1972).

Burdon was an avid proponent of American blues and marketing. For example, the Eric Burdon and War double album, *The Black Man's Burdon* (MGM, 1970), included a coupon that could be redeemed for one dollar toward purchasing a ticket for any live Eric Burdon concert.

Also refusing to perform was the Ike and Tina Turner Revue. "Proud Mary" had been released in January 1971 and by mid-March reached #4 on *Billboard*. It became their biggest U.S. hit and by May had sold one million copies. The record won Tina her first Grammy Award for Best R&B Vocal Performance, but her husband was always a problem. Ike was temperamental, volatile, and abusive because of his character and drug habit. In her autobiography *I, Tina: My Life Story*, Tina Turner watched cocaine destroy her husband:

> Things were getting bad around then, too, because the drug thing had started. The first time I remember seeing Ike do cocaine was in San Francisco. He was doing it on a hundred-dollar bill- that was supposed to be the classy thing, right? I didn't know. I thought to myself, 'I wonder why they're doing it on money?' I think he had been taking cocaine for a while, quietly, but then he started getting bold about it. He soon had the little containers of it around, and then people started giving him these little boxes. After a while, it became just like a pack of cigarettes in his pocket.

Ike demanded his money upfront, but because the promoters couldn't guarantee payment, he walked away. So what happened to Satsop's $210,000 in start-up money from interest-free and interest-bearing loans and other financial dealings? John Caldbick concluded:

> Money, lots of it, had simply disappeared, either through rampant petty filching or in large chunks. The situation was made worse by a flood of counterfeit tickets.

Nevertheless, additional funding was scraped up at the last minute, and the festival continued. Satsop performers including Delaney (without Bonnie) and Friends, Eric Burdon, Albert Collins, Spencer Davis, John Hammond Jr., Peter Jameson, Charles Lloyd, Steve Miller, Wishbone Ash, and Jimmy Witherspoon. Jesse Colin Young and The Youngbloods brought their universal message of love and peace to the crowd. "Get Together" reached #5 (RCA Victor, 1969) and became one of the anthems of the hippy movement.

Ed Jeffords, the press coordinator, said a total of 150,000 persons attended the event, with the largest crowd on Saturday, when the Buoys opened. Despite those numbers, losses were expected to reach $300,000, including $100,000 from ticket counterfeiting. The Federal Bureau of Investigation and the Internal Revenue Service were expected to investigate the counterfeiting case.

Counterfeit ticket seller arrested. (John Caldbick photo.)

20

DELANEY AND BONNIE & FRIENDS

An easterly drive from Satsop to Olympia, the performers' facility was The Westwater Hotel on Evergreen Park Drive. Built in 1970, the Westwater was the most excellent hotel in Olympia. It was surrounded by tall, evergreen trees and close to the water. It had an inviting lobby and entrance, a spacious restaurant and bar, and a private hot tub. John Caldbick was both an attendee and working journalist at Satsop:

> Many musicians who were supposed to play at the festival stayed at the hotel, although it's been so long ago now that I can't be positive. If I recall, it was sort of the off-site headquarters for the festival. Journalists could call in their copy from the farmhouse at the festival site, but still and moving pictures had to be ferried to somewhere they could be processed and disseminated.

Caldbick had to catch a ride down to Olympia several times to drop off film where it (and the film of other working photographers and filmmakers) was taken by either car or helicopter to Seattle. Finally, Caldbick's film was sent to the UPI bureau, located in the Seattle *Post-Intelligencer* building.

The trip from Satsop to the Westwater was a short half-hour drive. The hotel was top notch, said Carl Siracuse:

> Though I don't remember much of the layout of the rooms, I do remember the lobby area and the exterior and modern design overall being quite lovely even by today's standards. I recall being surrounded by tall evergreen trees with a view of the bay after a short walk down toward the water. Very nice.

The Westwater presented an exceptional opportunity for Hludzik and Kelly when they were asked to join thirty-two-year-old Delaney Bramlett for dinner. They were like old friends, for earlier in the year, The Buoys had played with Delaney's band and Sha Na Na at a free concert in Cleveland. Bramlett was larger than life and a meaningful connection. An animated Bramlett greeted Hludzik and Kelly with his Pontotoc County Mississippi drawl and trademark "Lord have mercy." The trio hung out until the early hours of the morning. Bramlett was drinking heavily and snorting cocaine as the night transformed into an amazing one of reverie, laughter, and stories of being on the road. Hludzic recollected:

> It was pretty exciting. Delaney told Kelly and me that we sang well. He was a real character and invited us to have dinner that night. We stayed in Olympia, Washington, at a place called the Westwater Hotel. Very nice place.
>
> We rarely stayed in fancy places. We usually stayed in shit holes, but that night I remember vividly eating lobster tail listening to Delany talk about other musicians, and repeatedly saying over and over, 'Lord have mercy!'

Seasoned and accomplished, Bramlett and Bonnie possessed an uncanny stage presence impossible to reproduce in the studio. Bramlett shared stories about his bandmates, legendary sidemen, including Duane Allman, Gregg Allman, Eric Clapton, Rita Coolidge, King Curtis, George Harrison, Dave Mason, Leon Russell, and Bobby Whitlock. He eagerly told story after story to an enraptured twenty-one-year-old Bill Kelly, who searched hard to uncover those ancient memories:

> I remember spending time with Delaney, who treated us well. He was great. Wishbone Ash was impressive, but really, I don't know who else stuck out at the time. It's been a while. Realize I was only twenty-one at the time and was way over my head.

Bramlett shared his accounts of playing with the Shindogs, the legendary house band of ABC TV's Shindig, which included guitar virtuoso and Rock and Roll Hall of Fame member James Burton, who played on Elvis, Roy Orbison, and Ricky Nelson sessions.

Hludzik and Kelly sat in awe of Bramlett in the restaurant. A cocaine-snorting, cigar-smoking girl hung on his arm. His estranged wife, Bonnie, was nowhere to be found. Kelly recalled:

> Jerry and I hung out with him and different people in the band. He snorted cocaine most of the time. He had it with him all the time. What I remember the most, he would do a blast of cocaine and go 'Woof! Lord have Mercy. Lord have Mercy.' And we'd get a giggle out of that.

The specter of Eric Clapton was omnipresent, and the cult hero may or may not have played with Delaney at the festival, according to photographer John Caldbick:

> As to Clapton, I believe that in my research, I found sources that went both ways on whether Clapton played with Delaney and Bonnie, and since I couldn't pin it down, I decided not to say one way or the other. I believe that he did, but I am not sure enough to state it as a fact. He wanted just to be one of the "friends" of Delaney and Bonnie at the time, and his presence was not emphasized in any of the materials I saw.

Still, the well-traveled Clapton believed that Delaney and Bonnie were light years ahead of his band, Blind Faith, and took Bramlett's band on the road in mid-1969 as the opening act. Clapton would often appear on stage with Delaney & Bonnie during this period, following Blind Faith's August 1969 breakup. Clapton brought Delaney & Bonnie to England and recruited musicians like George Harrison and Dave Mason to perform at their shows. Delaney, in turn, produced Clapton's self-titled debut solo album in 1970 and co-wrote most of the songs, including the gospel-tinged hit single "Let It Rain" (Polydor, 1972).

John Caldbick's clearest musical memories of Satsop, like those of Bill Kelly, were of Wishbone Ash (who did a Satsop reunion show back in 2010). However, he also was impressed with the high energy of Billy Preston, who did a knock-out show near the conclusion of the festival that helped it end on a relatively positive note. Preston, known as the Fifth Beatle, could, and did, dance like James Brown, bringing the house down.

BONNIE BRAMLETT

Bonnie Bramlett never showed up. Just before Sapsot, the couple had been entangled in a personal and professional meltdown, and their stormy marriage was dissolving. In 1970, on the eve of a concert tour, the duo's backup band abruptly quit. Bonnie told *People* magazine that marital woes were one problem, and drugs became another:

> Delaney and I were abusive to each other. We fought a lot, heavy-duty physical stuff. We were introduced to cocaine, and cocaine did to us what it does to people. It destroyed us.

Cocaine addiction can happen fast. Because the cocaine euphoria only lasts a short time, the user will snort it repeatedly to maintain the same high.

Unfortunately, chronic use often leads to physical tolerance, forcing the user to use increasingly higher doses. In his autobiographical book, *Street Player: My Chicago Story*, former Chicago drummer Danny Seraphine wrote about witnessing the destruction caused by this potent stimulant:

> More than ever, cocaine had gained a powerful hold on the band. The drug was everywhere in the 1970s, and nobody knew exactly how destructive it was. There were many times I considered coke a ninth member of the band. The guys thought they would be able to control its effects, but it often ended up controlling them. Over time, they became slaves to it.

Cocaine, a drug that induced energy and euphoria, was everywhere in the 1970s. People wore coke spoons around their necks, proudly proclaiming their user status. Tom Fox recalled when The Buoys crossed paths with someone who became a major cocaine dealer:

In the late 1970s, The Buoys began leasing planes from Factoryville's Seaman's Airport, flown by airline pilots including Frederick "Rik" Luytjes (pronounced Lie-chess). The charter service flew them to Iowa, Cleveland, Pittsburgh, and Nova Scotia. They also flew to Cumberland, Maryland, New York's Geneseo College, and frequently to Springfield, Massachusetts. On one occasion, they flew to Montreal for a TV show, and the following week, The Nitty Gritty Band flew in the same plane to perform on the same show.

Around 1980, Luytjes started Air America, operating out of the Wilkes-Barre-Scranton Airport. His main business was smuggling cocaine from Columbia to the U.S. using modified Cessna 310s to fly three thousand miles without refueling.

Mechanics spent thirty-three hours installing long-range fuel tanks, advanced radios, and navigation devices on twin-engine Cessna 310s. Air America then flew the hidden cocaine to remote airstrips in Pennsylvania and New York. Said Fox:

> They re-tooled Rik's plane with larger fuel tanks to transfer cocaine. That's where he got the idea to bring cocaine into Northeastern Pennsylvania and offload here. He had enough gas to fly all the way. Most people would stop in Florida and fuel up, but he didn't have to, and he flew low all the way to here.

In 1986, Luytjes and twelve co-conspirators were indicted on importing 7.5 tons of Columbian cocaine and laundering more than $25 million. In addition, $4.2 million in cash was uncovered, buried near Greentown, 45 miles northwest of Scranton. Luytjes maintained he was an informant working for the DEA and CIA.

Authorities claimed it was "the largest amount of cocaine ever smuggled into this country by a single drug trafficking organization," and according to Fox:

> I don't think he ever went to jail. He was going to Columbia, loading the cocaine, and coming back. All the competitors that he found he ratted out to the DEA and CIA. I think they let him work because he informed them about what was going on in Columbia.

Bill Stevenson, the owner of Delaware's legendary Stone Balloon, wrote that it seemed as if everyone was doing drugs at this time, and he "started doing more drugs in 1979." In *Stone Balloon: The Early Years,* he openly admitted his cocaine use:

> I do not mean to imply that all my business friends or even my close friends ever used illegal drugs. The story of my cocaine use is neither a sad nor a tragic story; it is simply the truth. People reading this might think I'm in denial and trying to spin the story to make myself look better, but the basic facts about my few years of cocaine involvement speak for themselves.

Stevenson estimates that he spent under $50,000 on cocaine during those six years and probably gave away half of what he bought. He said it was "a small cost of doing business." He noted that the Balloon grossed more than $10 million, all in cash, in those six years. Cocaine damages arteries and veins and causes the heart to race, resulting in cardiac problems. In August 2018, at the age of seventy, Bill Stevenson had a massive heart attack on the streets of New York City. He was severely obese and no longer the conditioned athlete he once was and almost died.

Cocaine experienced a surge in popularity in the 1970s, peaking in the 1980s. During this time, it was associated with celebrities, high rollers, and glamorous parties. Bonnie Bramlett told writer Jill McLane Smith that cocaine was part and parcel of rock and roll:

> Of course, it was the time. The people that were in control of the industry encouraged that behavior. Deals were made with ounces of cocaine on the table, and it was the suits who furnished it for us. An old joke in rock in roll says you can tell who has the best record deal by who has the best cocaine.

Bonnie didn't point fingers at the industry, charging that, "Nobody handed me a bag of cocaine but Delaney." The drugs, and specifically the cocaine, became worse. By late 1971, Delaney and Bonnie's often-tempestuous relationship had been damaged beyond repair, their love lost forever. It was then that they scored their most successful record. "Never Ending Song of Love" (Atco, 1971) reached #13 on *Billboard*. The couple divorced in 1973 after releasing their last album *Together* (Columbia, 1972). In 2008, Delaney died in a Los Angeles hospital following gallbladder surgery. He was sixty-nine and one of the most significant musicians that Hludzik and Kelly would encounter.

Although it was somewhat trendy to write songs about recreational drug use, The Buoys and Dakota never addressed drugs, either pro or con, in their songs. They felt that the all-prevalent drugs and groupies were just a distraction. They were serious about what they were doing. "Our songs had depth, and drugs never got a foothold," Kelly said about why they never focused on them.

21

SATSOP'S SWAN SONG

Road Manager Tom Fox said that being a part of the West Coast road trip, taking The Buoys to the famed Whisky-a-Go-Go and the four-day Satsop "people's festival," was among the high points of his career. Passing through California, Oregon, Washington, Idaho, and Montana presented the band with an opportunity to showcase their songs, harmonies, and stage presence. Bill Kelly said they did not disappoint, as indicated by favorable Satsop reviews:

> I know we were mentioned in the trades as delivering a near-flawless imitation of Crosby, Stills, and Nash. I'm not sure if it was a slam or a compliment.

It was indeed a compliment that Kelly would repeatedly hear during his time with the group. The Buoys had perfected the vocal delivery of CSN&Y,

Satsop's bad weather. (John Caldbick photo.)

offering note-for-note renditions of those intricate harmonies. That was what the Satsop crowd was screaming about. Satsop gave them exposure as it afforded them the opportunity. Leann Paul, the site owner, viewed the festival as a grand opportunity for fledgling bands. She said:

> I've never known anything about The Buoys or the Sheppton mining disaster. I will say, and you can quote me, that every person who took the stage at Satsop deserved to be there. Rock Festivals, by nature, were a 'Peoples' platform, and all of the up-and-coming artists of the time were excited to get the exposure. It was kind of like our modern-day X Factor, but the audience was the judge. Many of the bands, including The Buoys, became household names after Satsop.

The Buoys' appearance at Satsop inspired concert attendee and song-writer Irven Lorance to connect Sheppton, Pennsylvania with Carbonado, Washington:

> I saw the Buoys at Satsop River Fair & Tin Cup Races in 1971. They per-formed 'Timothy,' and I bought the album it was on. I thought Timothy was a mule or a donkey. The song helped inspire me to write a song about an 1899 mine disaster in Carbonado, Washington, called 'Black Diamonds.' The song was about the reflection of coal in the eyes of a mule.

Inspired by "Timothy," Lorance wrote about Carbonado, the largest coal mine in Pierce County. Located forty miles east of Tacoma, it was the worst coal mining disaster in Washington when an explosion in the Carbon Hill coal mine killed 32 miners.

NEW WASHINGTON STATE LAW

Satsop was the first rock festival organized under a new Washington state law requiring promoters to obtain a permit endorsed by local health officials ap-proving water supply, sewage disposal, food preparation facilities, and lighting. In addition, law enforcement had to certify good crowd and traffic control. It was an example of cooperation between rural communities and big-city concert promoters.

The Satsop River Fair and Tin Cup Races attracted over 100,000 music fans but resulted in only nineteen accidents, including the angry watermelon driver who plowed unto the crowd. One unnamed attendee recalled the meteorologi-cal, Woodstock-like event:

> It rained most of the time. We dried out our sleeping bags in a local laundro-mat, and I remember spending two nights sleeping in the front seats of a VW

(John Caldbick photo.)

bug. The car belonged to my friend, so he got the backseat. I don't remember much about the music. Delaney and Bonnie and Friends were there. We were more concerned about keeping dry.

Satsop still reverberated in their ears. The members of the band all shared in the "inside joke" after they saw the Satsop concert poster that misspelled their names as "The BOYUS." With Satsop behind them, additional tour dates took them further east into Missoula, Montana, and Twin Falls, Idaho, where they performed the first concert of the season at the College of Southern Idaho Fine Arts Center.

The group members flew back home from Boise's Gowen Field. The Buoys' equipment was packed into a Ryder truck and driven on I-80 through nine states and over 2000 miles by the band's capable roadies, Frank Colosimo, Alan "Bear" Eckert, and Joe Van Loon.

The adventure continued: more places, more exposure. Much of the Midwest was flat and predictable, with its natural beauty, but worlds apart from Pennsylvania's mountains and rivers. On Wednesday, October 20, 1971, the Buoys performed at the Green Onion in Indianapolis. A promotional ad in the Indianapolis *News* read:

> The Onion offers you the Biggest Night of entertainment ever. National Recording Stars, The Buoys will be at the Onion in concert with a Ninety-Minute Knock-out-Show featuring their Gold Record "Timothy." Also, in concert, The Force, the Onion's exciting head group that plays what's happening now.

Going home through the mud. (John Caldbick photo.)

So, come in and dig a musical happening. The Green Onion, the Club that brought you The Archies, The Zombies, The Outsiders, and the Animals.

The Buoys were developing a reputation for musicality and solid stage performances. They were more polished, more rehearsed, and more confident. They had practiced their stage act over and over again, realizing what worked and what didn't, what got them standing ovations, and how best to sequence their list of songs. Also, if imitation is the sincerest form of flattery, then the Buoys acknowledged the Beatles and other musical influences.

The group returned home in the fall of 1971. They performed at the King's College Auditorium on November 18, "in their first area appearance in three months." The opening act was folk artist Ted Bird. Tickets were $1.50.

That same month they performed with Mutt Lee, Eighth Street Bridge, and Gardner at Serge's Cabaret, East Mountain Road, in a fund-raiser for the non-profit Peace and Freedom Center.

Satsop was a magical moment, the pot of gold at the end of the rainbow. It was the secret city within our 42nd state, hammering home the fact that the Buoys were good enough to open the festival for two days straight, in front of thousands, and command the same stage as Delaney Bramlett, Eric Burden, and Jesse Colin Young. The Satsop River Fair will be remembered as one of the last utopian events of its kind and something that could never have been envisioned by The Moffats, jamming in the West Wyoming Hose Company just a few years before.

★ PART VI ★

HOT FUN IN THE SUMMERTIME

22

SLY STONE'S POCONO SUMMER TRAFFIC JAM

The Buoys crossed paths with Sly and the Family Stone just after that supergroup scripted a rather personal chapter in local rock & roll history.

Twenty-three months after the hot fun of the Woodstock summertime, Sly Stone brought his electrifying act to the region, creating a massive, five-hour traffic jam on Luzerne County's backwater country roads. In a word, it was a mess, but it could have been a calamity.

THE POCONO SUMMER CONCERT

Panicked racetrack owners forced the Pocono Summer concert to change locations from Wilkes-Barre's Pocono Downs Raceway after advanced sales tallied over 10,000.

They chose Palace Park, a rural twenty-six-acre recreational area long past its glory days, and set the date of Sunday, July 11, 1971. In hindsight, it wasn't the best of plans. Palace Park was nestled in the village of Hunlock Creek and had only one tiny access road. Concert goers immediately created a winding nine-mile traffic jam beginning at Palace Park and continuing beyond West Nanticoke. Frustrated drivers pounded on their horns in a harsh screeching, triggering incidents of road rage. Traffic had virtually stopped on the three-mile Hunlock Creek Road leading to the concert site and several miles on Rt. 11, and the cavalcade of cars just kept on coming.

Groups of youthful hitchhikers, bound for the concert, clogged Route 309 from Hazleton to Wilkes-Barre. Thousands arrived earlier in the day, while many others camped out Saturday night. Crowds were estimated at "well over 15,000," many without tickets, quickly slipping past security through the surrounding woods. Approximately fifty bonfires, made from broken picnic benches and timber taken from a nearby storage shed, helped take the chill out of the summer's nighttime air.

Promoters could have averted the traffic jam if seasoned Pocono Downs personnel handled the crowd. But, instead, groups of inexperienced and cheaply hired college students directed traffic into the fields around Palace Park.

Being late for concert appearances was a notorious and expected part of the Sly Stone tradition. An ad in the Madison, Wisconsin *State Journal*, promoting an upcoming Dade County Coliseum concert, considered that:

> The performance of the rock group is guaranteed. There will be full refunds if Sly and the Family Stone do not perform for the contracted time. The group failed to appear for a concert here previously.

The Pocono Summer concert was different, as the band's entourage could not avoid or circumvent the messy Rt. 11 and Hunlock Creek Road quagmire. Still, true to form, Sly missed his scheduled time to be on stage. So instead, local musicians Lex Romane and Patti Lewis performed. Dr. Hook and Ruth Copeland also soothed the crowd; their sets interspersed with announcements that "Sly is coming," "Sly is coming."

DR. HOOK

Dr. Hook was just starting out and far from his peak of popularity. Nevertheless, the New Jersey band, formed in 1968 as Dr. Hook & The Medicine Show, charted with "Sylvia's mother" #5 (Columbia, 1972). They returned to the area, performing at the Bloomsburg Fair, on September 23, 1980. (Note: These were exciting times for me. As a Rock Journalist, I received coveted Backstage Passes to interview Dr. Hook on Tuesday and Rupert Holmes on Friday. The easy-going lead singer Ray Sawyer (with the eye patch) offered me a beer, and we drank while I interviewed him in his R.V.) Sawyer sang lead on their #6 hit "The Cover of the Rolling Stone." (Columbia, 1972.)

Dressed like Supergirl, Ruth Copeland, from Newcastle, England, came on stage in red tights and swirling cape. She evoked the late Janis Joplin, with hair flying and feet stomping. Copeland, an exciting blues singer, performed her single "Gimme Shelter" (Invictus, 1971), the well-known Stones' classic, to an enthusiastic crowd.

Sly was over four hours late. He was supposed to start at 7:00 P.M., but his five limousines didn't arrive until 11:20 P.M. The band appeared on stage at midnight. State Police officials reported that the concert broke up around 1:00 A.M. Five squad cars, with two troopers each, policed the area, ensuring the safety of local citizens, mainly directing traffic and helping dazed and confused fans get out of town.

In the aftermath, concert critics cited the usual litany of drugs, litter, congested traffic, and the end of the world as we once knew it. But, even worse, after the Pocono Summer concert, Sly's Day of Armageddon and well-publicized struggles with substance abuse would sadly catch up to him.

SYLVESTER STONE'S FALL FROM GRACE

While Hludzik and Kelly were hanging out with Delaney Bramlett at the Westwater Hotel, Tom Fox was shooting pool at a local Olympia bar. Both places were a short drive from the grounds of the rain-soaked and chaotic Satsop Festival. Several musicians had gathered there, drinking, unwinding, and trading stories. Fox was about to meet a genuine Rock and Roll Hall of Famer. One of the band members introduced him to twenty-eight-year-old Sylvester Stewart, the Family Stone's prolific architect. Stone, at 6' 2", towered over Fox.

Sly was spending time in the area before several concerts in Inglewood, California's Forum. He had racked up monster hits: "Everyday People" #1 (Epic, 1969), "Hot Fun in the Summertime" #2 (Epic, 1969), and "Family Affair" #1 (Eric, 1971), and recorded acclaimed albums including *Stand!* (Epic, 1969) and *There's a Riot Going On* (Epic, 1971). They were paid $7000 for their Woodstock performance, not as much as Hendrix, but worth every penny.

Sly was larger than life, confident, imposing. And loud. He wore a glittering jumpsuit, like Elvis, only with more glitter. Sly chided Tom Fox into playing a game of pool, but the highly competitive Fox was terrible at pool. It wasn't going to end well. The jukebox played "Hot Fun in the Summertime" as Sly chalked up his custom-made pool cue and got down low. He was a natural with a loose wrist and grip. He used a short, snappy follow-through. His balls, like rounded magnets, went straight into the called pockets. His stroke was fast, and his shots dangerous, straight through the cue ball, like an explosion. Crack! Every time Sly made a shot, Family Stone musicians Freddie Stone and Larry Graham went wild. The place was crazy loud. Finally, drawing back the stick, Sly sank his best shot. Nothing tricky, just laser-sharp accuracy, followed by a flash of teeth and a mumbled challenge. Fox stood against the wall, feeling foolish as Sly lined up his next shot. The clacking of balls exploded along with the cheers of his minions.

"Loser buys. Rack 'em up," he barked, not so much to Fox but to anyone in the room watching the unfolding drama. Fox never had a chance. All eyes were on Sly, the quintessential showman, running the table, monopolizing the game, hustling Fox. Years later, Fox admitted that, despite his embarrassment, he would always cherish those exciting Satsop days of laughter and shared memories.

TRANSFORMATIVE MUSICAL LEGEND

Sylvester Stone had been a transformative musical legend who blended musical genres into one. Moreover, his appeal crossed cultural lines. With his Family Stone, he turned Max Yasgur's farm into a dance party, traded rock for funk, and was among a handful of acts to emerge from Woodstock as a bona fide "superstar." Before his fall from grace, the former disk jockey and San Francisco record producer was one of the hottest acts of the era. Then, slipping into drug addiction and withdrawing from the spotlight, he retreated into the inner-city slums as a ghostly non-person.

Arriving late for concerts became a notorious aspect of the Sly Stone tradition. Stone canceled twenty-six of the eighty dates he had committed himself to in 1970 and roughly half of the following year's shows. Tardiness wasn't the problem, but his struggles with substance abuse, like a raging riptide, were. After an arrest for cocaine possession, the singer entered a drug diversion program in Los Angeles in October 1979. He was arrested two years later in Hawthorne, California, for possession of a controlled substance and arrested again on July 27, 1982, after Los Angeles police found cocaine and a handgun in his attaché case.

It only got worse. In June 1983, Stone was unconscious, with a female companion, at a Fort Myers, Florida hotel. Officials stated that he "was in a narcotic trance or semi-conscious state" when deputies arrived to arrest him. Police found what appeared to be a freebasing glass kit, three propane tanks, a torch, and a razor with white powder still on it. Officials charged him with third-degree felony possession of cocaine, possession of drug paraphernalia, and attempting to skip out on a bill for food and drinks. Then, as Woodstock celebrated his coronation, Fort Myers witnessed his fall from grace. He refused to go to the hospital and, after posting a $5,750 bond, was released from the Lee County Jail.

COCAINE

Long associated with the rich and famous, cocaine (Cocaine hydrochloride) is a water-soluble salt that the user can snort, eat or inject, but not smoke. In his book, *Street Player: My Chicago Story,* Chicago drummer Danny Seraphine watched as cocaine, ever-present in the 1970s, gained a powerful hold on his peers:

> The beauty of the hippy movement had long since turned ugly. The drug culture had cast a shadow over everything. People like Jimi Hendrix and Janis Joplin had already succumbed to their addictions. Nobody simply experimented anymore. Drugs were being used for daily maintenance, not recreation and exploration.

An alternative Rock and Roll Hall of Fame sadly lists the musicians who have succumbed to cocaine's allure: Steve Clark (Def Leppard), Kevin DeBrow (Quiet Riot), John Entwistle (The Who), Shannon Hoon (Blind Melon), Johnny Thunders (New York Dolls), David Ruffin (The Temptations), and Ike Turner (Kings of Rhythm).

FREEBASE COCAINE

Cocaine, also known as "base," is made from hydrochloride and alkaloid. In the 1970s, ether, a highly flammable liquid, was used to "free" the base from additives and impurities. A heat source, like a lighter or torch, heats the freebase, and the user inhales the vapors. A powerful rush is felt within seconds, coupled with an orgasmic, long-lasting high. With a 75% to 100% purity, freebase can trigger psychosis, hallucinations, paranoia, and violence. The high is often followed by depression, anxiety, and uncontrollable drug seeking, as the user craves freebase again and again.

Freebasing caused numerous burns and accidents whenever the heat source set off the incredibly flammable and unstable ether. Around that time, another reworking of freebase, known as crack, hit the streets. Crack is made by boiling cocaine in a water and baking soda mixture, creating a waxy, rock-like crystal. The rocks, sold in vials, are heated and inhaled into the lungs. The term "crack" referred to the crackling sound the rock made when heated.

Although the terms "freebasing" and "smoking crack" are used interchangeably, crack is less dangerous because the user does not have to heat ether to free the base and is generally less expensive than freebase, which is almost pure. Crack has the reputation of being the "poor man's drug." Still, it has appealed to many accomplished personalities like Toronto Mayor Rob Ford, Washington,

D.C., Mayor Marion Barry, Whitney Houston, Amy Winehouse, and musician Gil Scott-Heron. Crack plays no favorites.

NARCOTICS VIOLATION

Several individuals were responsible for raising awareness of the drug's dangers. For example, Richard Prior was severely burned while freebasing in 1980, and that same year, Sly Stone publicly boasted that freebasing was superior to snorting cocaine.

With mounting legal troubles, and lawsuits against his former manager, Stone's difficulties continued. The millionaire was now bankrupt. Stone was charged with possession of cocaine in November 1987, the second time in less than a year. In 1989 he spent Thanksgiving in a California jail, and in 2011, he was reportedly homeless, living in a white van parked in the rough Crenshaw neighborhood of L.A. Finally, he was arrested in 2017 (once again) for cocaine possession. It was a sad ending for someone who had created such a brilliant and innovative career.

One of the most positive signs of individual wellness is when someone asks for help. For example, in Mychal Denzel Smith's article "Why did we let Sly Stone slip away?" the author uncovered an obvious truth:

> It's easy to draw the line from genius to a dark and troubled soul, but something about Sly suggests that he simply enjoyed getting high more than he enjoyed performing and being fawned over. And that's just Sly, the main reason we haven't heard from him in so long and the main reason we haven't been able to be there for him the way we may have been for other fallen legends who needed our support: he just didn't want it.

"I wanna take you higher," Sylvester Stone sang out to the masses, but the higher he climbed, the harder he fell. Stone chose freebase over powder cocaine because the effects were more intense and immediate and more potent than the adoration of his fans. For this former superstar, who had attained magnificent heights of greatness, freebase symbolized his fall from grace and a possible cautionary tale for the rest of us.

★ PART VII ★

POLYDOR RECORDS

23

TWO-MILLION COPIES SOLD

The end of the Scepter chapter wasn't pretty. Scepter had lost heart and was going out of business. Additionally, some felt the label wasn't being straight up about its bookkeeping.

Carl Siracuse joined the band in November 1970, right after Scepter re-released "Timothy." Scepter took out several full-page ads in *Billboard* and *Cashbox*, but, other than that, the label was not doing much to promote the band. One of the technical snags was that C. Michael Wright was under contract to Scepter Records, but The Buoys were under contract to him. Because of that caveat, Scepter treated them like orphans, observed Siracuse:

> We were being ignored by Scepter. That was one of the problems with them. We complained that we needed more promotional support and were itching to get out on the road to promote the record, but nothing was done on Scepter's end. They were tight.

Chris Hanlon was involved in one specific incident. Hanlon sat on a glass table at one of the meetings and unintentionally cracked it. He had been agitated at the time, and negotiations were not going well. Nevertheless, Scepter added the cost of the table to The Buoys' dwindling account. Kelly remembered Hanlon's accident during the Scepter meeting with Stanley Greenberg and his mother:

> How he did it, I'll never know, but Chris leaned on a glass table, and it shattered. Scepter charged us for that, and the damage showed up on one of our royalty bills. It was less than a hundred dollars, if that, and as artists with a Top Twenty record, Scepter actually charged us. What kind of a small-minded pea would do that? We left on a sour note. We didn't like them, and they didn't like us.

And during their Western road trip that included Satsop, Scepter arranged for the Ryder van to haul their equipment and a Scepter credit card. As a result, the band was able to call long distance to talk to their parents and girlfriends, the charges then meticulously added to their account. The Buoys were not profiting from "Timothy"'s success, recollected Siracuse:

> We weren't receiving any kind of royalties. During one meeting, Scepter told us that 'Timothy' sold 400,000 copies but that the production costs were more outstanding than what we were going to get. They said there wasn't enough money left to divvy up. We didn't believe them because Tom Fox was told by a distributor from the Atlanta / Southeastern U.S. market that he had personally sold, or was responsible, for well over another 400,000 copies.

The numbers from Scepter just didn't add up. In February 1971, at a Wilkes College concert, producer C. Michael Wright formally presented the Buoys an award for "Timothy," selling 500,000 copies. The audience went wild, filling the auditorium with an explosive celebratory roar that, months later, was silenced.

"Timothy" became one of the slowest-developing hit singles in recording history, but the actual amount of record sales depended on who was telling the story. For example, Scepter president Florence Greenberg told Cash Box:

> Sales are now over 700,000, and we consider only 50% of the country has ever heard the record. Projecting on this, "Timothy" could become a two-million seller.

Kelly joined in the chorus of those suspicious of Scepter's accounting methods:

> Well, we only knew what Rupert told us. As far as being undercounted, we didn't have the financial backing to go and pursue it. Rupert knew more about the business than we did, and he pretty much said, 'Yeah, we were undercounted.' He said that he had done a count, at some point, and the record sold a million and a half copies, but we never got credit for that many copies.

Scepter's questionable bookkeeping led to several of the label's most prominent acts suing for nonpayment of royalties. In 1963 The Shirelles learned that the Scepter trust holding their royalties (that they were supposed to receive on their twenty-first birthdays) did not exist. They left the label and filed a breach of contract suit against the company. On November 9, 1998, after lengthy litigation, The Kingsmen were awarded ownership of "Louie Louie" and other

Wand recordings because they had not been paid royalties since the 1960s. To this day, The Buoys can only speculate what their bottom line looked like and how many recordings of "Timothy" were sold.

In June 1971, Scepter announced a new retail and distribution price schedule. Executive vice president Sam Goff and national sales director Ed Kushins said that the Scepter 500 series (Dionne Warwick, B.J. Thomas) would retail at $5.98. In contrast, the 24,000 series (Brethren, The Buoys, and Allen Toussaint) would remain at the $4.98 list price. So again, lots of people were making money on lucrative vinyl albums.

DINNER MUSIC

The promotion could have been smoother. First, Scepter should have released *Dinner Music* earlier to capitalize on the three singles. Then, "Timothy" was banned on some major radio stations, and the lyrics changed to appease irritated station owners. Explained Chris Hanlon:

> If it hadn't been for that timing, 'Timothy' would have been a million-seller. But, unfortunately, we had terrible coordination with the song's release throughout the country. If it had all hit everywhere, at once, we feel it would have been bigger.

For road manager Tom Fox, the timing was about as bad as it could get:

> When 'Timothy' was hot, it took us so long to get the album out. It took too long. It wasn't our fault. It was Scepter's fault. They weren't convinced about how strong the song was, and, all of a sudden, we're in the Top Twenty and being played everywhere. But, unfortunately, they dropped the ball on this one.

As the sun's rays faded, it signaled the end of a once vibrant record label. Scepter folded. The Buoys moved on. Ed Socha, writing for the Hazleton *Standard-Speaker*, reported:

> After another release, "Give Up Your Guns," and another album, the band and Scepter Records became a part of a series of lawsuits that prohibited the Buoys from recording for two years.

"HOLLYWOOD & VINE"

Harold Vealer, a long-time friend of C. Michael Wright, organized the western tour. Vealer, a.k.a. "Hollywood & Vine," was a former record distributor and disc jockey and an invaluable asset. He booked the Buoys into the Whisky-A-Go

Go and several other gigs on the West Coast. But Vealer was someone Fox had his eye on:

> Vealer's the one who was double-booking us. He was taking the deposit and not telling us, and we were picking up the balance. We thought we were just making the money we were getting, but it turns out, a significant percentage of the capital, maybe as much as half of it, was being sent back to New York to Vealer as his commission. We all flipped out. We were upset.
>
> We were struggling. We weren't making a lot, maybe a thousand dollars a night. It wasn't a lot of money. With the tour, we wanted to get our name out there, but we found out later that Vealer was getting another thousand dollars more than us. If we had gotten that, we would have been filing a couple of thousand dollars a night.

Something stunk at the label, beginning and ending with disputed book-keeping. Compounding the situation, The Buoys committed the cardinal sin of young artists by not seeking legal advice. Hanlon recollected:

> 'Timothy' should have made $80,000 for us, but our contract was terrible. So we got a lawyer, Jerry Margolis, who is also the attorney for the Rolling Stones, and it's the best thing that's ever happened to us. So now we have a good contract with Polydor Record. If it weren't for Margolis, the group would have folded up.

Fox was angry at the financial gremlins plaguing his group, having detected irregularities with monies owed and Vealer's so-called "commission." Money was the dirty part of the business. So it made sense for Fox to step up and take charge, to keep things on the up and up:

> When we finally completed that West Coast trip, we immediately fired Vealer. That was when Michael Wright asked me to be their manager. We weren't that sophisticated back then, just starting, and then we hired Gerry Margolis.

Their association with entertainment attorney Gerry Margolis would lead to their next chapter, a new record deal, and the promise of more extraordinary things.

24

LIZA'S LAST RIDE

As Scepter retreated in their rearview mirror, Brozena, Hanlon, Hludzik, Kelly, and Siracuse's big adventure continued. At this point, the band had severed ties with C. Michael Wright and came up with another plan. They would write the songs, Rupert Holmes would handle the production and, with luck, the magic would continue, as recollected by Tom Fox:

> Rupert ended up negotiating our album with Polydor and produced the whole thing. Rupert's a very qualified producer and knows music well, but I think his biggest problem is that he overproduces. He over arranges. He loves strings and orchestration, and his type of music is current.

The Buoys didn't have to worry about overproduction because Holmes took a different approach from *Dinner Music*. Although there was discussion about overdubs and additional embellishment, they agreed that the songs needed to be "clean" to be played live without other musicians. With that in mind, Holmes departed from the multi-layered instrumentation heard on *Dinner Music*, producing a more stripped-down sound. Said Siracuse.

> I think it was intentional not to embellish the songs with other instrumentation. Some of the guys, like Bill and Jerry, and I'm not sure about Fran, didn't like the idea of adding all of the instrumentation. They wanted the songs to be ones we could do live because we didn't want to hire five backup people doing strings.

(L-R) Manager Tom Fox, author Maxim Furek, Carl Siracuse. (Marlyn Kauffman photo.)

Siracuse preferred Howard Reeves' instrumentation that brought life into both "Timothy" and "Give Up Your Guns," but, with apologies to Chairman Mao, there's was a democratic process and, despite varied opinions and dissenting voices, the majority ruled.

GERRY MARGOLIS
Another invaluable team member was Gerald Alvin Margolis, a skilled surfer and entertainment attorney who became the bridge between The Buoys and Polydor Records. Kelly thought that Margolis was a bit of a genius:

> Gerry was just a great attorney. He guided us. He told us what to accept, what not to accept, when to take a dice roll, or how to be strict with the label. So he was a significant influence.

Entertainment lawyer Margolis earned a law degree at Fordham University and, after joining a New York law firm, founded a California branch in the mid-1970s. As a partner in the Los Angeles law firm of Manatt, Phelps, and Phillips, Margolis helped build the firm's music practice with many high-profile celebrities. Among their entertainment clients were Lyle Lovett, Jennifer Nettles, and Neil Young, in addition to Death Cab for Cutie, Earth, Wind & Fire, and Papa Roach.

Margolis was in high demand. He later took on tough high-profile cases, such as defending R. Kelly in a lawsuit involving the allegation that he had sex with a minor and successfully defending Mick Jagger and Keith Richards over alleged copyright infringement.

Mark Gaillard and Mary Anderson sued The Rolling Stones, claiming that the song "Saint of Me" (Virgin,1997) plagiarized a song they wrote and recorded in 1996 called "Oh Yeah." They claimed the engineer for the Stones album, John Bernard, was in the studio when they recorded the song in 1996. The Stones countered that "Saint of Me," on their *Bridges to Babylon* album, was written as a tribute to R&B performer Billy Preston, who played keyboards on the track.

BLAXPLOITATION GAME

Polydor was a new chapter for The Buoys. It was an opportunity to jumpstart their careers. The German-British record label, Polydor Records Ltd., was established in London in 1954 as a British subsidiary of German company Deutsche Grammophon GmbH. Polydor entered the U.S. market in 1969 and in 1972 was renamed Polydor Ltd. Music critic Randall Davis observed that, even back in 1972, the label was taking a different approach:

> Polydor Records is beginning to make inroads into the popular music market by releasing fewer albums and by issuing, for the most part, only top-quality music.

The first time The Buoys walked into the Polydor studios, they saw a life-sized cardboard cutout of James Brown prominently displayed in the center of the lobby. James Brown, The Godfather of Soul, was Polydor's overachiever, but the label was also home to The Bee Gees, Manfred Mann, John Mayall, and The Moody Blues, Slade, and The Who.

Despite that fantastic talent, Polydor had built a bridge over troubled waters. They were active participants in the Blaxploitation game, a film genre that exploited black youth by stereotyping them in questionable roles, such as pimps and drug dealers. Polydor issued soundtrack LPs for urban films; *Black Caesar*, featuring Fred Williamson, with music by James Brown; *Coffey* featuring Pam Grier, with music by Roy Ayres; and *Slaughter's Big Rip-Off*, featuring Jim Brown, with the score composed by James Brown and Fred Wesley, with Brown doing the vocals.

Writing for the New York *Daily News*, Jim Farber's "Hymns to The Bad Old Days of Blaxploitation" asked:

> Was there ever a genre more gloriously perverse than early '70s blaxploitation films? Loathed by liberals but lionized by inner-city youths and outer-limit,

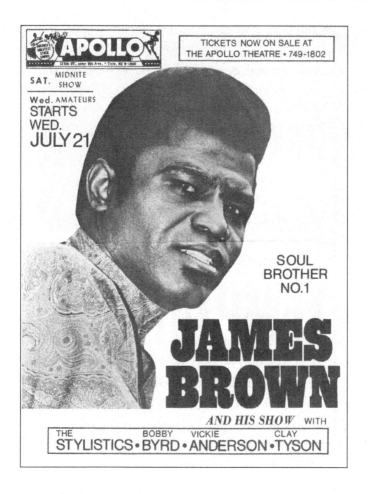

campy whites, movies like *Shaft's Big Score* or *Sheba Baby* presented black
empowerment as an exhilarating cheap thrill.

The controversial era of Blaxploitation was roughly from 1971 to 1974.
Films that used Polydor soundtracks were modestly successful, as evidenced by
Black Caesar (1973), $2 million rentals and ticket sales; *Coffey* (1973), $2 million; and *Slaughter's Big Rip-Off* (1973), $1 million. Other blaxploitation films
were lucrative motion pictures, often shot on shoe-string budgets. Among the
notable successes were *Shaft* (1971), $12 million, scored by Isaac Hayes; *Shaft's
Big Score* (1972), $10 million; followed by *Shaft in Africa* (1973), $1,395,000;
and *Shaft* (2019), $21.4 million. *Superfly* (1972), with the soundtrack com-
posed by Curtis Mayfield, netted $30 million in sales, and the 2018 remake
earned $20.8 million.

Both Florence Greenberg and Polydor courted the profitable African-American market. Scepter did it with black crossover artists like Dionne Warwick and the Shirelles' highly successful girl group. As manager of the Shirelles, and with co-owner Luther Dixon, Greenberg was able to navigate the black pop market, amassing an impressive catalog of black artists, including Maxine Brown, the Esquires, Tommy Hunt, the Isley Brothers, and Chuck Jackson. Then, too, Scepter gave The Buoys a white rock act, their first taste of success.

"DON'T TRY TO RUN"

With Holmes replacing Wright as producer, a new album, written entirely by The Buoys, was recorded at Manhattan's Media Sound Studio. Manager Tom Fox was excited about the possibilities:

> When they signed us, Polydor wasn't a big player in the States, but they wanted to get into (the American market) more. They were a big European company just gaining a foothold in the States. James Brown was their big star. At that time, everybody was writing their own songs. The Beatles, Dylan. So were The Buoys.

The proposed Polydor LP included an entire slate of original Buoys' compositions, including "Streams Together," "Pittsburgh Steel," "Dreams," and "Look Back America." "Don't Try to Run" and "Liza's Last Ride" were the first single releases. The songs were co-produced by Holmes, Billy Meshel, and Danny Jordan and pressed by Scranton's Capitol Records Pressing Plant.

"Don't Try to Run" (Polydor, 1973), written by Brozena, Kelly, and Hludzik, was a harmony-laden gem that evoked the nostalgic transition when "electric trains and childhood games make way for something new." It began with a majestic buildup and Hanlon's pounding drums before segueing into a slower tempo with Hludzik and Kelly trading lead vocals on the infectious and convincing "Don't try to run, don't try to run, run" chorus. On the second stanza, Kelly is on the lead. They meet again with the chorus before a fadeout; Kelly's voice is bursting forth, traveling through a reverb time machine and whipsaw lead guitar. An optimistic mention in the Hazleton *Standard-Speaker* projected, 'The group's new smash single, 'Don't Try to Run,' is predicted to outdistance their last big hit, 'Timothy.'

The flip side was called "Dreams." Listening to this song, one hears the spirit of David Crosby, shapeshifting into Media Sound and lending his voiceover to the mix. The soft, well-paced song, with unbounded possibilities, could have easily been included on CSN&Y's *Déjà Vu* LP It has a beautiful piano interlude and proves that The Buoys were apt students of the genre.

"Look Back America" owed much to Neil Young's "Cowgirl in the Sand," with Kelly's vocals floating over the track, soon met with the added voices of the others, keeping true to Young's creative spirit.

The songs included the dark, revenge-song "Pittsburgh Steel" about foundry workers who dispose of their cruel and heartless boss by dumping him into a vat of molten steel, which was possibly a variation on the melancholy theme of either "kill him or eat him."

A particular composition was "Liza's Last Ride" b/w "Downtown Singer" (Polydor, 1973). "Liza" was co-written by the Buoys in honor of Holmes' wife Liza (actually attorney Elizabeth Wood). Air Personality Mike Naydock, host of the *Cellarful of Noise* (King's College Radio 88.5 WRKC), and composer of The Badlees' "Angeline is Coming Home," observed that the song "was a great little jaunty break-up song with a nice Guess Who-ish feel to it." The song featured Hludzik's strong lead vocals. Siracuse suggested adding a baritone sax to "beef up" Hludzik's bass line and began to compose a simple sax part.

25

LIVING FOR THE CITY

Opening in 1969, Media Sound Recording Studios, once the home of the Manhattan Baptist Church, was a cluster of state-of-the-art recording and mastering studios and one of the most successful recording studios in the business. Echoes of Aerosmith, Billy Joel, Lou Reed, the Rolling Stones, Streisand, and Sinatra were among its hallowed vibrations. The studio retained part of the Baptist ambiance, and soft patterned light flowed through the ornate stained glass. Yet, there was something special about Media Sound's "Studio A." According to Mixonline's Bobby Bank:

> Studio A became the talk of New York; it was architecturally flamboyant and the scene of many hit sessions. Hank Meyer, booking manager, remembers Mick Jagger wearing a mink coat and sporting a beard, just coming off 57th Street wanting to take a look at Studio A.

Bass guitarist, Bob Babbitt, was familiar with Studio A. His group, the Funk Brothers, were considered among the most successful studio musicians in music history. They played on Motown hits such as The Temptations' "My Girl" #1 (Gordy, 1964), Marvin Gaye's "I Heard It Through the Grapevine" #1 (Tamla, 1968), and Martha and the Vandellas' "Heat Wave" #1 (Gordy, 1963). Babbitt perceived that:

> Media Sound was a studio that had everything going for it. I was able to get great bass sounds, especially from Studio A. It had a sound that no other studio had, complete with stained glass that was kept intact.

The actual creation of Media Sound Studios resulted from a one-of-a-kind ad that fortuitously ran in the March 22, 1967, issue of the New York Times. It read:

> Young men with unlimited capital looking for interesting, legitimate investment opportunities and business propositions. X1739 Times.

Those young men were Joel Rosenman, twenty-four, and John Roberts, twenty-two, well-to-do Ivy Leaguers. Roberts had just inherited "several millions of dollars" from his family's pharmaceutical business, and the partners were searching for ways to turn their windfall into additional profit. The ad sparked several momentous business venture ideas.

The first was the creation of Media Sound Studios and then Woodstock. Rosenman co-created the three-day Woodstock Festival. Together with Roberts, Michael Lang, and Artie Kornfeld, he formed Woodstock Ventures, Inc. After being heatedly debated and rejected in Woodstock and Walkill, New York, Max Yasgur invited them to his Bethel dairy farm. The Woodstock Music and Art Fair drew over 400,000 attendees on August 16, 17, 18, 1969. Rosenman and Roberts later co-authored *Young Men with Unlimited Capital*, later published as *Making Woodstock*.

STUDIO A

Almost overnight, Media Sound attained legendary status and a special mystique within the recording industry. The Buoys recorded their Polydor songs while Stevie Wonder's people were finishing up "Living for the City" and inadvertently became part of rock history.

The recording of "Liza's Last Ride" was rudely interrupted when two men walked into the control booth in the middle of the session. The Buoys looked at each other in confusion. The men explained they were recording upstairs in Studio A and needed someone with a low, gravelly voice to do a voiceover for Stevie Wonder's upcoming album. (Stevie wasn't there.) Everyone turned and looked at Siracuse, who recalled:

> Everyone immediately pointed to me. I initially resisted because my attention was on our song. The guys from Studio A told me it would only take a minute, but I knew it would take long enough that our session would be pretty much over by the time I returned. But I was very interested in the Wonder project. Remember, Stevie had just negotiated a new contract that gave him complete artistic control over his product. Unheard of at the time. So, upstairs I went.

Siracuse entered Studio A, immediately bathed in light patterns, radiating through stained glass windows. He was handed a set of headphones and positioned in front of a microphone. Someone told him the racist vulgarity they wanted him to say, as Siracuse recalled:

I told them I wasn't comfortable saying, 'Come on, come on. Get in that cell, Nigger,' but they said that was part of the dialogue. The engineer rolled back the tape revealing Stevie Wonder singing, 'Living just enough, living for the City,' followed by his synthesizer work. God, it was so fresh and different. It was great.

Siracuse recited his lines several times. The third time they insisted that he push against a large man, standing next to him while repeating the repugnant words.

Carl Siracuse had unintentionally found himself part of a historic moment. The N-word represents a horrible past, and, unfortunately, the racial slur is still used by some to insult persons of color. Most people condemn the word, refusing to use it. It is objectionable and unacceptable, yet the word lent stark authenticity to Wonder's hit record. Siracuse reflected:

I thought that I would only fill in a voice until a professional put the actual part on. Imagine my surprise when the album was released, and I heard myself.

In reviewing the song, *Song Facts* erroneously stated that "Wonder asked one of the janitors at the studio to say the "Get in the cell, n----r" line. They were wrong because Wonder wasn't at that particular session, and Siracuse certainly was no janitor.

"Living for the City" was released on the *Innervisions* LP, Wonder's 16th album release. In 2001, VH1 named it the 31st greatest album of all time with the following statement:

The whole message of this album seems to be caution—Wonder seems to be warning the black community to be aware of their own plight, strive for improvement, and take matters into their own hands. But this is all against the backdrop of the harsh social realities of America circa 1973, and nowhere does this conflict hit home more than in Wonder's magnum opus, 'Living for the City.'

"Living for the City" #8 (Tamla, 1973) took a contemporary look at urban struggles as it addressed America's systemic racism. It was visionary, later described as "a raw piece of modern blues." The song incorporated street sounds of traffic, voices, and police sirens as a backdrop to the driving music. The song won two Grammy Awards, and *Rolling Stone* ranked it number 105 on their list of the "500 Greatest Songs of All Time."

Carl Siracuse contributed his numerous talents to the Polydor session but, in the process, became part of a rather bizarre rock aesthetic, an obscure factoid of rock trivia. He concluded:

Yeah, I have the distinct pleasure of being the one person to utter the N-word on a Stevie Wonder song, me, the last one who'd want to say such a thing or offend anyone like that, least of all Stevie Wonder. You get my point. But, ah, acting.

On "Living for the City," twenty-three-year-old Stevie Wonder played every instrument (Fender Rhodes electric piano, drums, Moog bass, T.O.N.T.O. synthesizer, handclaps) and did all the vocals. In 1989 he was inducted into the Rock and Roll Hall of Fame alongside The Rolling Stones, while The Buoys provided an interesting footnote to rock and roll history in their moment of infamy.

BIG SHAKEUP

The Buoys were excited about their new Polydor single, "Liza's Last Ride." Bill Kelly told *Times-Leader* writer Barbara Stevens Loftus:

> All the local stations have it, but some play it, and some don't. It could take weeks or months to make it. 'Timothy' took 14½ months before it made it nationally, and when it did, it went to number 17. In Canada, it was number one, and it was number one in Buffalo and Syracuse two years in a row.

The Buoys distributed the song in the immediate region. An advertisement for Scranton's Spruce Record Shop in November 1973 offered a Single Special of "Liza's Last Ride" for only 69 cents. Even as the song attempted to get traction, a bad moon was rising over Polydor. On one occasion, the band went to the New York office with Rupert Holmes. They wanted the national promotional manager to help "put something together" but found that Polydor did not have such a manager on staff. Something terrible was happening. The Buoys felt it coming, recollected Tom Fox:

> There was a big shakeup. Polydor hired a new A&R guy and a new president for the American division. They wanted more storytelling songs and liked Rupert more than they wanted The Buoys. They weren't really into us, didn't get behind us. So we had a meeting and met with some of their people, but they had a change of executives, and somebody different came in. It wasn't anyone we had negotiated with before.

The Polydor president was Jerry Schoenbaum, the former General Manager for Verve Folkways, responsible for launching Tim Harden, Janis Ian, Ellen McIlaine, and Laura Nyro. Other key execs were Jon Sagen, director of Artists and Repertoire, and former sound engineer Ed Kollis. Sagen and Kollis were the A&R guys in charge of discovering new talent, assisting with song choices, and selecting personnel to produce marketable albums. But unlike Mandrill and Slade, The Buoys were ignored by Polydor's Artist Development, Marketing, and Publicity Departments. Polydor's lack of support amounted to a betrayal. It left a bitter taste in their mouths, acknowledged producer Holmes:

> I've never really understood what was on their mind. Why they signed The Buoys and got excited about them, and then never released the album, they had no grasp of what to do with the album. I think they were looking for the group to do another cut like 'Timothy,' but the stuff they got was much better, frankly. I produced only their material and felt that it was the time people realized that Jerry and Bill were superb writers in their own right. I thought the Buoys deserved the chance to showcase their songs.

Their showcase was more like the Bataan Death March as they suffered the anguish of being herded into a conference room with Polydor executives, their faces distant and condescending. The Buoys felt like squashed bugs. Holmes explained how it all came crashing down:

> One awful day when all of us were in the (Polydor) office and (the label) said they couldn't release the album because there wasn't any cover art. And the guy who signed them said, 'Don't you have a generic photo of a rock band where you can't see their faces? Can't we just put any group on the cover?

As the company experienced an executive shakeup, the new chiefs were reluctant to complete projects initiated by former Polydor staffers. Everyone seemed to be looking in other directions. Despite the professionalism of the songs, there was no interest from Polydor, and having no cover art was a flimsy excuse. They had been rejected and tossed aside by dismissive executives, and there was nothing they could do. Says Kelly:

> Lol! They hated it. They thought they were getting an album of Rupert Holmes songs. When we delivered the original album, they were pretty upset.

Part of their predicament was horrible timing and competition from Slade, a juggernaut of English skinhead rockers. Slade exploded onto the scene with headbanging assaults such as "Cum on Feel the Noize" #98 (Polydor, 1973), "Gudbuy T' Jane" #68 (Polydor, 1973), and "Mama Weer All Crazee Now" #76 (Polydor, 1973). In the early 1970s, they scored seventeen consecutive top 20 hits and six number ones on the UK Singles Chart. The British Hit Singles

& Albums names them the most successful British group of the 1970s, and they were the first act to have three singles enter the charts at number one. According to the 1999 BBC documentary *It's Slade*, the band had sold over fifty million records worldwide at the time.

The reality hit The Buoys like a mine cave-in. Polydor had deep-sixed any possibility of putting out an album of the band's original songs. The LP was an ill-fated endeavor from the start and never seriously considered by industry executives. Siracuse observed:

> They never released our album, and I still don't know why. We were never actually told that they were not going to release the album, to my recollection. It was hard to get an answer from them because they were in such a transition, and they were more intent on getting sales.

Holmes also felt that Polydor was going through many transitions, and the people running the label didn't know quite how to do it. Brozena thought that Polydor was only looking for a winner like Slade:

> 'Don't Try to Run' was the first single released, followed by 'Lisa's Last Ride.' My guess is the album never was released because the two singles did not get any chart activity.

Sometimes life isn't fair and doesn't break your way. Unfortunately, Polydor was one of those times. Because tunesmith Holmes didn't contribute to the writing, Polydor viewed the songs as second-rate. In any event, the bottom dropped out like a Wile E. Coyote cartoon, and they just stood there with their hands in their pockets. It was another punch-in-the-gut heartbreak and another old lonesome feeling on the poor side of town.

Polydor could have been a better partner. It would have been a relatively straightforward matter to have penciled The Buoys in as an opening act for any number of Polydor rockers like Slade, Mandrill, or Manfred Mann. That would have increased their visibility and improved their record sales. Polydor chose not to. After "Don't Try to Run" and "Lisa's Last Ride" experienced disappointed chart action, all hopes of an LP vanished.

The Polydor recordings were shelved for almost thirty years until Collectibles Records released the "Timothy" CD, aka *The Buoys Golden Classics* (Collectables, 1993). The CD included all songs from the Scepter and Polydor albums, plus "These Days" and "Smackin' Good Lovin'," mistakenly titled "Good Lovin'," which were not on the original Scepter album. In addition, "Sunny Days" was included twice, as a single composition and again as the clever "Sunny Days/Memories" suite. The Collectables release was an essential contribution for fans of The Buoys.

At some point, it did get better. The Buoys would emerge stronger for the experience, but, at that time, they walked the streets with ghosts and the undead. Their story was as grim as Dostoyevsky's *Crime and Punishment*, and, in a cruel sense, it was all part of the corporate game of winners and losers. But then, in a simple karmic twist of fate, another chapter opened in the Polydor saga when federal investigators began to look into irregularities at several music corporations.

26

THE 1975 PAYOLA PROBE

Polydor National Promotional Director Joseph Medlin was among the nineteen industry officials and six corporations indicted during the 1975 "Payola Probe." Medlin, an employee of Associated Music and former promoter for Philadelphia's Gamble-Huff Records, was charged with conspiracy.

He had enjoyed an early solo career singing with The Ravens before working for Decca, Brunswick, and Mercury records. In the 1960s, he became United Artists' A&R man and then Regional Promotional Representative. Medlin was the first Black Vice President employed by a major label.

The federal grand jury investigation leveled payola charges, including conspiracy of tax evasion, fraud, theft, and bribery of disc jockeys and radio station executives in 1973. Sham companies had funneled tens of thousands of dollars to disc jockeys in New York, Los Angeles, and Philadelphia. California, Illinois, Michigan, New York, and Pennsylvania radio stations were involved.

The trail of breadcrumbs led directly to "The City of Brotherly Love" when Philadelphia's Kenneth Gamble and Leon Huff, founders of Philadelphia International Records (PIR), were indicted. Gamble was the multi-tasking head of Associated Music, Gamble-Huff Records, North Bay Records, Huga Management, and Cheyenne Records. Associated Music issued records with the Neptune and PIR labels, made, distributed, and sold by CBS Records. Some of the label's monster hits included The O'Jays "Love Train" #1 (PIR, 1972), Billy Paul's "Me and Mrs. Jones" #1 (PIR, 1972), and Harold Melvin and the Blue Notes' "If You Don't Know Me by Now" #3 (PIR, 1972). Others indicted were Clive Davis, president of Arista Records, and Nat Tarnopol, president of Brunswick Record Corporation.

ALAN "MOONDOG" FREED

After a 1959 congressional investigation revealed the widespread use of bribes by recording companies, Payola entered the English lexicon. Radio executives discovered that the best way to generate sales was to pay disc jockeys and station officials to place their songs on heavy rotation, spinning them numerous times within twenty-four hours.

Two Pennsylvania individuals, perceived opposites, were at the center of the storm. Alan Freed was born in Windber, Pennsylvania, in Somerset County and was an innovative pioneer in the record business, promoting Black R&B to mixed-race audiences. In 1951, he began hosting a rhythm and blues program on Cleveland's WJW, using the nickname "Moondog." He called the music he played "rock & roll." Moondog hosted the first live rock & roll concert in 1952, and The Big Beat was America's first prime-time TV rock show, premiering on May 4, 1957.

But on November 20, 1959, Freed was fired by WABC. The disk jockey, scandalized as payola's poster child, was blacklisted from broadcasting, effectively ending his career. Called "the father of rock 'n' roll," Freed was one of

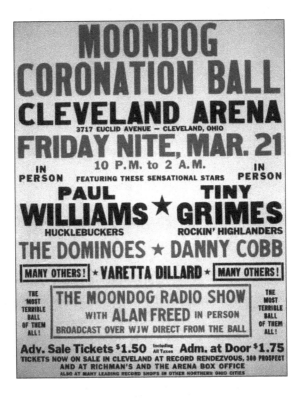

The Jordan Brother's were inadvertently caught up in Dick Clark's conflict of interest.

the first people inducted into the Rock and Roll Hall of Fame but sadly died of alcoholism at forty-three.

If Freed was the scapegoat, Dick Clark represented the charmed "Golden boy." American Bandstand's Clark told a congressional committee he was unaware performers in whom he had interests (record companies, song publishing houses, and artist management groups) had received disproportionate play on his programs.

Clark was a shareholder in the Jamie-Guyden Distributing Corporation, which nationally distributed Jamie and other labels. Frackville's Jordan Brothers were inadvertently caught up in Clark's conflict of interests, were dropped from the label. The Jordan's had recorded six Jamie singles and appeared on Dick Clark's legendary "American Bandstand" three times. They were headliners on Clark's forty-nine-day "Caravan of Stars" that toured the United States and Canada.

In 1960, when charges were levied against Clark by the Congressional Payola Investigations, he quietly divested himself of interests in thirty-three businesses. ABC suggested that his participation might be considered a conflict of interest, so Clark sold his shares to the corporation and signed an affidavit denying involvement. After suffering a stroke, Clark continued his highly successful career, with reputation and integrity virtually unscathed. The "world's oldest teenager" died in 2012 at the age of eighty-three.

CRUCIAL INFLUENCERS
During the 1970s, Bobby Vanderheyden (later known as Bobby V, the Duke of Doo Wop) was Program Director at CBS FM in New York and had the "great joy" of hiring Harry Harrison and Cousin Brucie, among others. He became National Program Director for the seven CBS stations and then the twelve CBS stations. Because Bobby V and his wife are the godparents to Alan Freed's godson, he was able to address payola through a personal and professional lens:

> Payola's not illegal. The problem was that the jocks weren't reporting the income and the cars, whatever they got to play the music, to the IRS, and the IRS was not collecting their taxes on it. But if you take money to play a record and report it to the IRS, that's not payola. Nobody's going to do that anymore because of what happened. The fact of the matter is, in today's world, record companies pay radio stations that are playing current music to play the songs, and they report it. As long as it's all above board, it's not payola. That was a very dark period, but look, rock and roll survived.

Program Directors like Philadelphia's Joe "Butterball" Tamburro at WDAS became essential players in the payola—plugola investigations. They were the crucial influencers who could easily "make or break" a hit record and were constantly being wined and dined and offered free "sold out" concert tickets and other gratuities to make that happen. According to former KRZ "Saturday Night Live at the Oldies" host Shadoe Steele:

> The way it worked at urban contemporary radio is that middlemen or indies gave cash under the table to a station's Program Director, then kicked back buried money to the Vice President of promotion at the record label. Insiders of R&B/Urban stations in 1975 later reminisced that trips, jewelry, and even automobiles (in top-20 markets) would show up in Program Directors' driveways overnight. It was very difficult to 'sting' payola sharks as these 'gifts' would be three levels down in accountability and very tough to trace a bottom-line name.

One individual who traced those bottom-line names was U.S. Attorney Bob Romano, who directed the year-long Gamble-Huff investigation. As a result, federal payola indictments were handed down on June 24, 1975, by four Federal grand juries. Count 1, paragraph 20 of the indictment, charged that:

> The defendants would provide United States currency, clothing from Krass Brothers, and other goods and services to disc jockeys, music directors, program directors, and other employees of radio stations in Philadelphia, Pennsylvania.

The unidentified disc jockeys and program directors allegedly received plane tickets and more than $6,000 worth of clothing from Krass Brothers Clothes "as consideration for promoting songs produced by companies owned by Gamble and Huff." Along with Gamble and Huff, their former partner Ben Krass, and four promotional associates, Earl Shelton, Edward Richardson, Harry Coombs, and Joseph Medlin, were named. In addition, some radio station employees received immunity in return for their testimony.

The Philadelphia *Daily News* "Pop Music," noted that Kenny Gamble and Leon Huff, just before their payola trial, acknowledged that "friendship" with deejays could boost their cause:

> But only in the sense that personal contact helps the jocks to better understand the underlying black consciousness of Gamble-Huff songs like 'Wake Up Everybody" or "Love Train." Raised in praise in this regard were the names of 'good friends' Georgie Woods and Jimmy Bishop. Bishop recently exited WDAS radio to become an executive with the Gamble-Huff team.

Both Georgie Woods and Jimmy Bishop were fellow WDAS staffers, along with Joe "Butterball" Tamburro. "Butterball" was a white Italian American at black radio station WDAS 105.3-FM. He worked at the rhythm and blues station for nearly fifty years, hosting "The Butterball Show" and later "Oldies with Butter" alongside legendary DJs Jocko Henderson, Hy Lit, and Georgie Woods. But back in 1973, Butterball was known as Kenny Gamble's "right-hand man," respected for having a "golden ear" that could detect a potential hit record. Butterball became DAS's Program Director and General Manager. The Philadelphia Music Walk of Fame inducted him in 1997.

Shadoe Steele believed that "The Sound of Philadelphia" by Mothers, Fathers, Sisters and Brothers (PIR, 1974) was the first of many "alleged" "pay for play" hits that the well-connected and influential "Butterball" Tamburro helped push over the top. Steele observed:

'The Sound of Philadelphia' was everywhere and hit #1 on *Billboard*, *Cashbox*, and *Goldmine*. Because it was instrumental, it crossed all boundaries of format, including R&B, Top-40, Adult Contemporary, and 'Disco.'

"TSOP" ("The Sound of Philadelphia") was a massive 1974 hit recording by MFSB featuring vocals by The Three Degrees. It was written by Gamble and Huff as the theme for *Soul Train*, selling over a million copies. It was the first television theme song and arguably the first disco song to reach number one on *Billboard's* #1.

The payola scandal brought out accusations of corruption on both sides, and, as with any debate, opinions hovered like vultures. However, *Daily News* writer Jonathan Takiff charged that radio station personnel—station managers, music directors, air personalities- were the true villains:

> The name of the game isn't bribery. It's extortion. As practiced, not only newcomer acts but also established artists will be shut out from radio play unless the record company comes across with bucks. It doesn't matter if the record is already a 'hit' in other markets. No grease, no play. So, if a record company expects just a fair shot for its product, good business sense demands playing by the 'rules.'

Acceptance of payola isn't a federal crime, only the failure of the recipient to report it to the station's license holder. The Federal Communications Commission requires the licensee to exercise reasonable diligence in guarding against payola and, if it discovers it, to announce on the air that a payment-for-play was made and who made it. The Recording Industry Association of America said in a statement that most persons employed in the industry "follow ethical and lawful" practices and that "it would be wrong and unfair to suggest that the practices alleged in these indictments represent typical business behavior in these industries."

In the aftermath of the '75 payola scandal, Gamble, but not Huff, was ordered to pay a fine of $2,500. Shadoe Steele offered the final word on the Federal investigation leading to the Gamble-Huff and Joe Medlin affair:

> Medlin and nineteen others received a slap on the wrist after a Grand Jury conspiracy charge in the mid-70s. Very little is known about life in the next few ensuing years after that, as record labels usually police themselves. Payola is the smallest big business, and many of the same names implicated with Gamble-Huff, Sigma Sound, and Philadelphia International Records/CBS survived well into the late '90s.

Shadoe Steele and countless others concluded that "payola is still considered, by many, a victimless crime," or, as William Shakespeare quipped over four-hundred years ago, "Much ado about nothing."

★ PART VIII ★

THE JERRY-KELLY BAND

27

GIVE UP YOUR GUNS

One of the biggest thrills for The Buoys was watching another of their songs, "Give Up Your Guns," land on the charts. WABC's Chuck Leonard premiered the song on his Sneak Preview late-night show. Leonard, the first Black D.J. to be hired at the station, introduced new songs to millions of listeners across the country. "Give Up Your Guns," b/w "The Prince of Thieves" (Scepter, 1971) peaked on *Billboard* at #55 on July 3, 1971. "Guns" was the follow-up hit to "Timothy," providing them with all-important national exposure. Fran Brozena explained the machinations behind the corporate thinking:

'Timothy' became a hit, and then Scepter wanted another song like it. The record label wanted a song called "Bloodknot" as the next single. We didn't want that and thought 'Bloodknot' was too hokey. We didn't want that formula, so we did 'Give Up Your Guns,' which was much more different.

"Guns," the four-minute-and-fourteen-second song, co-written by Rupert Holmes, embraced an apparent western influence. That inspiration may have been precipitated by the MGM motion picture *The Animals* (1970), starring Keenan Wynn, a film Holmes was scoring during that period.

According to the website *Mental Itch*, "Guns" was a lot different than "Tim.":

Holmes went on to write the Buoys' follow-up single 'Give Up Your Guns,' which tells about a bank robber who's at large. The song had a more serious and darker tone (and less humor) compared to 'Timothy.' It was a bigger hit in Europe (not only on one occasion but twice).

The Buoys recorded the song in November 1970, and it reached its peak eight months later. Scepter included it in *Dinner Music*. An ecstatic Carl Siracuse recollected the sessions:

> We had put down some of the tracks for 'Give Up Your Guns.' Michael and Rupert were putting the strings on, and it knocked me right off my feet. We did 'Give Up your Guns' many, many times using synthesizers for the string sounds. Kelly's voice was perfect for it. The arrangement was great.

"Guns" was a clever composition with nice chord changes and chorus and keyboards by Rupert Holmes. It told the tale about a man who robbed a bank in Tampa and then tried to escape through the Florida Everglades, with the hounds on his trail. His girlfriend pleads with him to "give up your guns and face the law." Kelly's superb vocals, instrumentation, and strings make this a wonderful song in message and execution. It was a song of peace during a time of conflict, a song that, years later, resonated in a European country embracing pacifism with nationalistic pride.

Fred Beldin's critique of the *Dinner Music* LP withheld praise for everything except "Timothy" and "Guns," noting:

> The rest of the album's material is relatively faceless, though the second single, 'Give Up Your Guns,' is a good country-rock number and strives for an "outlaw on the run" vibe that almost convinces. Nothing else on the album matches "Timothy" in either content or euphony, dispensing with the gallows humor and catchy refrains in favor of a rustic rock sound laced with a few contemporary psychedelic elements.

But not everybody liked "Guns." Terry Hazlett's "Disc Talk" in the Canonsburg, Pennsylvania, *Daily Notes* criticized the side, suggesting that The Buoys were not allowed to stray far from their successful formulae. Hazlett charged:

> A complete change of pace for the 'Timothy' crew, and unfortunately, it may have been a bad switch. This one is slow, with little to comment [on] it, except that it is different than the big hit of a few months ago. 45 percent.

Still, 45 percent was better than nothing, and with precision vocals and smooth orchestration, "Give Up Your Guns" found a wider audience. The Pick Hit of the Week on numerous radio stations such as WETB (Johnson City,

Tennessee) and KEYS (Corpus Christi, Texas) and premiered at #95 on *Cashbox*'s Top 100 Singles Chart the week ending June 12, 1971.

Shadoe Steele, former host of Saturday Night Live at the Oldies, called "Guns" "a brilliant piece of music with a long trail-out more appropriate for AOR album rock stations," like his direct competition, WEZX Rock 107." Steele did his part to promote the song to the masses and interviewed members of The Buoys numerous times.

TROUBLE IN AMSTERDAM

There was more to the unbelievable story. After being sold to Springboard Records by the defunct Scepter, "Guns" was re-released in Europe on the EMI label and given another chance eight years later. EMI thought the album had remaining life, and in 1979, *Dinner Music* was re-issued in Europe where "Give Up Your Guns," surprisingly, climbed the Holland charts to the lauded #6 position.

In a sense, "Guns," with its pacifist lament, was tailor-made for the Dutch. The Netherlands, or Holland, is unique among its neighboring states. When World War I broke out, Holland remained neutral, priding itself as an island of peace in a world of horrible bloodshed. For over three

Hludzik and Kelly.

centuries, the Dutch foreign policy opted to keep out of world problems and avoid spending money on defense. "Guns" easily fit into that antiwar philosophy, and, years later, the European market embraced the music of Dakota more passionately than did those residing on the American shores.

As the gentle citizenry embraced the song, Buoys Manager Tom Fox figured out the secret to the song's success:

> The Netherlands was hot on pretty songs and anything with falsetto and high pitch in it. Most people are bilingual over there, and it seems that they're interested in lovely, easy listening songs.

The Buoys shared a possible history with Holland's rock fans. *Rolling Stone's* Paul Gambaccini recognized a similar musical structure between "Venus" and "Timothy." "Venus" by the Dutch rock quartet Shocking Blue shot to the # 1 position on the *Billboard* charts in 1969. The Buoys' "Timothy," two years later, had a similar approach which, mimicking the success of "Venus," was not accidental. It was intentional.

There were other factors, as well. For example, on their 1984 Dakota liner notes, MCA Records suggested that the song received an unexpected bounce from a surprising place:

> 'Guns' was a modest hit in both the United States and Europe, and it had a long instrumental coda which ended up being used throughout Europe as an introduction to the news long after the single died. Then, in 1980, ten years after the tune's original release, it was re-issued in Holland, reaching #6 due to listener familiarity with the news theme.

Fox, Hludzik, and Kelly went over to Holland to capitalize on this good fortune in separate ventures. They looked for connection, past the howl and the hum, the hype, and the spin. They walked over cobblestone streets, past windmills, corner cafes, and boathouses anchored on the canals, past the wafts of marijuana and hashish, and discovered that, yes, there was a European audience attuned to the music of The Buoys.

It was an unexpected door opening and an opportunity that came a-knocking. To take advantage of the situation, Fox immediately flew over to the Netherlands, setting up meetings with record officials:

> They were playing "Give Up Your Guns" over there. It was a big hit, and I went over to Holland and negotiated with them. I ended up meeting with the president of Polydor in Amsterdam. They were high on the band, but it did not translate back to the States.

Fox spent two weeks investigating the uncanny success of "Give Up Your Guns" by visiting record shops and recording studios. "Guns" hit the Holland Top Ten almost a decade after its initial release. According to Fox, the song was selling for ten Gildas, or $5.00 American as a single. It sold over 50,000 copies. Fox looked to broker a deal with EMI in Holland and to talk with Polydor about releasing their second album:

> 'Give Up Your Guns' did a lot of business over there for EMI. It grossed over a million and a half dollars. EMI re-released the old *Dinner Music* album. They didn't even have to do any recording and used the same album cover. Everything was the same.

EMI Records Holland B.V. re-released "Give Up Your Guns" (EMI International, 1979), and the song made the Dutch Top Ten with its message of peace and social order. Unknown to Fox, Hludzik and Kelly were also in Holland promoting the song and their Jerry-Kelly Band LP at the request of EMI Records. Hludzik and Kelly spent four days plugging the music and appearing on leading Dutch TV programs like *Rock Planet*, *Teen Scene*, and radio talk shows originating from the government-owned Hilversham facility in Amsterdam. The renewed success of "Guns" was one of those abstract, out of the blue, variables that no one could have predicted. Said Kelly:

> 'Give Up Your Guns' took everyone by surprise. It just came out of nowhere. The people at EMI called us and asked if we would like to come over to Holland and do some promotional things. We saw a perfect opportunity to promote that record and promote some of the new stuff.

Europe, and Holland, in particular, loved the sound of The Buoys and Dakota. Years later, Hludzik was interviewed by Vincenzo Ferrara, of the Italian *Hardnheavy* site:

> Kelly and I went to Holland to promote the song, doing radio and TV shows; one, in particular, was the famous *Top of The Pops*. In the Netherlands, still to this day, "Guns" is #50 of All Time!

But Fox was upset with that, sensing that Hludzik and Kelly had betrayed their former group in word and deed:

> I was pissed off because Jerry and Bill went over representing the band. They went over as The Buoys, but they said they didn't have anything to do with us after they left the group. It was very frustrating.

Far removed from the drama in Amsterdam, composer Rupert Holmes, who co-wrote "Guns" with Danny Jordan, reflected on the song's good fortune:

> It's incredible. I'm still trying to accept that that happened. It's amazing when a record that you've given up on for seven years suddenly surfaces again, and the idea that it would do so in a country where English is not the first language is amazing. I've always felt that 'Give Up Your Guns' was better than "Timothy" and had more of what The Buoys, as a group, were about.

CBS European representatives were impressed with advance copies of the new Dakota album, with a simultaneous release scheduled for Holland, Belgium, and France. Columbia was also planning to re-release the Del Shannon classic "Runaway" and "Settle Down" (both on the Jerry-Kelly Band album) in Holland, possibly to coincide with the release of the Dakota LP.

"Bloodknot" b/w "Tell Me Heaven is Here" was released as the final Scepter single. "Give Up Your Guns" was another story as the song refused to go away. American rapper and songwriter Royce da 5'9", best known for his longtime association with Eminem, sampled the intro from "Give Up Your Guns." According to Lakeyta M. Bonnette-Bailey, Associate Professor at Georgia State University and author of Pulse of the People: Political Rap Music and Black Politics, Royce da 5'9" gave the song a new meaning:

> This song by Royce da 5'9", is talking about not giving up your guns because they are needed for protection. Each rapper (Royce da 5'9", Talib Kweli and Raekwon) presents a different reason for the need for protection either from individuals or the government.

The rapper's rationale was that, on the street, you need to own a gun to protect yourself and your family from the bad guys. Their message was, "Don't give up your guns." There were other changes. Bill Kelly's original vocals were sped up to create a high-pitched squeaky voice, sounding more like Alvin and the Chipmunks. The song was part of the hardcore/ underground rap LP, *The Album* (M.I.C., 2008), released on November 10, 2008.

And according to the *Standard-Speaker's* Jim Dino, "Give Up Your Guns" is still played on Euro-radio to this day and is the #50 all-time song on the Top 100 in the Netherlands, an impressive tribute to the legacy of The Buoys.

Memories have faded over the years. John Buckley said they performed "Give Up Your Guns" for about a year while hot in Holland. He played the orchestral parts on his Mellotron and synthesizer while Steve Furmanski sang the lead, but Siracuse and Brosena said they never played the song after Kelly left.

TOM JANS

After their trip to Holland, Danny Seraphine asked Hludzik and Kelly to do background vocals for his friend, Los Angeles singer-songwriter Tom Jans (1948-1984). Jans wrote "Loving Arms," recorded by over 100 singers, including Elvis Presley, Millie Jackson, Kris Kristofferson, and Rita Coolidge (A&M, 1973.) Kelly said they met Jans around 1982, about the time they were recording *Runaway*:

> He was a good friend of Danny but was having some difficult times. Tom had some difficulty with drugs and alcohol and was recently sober. Danny had decided to help Tom by working us into recording one of his songs, "When the Rebel Comes Home." Danny also worked out a publishing deal of some sort with Tom to help him along. We met Tom several times while working in the studio. He seemed like a great guy, and we got along really well with him.

The members of Dakota were impressed with the talented Jans, who referred to his music as "laidback country-rock with an Eagles influence." (NOTE: I first heard about Jans after an enthusiastic Jerry Hludzik told me that they were going to record "When the Rebel Comes Home," co-written by Jans and Seraphine, and featured on *Runaway* (1984), and 'Working Hot" on *Little Victories* (2000).]

At the time, Jans was recording Champion and asked Hludzik and Kelly to contribute their distinctive bright harmonies on seven of the nine tracks, including "When the Rebel Comes Home" and "Working Hot." The album was recorded in 1978 and released in 1982, but only in Japan. Kelly said:

> Jans had heard our sound and liked it. He knew that we were fast and good with background vocals. In this day and age, when you want to save money in the studio, you need players and singers who can come in and cut the parts quickly and know what they're doing. Vocals are probably our forte in the studio. Once we know what we're doing, Jerry and I can go through them like a shot. I think that's the reason we were chosen.

Jan's career had been sadly overlooked and, his albums, such as *Champion*, were hard to find. After college, Jans joined Mimi Farina (Joan Baez's sister), whom he later married, to tour the U.S. with James Taylor and Europe with Cat Stevens. Jans would go on to record several respectable albums, as *Santa Maria Times* writer Tom Leyde observed:

> Jan's songs are simple, gentle, and poignant. He sings about loving, lost love, and about people lost and lonely. The latter two subjects are revealed quite

clearly in his song 'Hart's Island,' a place where paupers are buried. 'That's where you go when you're someone no one knows, just a plastic rose on Hart's Island.'

Dakota traveled in circles beyond circles, their association with Danny Seraphine and Tom Jans just another paradigm of interconnection. Mark Hartley and Larry Fitzgerald, the company that handled Chicago, Rufus, Tom Jans, and Toto, also managed them. Synchronistically, everyone listened to the same orchestral maneuvers in their heads, tapping to the same beat and dancing to the same *paso doble*.

28

LOOK BACK AMERICA: THE BUOYS BREAK UP

Michael Kamen of the New York Rock and Roll Ensemble produced their final effort. Kamen was a highly sought-after arranger who worked with Pink Floyd's David Gilmour and Roger Waters, David Bowie, and Eric Clapton.

"Don't Cry Blue" (Ransom, 1975) b/w "Borderline," was released on their short-lived private label. The song was a piano-driven, countrified tune with Poco influence and Bill Kelly's lead vocals. Earl Slick added guitarwork and Bryan Madey, the drummer from Stories, played drums on one of the tracks. Stories from New York had a hit with a cover of Hot Chocolate's "Brother Louie" #1 (Kama Sutra, 1973).

THE WRITING WAS ON THE WALL

Towards the end of the decade, the writing was on the wall. Kelly quipped that The Buoys "were all out of gas," and friction between group members signaled that it was the end of the band's Grand Experiment.

Chris Hanlon had lost interest during the Polydor sessions. First, he doubted his drumming abilities and thought the recording process was too grueling and drawn out. Then, too, he disliked the substance abuse:

> I had a lot of fun playing drums and touring, but I hated the smoky bars and excessive drinking, and, later, the drug use. That was the part of the business that I hated when drugs came into the picture.

Still, he remained with the band, pounding his drums and twirling his sticks, until they broke up in 1987. Hanlon now owns Chris's Western Beef in Meshoppen, Pennsylvania, that features, of course, a "Timothy" Burger.

The revamped Buoys (L-R) John Buckley, Steve Furmanski, Fran Brozena, Carl Siracuse, Chris Hanlon.

SEPARATE WAY

Each faction wanted to go their separate way and follow their dreams, so they broke apart, and every Northeastern Pennsylvania reporter and music critic wanted to know their feelings about "The breakup." It seemed to be the single-most burning question, and it followed them everywhere, as Kelly told *Citizen's Voice* Jack Smiles:

> Jerry and I complemented each other perfectly. If you listen to our harmony, the tone of blend when we sing together, there wasn't anything quite like it for our time. Jerry and I were driven. We didn't know the meaning of the word 'no,' and that's one of the things that separated us from the other members of The Buoys. We knew we had something, and we were not going to give up no matter what. Our success was born out of our commitment and determination and our love for what we do.

Tom Fox had been with them since the early days. They had forged a strong bond shaped out of trust and mutual affection for each other. They became part of an extended family unit. As the Buoys' manager and business agent, the worst moment of Tom Fox's career was when they told him they were leaving. Fox remembered that hard fist in his gut:

> It was awful when Bill and Jerry said they were leaving the band. It broke up the family. I can remember exactly where I was when they told me they were going.

Storm clouds were forming. They were all feeling the stress and the anger of hearing too many conflicting opinions. Finally, Kelly explained to *Times Focus* Editor Lance Evans that "we just couldn't reconcile our differences" regarding the inevitable split:

> Certainly, there were some hard feelings left. Jerry and I don't hate them, and we hope they don't hate us. But they weren't happy when we left. It also seemed that the other guys were quite content with the pattern we had fallen into. They didn't see the need to keep reaching out.

Hludzik and Kelly felt the same sentiment as superstar Eric Clapton while playing with John Mayall and the Bluesbreakers. Michael Schumacher, in his book *Crossroads: The Life and Music of Eric Clapton*, wrote that Clapton felt that he had reached his potential with Mayall's band:

> The ambition wasn't really going. John was quite happy to stay on the club circuit and play the same kind of music, changing a few numbers here and there. But there was something inside me that said there was more to do or different places to go.

For Hludzik and Kelly, the painful decision came after much soul searching. The pros and cons swirled in a dance of mental probing. It's wasn't easy. They were like brothers. Hludzik told Scranton's Lance Evans:

> Kelly and I have wanted to make it nationally for many years. To do that, there are a lot of sacrifices that have to be made. It didn't seem as if the rest of the group wanted to do the things that had to be done. To Bill and me, it appeared as if they were satisfied. We weren't, though, so something had to give.

Hludzik and Kelly wanted to take The Jerry-Kelly Band out to the coast, but the record company executives dismissed them, Hludzik said:

We feel saddest about our fans. A lot of them didn't seem to comprehend the
need for us to do what we did. It appears that some of them thought it was
etched in stone somewhere that The Buoys would always have to stay together.

There were two distinct camps, and Tom Fox had his feet firmly planted in
one of them. Fox thought that the band needed to rethink their strategy and
place their focus elsewhere:

Jerry was a very talented and hard-driven guy, and Bill's voice was exceptional.
We all knew it, but if they would have done other people's songs and had songs
written for them, like Rupert's, they would have gone further.

Fox remembered a big argument they had over one of Hludzik's original
songs. They kept on practicing it, over and over, but it wasn't working out.
Siracuse didn't like it and said it's "not in the groove. The song's not going to
make it." Hludzik flipped out and said, "that's ridiculous." That disagreement
was difficult for everyone, said Fox:

I loved all those guys, but how do you tell someone that you love that you
don't particularly like the song they just wrote? It's hard to do because they take
it personally. In my personal opinion, of all the guys in the band, Fran was the
best writer and wrote some outstanding original songs.

It was a classic *Tale of Two Cities*. The Buoys wanted to continue their successful shows doing cover songs and hits from their Scepter/ Polydor catalog.
But Hludzik and Kelly, after tasting the high life of limos, spacious auditoriums,
and high-tech sound equipment, craved more, compelled to keep reaching out
and writing new material. Hludzik and Kelly were already playing as a duo at
places like the Heartstone Pub in Dallas. They were also making demo tapes at
WVIA with some Hazleton-area musicians. Brozena, too, saw the writing on
the wall:

We thought, this just isn't going to work. Once Bill and Jerry found out that
we had tried out Steve and John, that's when they knew they had to come in
and say they were leaving. There were no if's, and's, or but's. That's how that
ended and was risky for both of us. I believe they should have stayed a little
longer before they left us until they had a record deal. The Buoys were our live-
lihood, and we were still making money. We kept the name, which I thought
was very important because the name had quality behind it.

Bill Kelly was proud of the compositions he and Hludzik had written that made their way over to Epic's Jerry-Kelly album:

> It's great to be a cover band, but at the end of the day, that's all you are. Jerry-Kelly Band came out of the fact that The Buoys would not play our original music. They were not interested. They did not like the songs we were writing, so we put together a demo band and did our demo at WVIA. Out of that demo, Danny Seraphine heard us, loved our sound, got in touch with us, and started the Jerry-Kelly Band. It was tough on The Buoys because all those songs on the Jerry-Kelly album were songs they rejected. So they didn't want to be a part of it. They had a little egg on their face for a while.

The formal ending occurred at the Carbondale Armory after the breakup was articulated and finalized. Brozena remembered what that was like:

> The breakup was happening entirely before that, and it was a bad breakup. We were still super popular locally, but we were tired of trying to make it big. We just wanted to have some fun and play some clubs. In reality, that's what we wanted to do. Jerry's drive to hit the big time continued, and that was fine. And, at the end of the day, if you take all of the emotion out of it, Bill and Jerry did what they wanted to do, and we did what we wanted to do, and we both, I think, were somewhat successful.

Nobody expected that to happen. However, the "breakup" proved to be a "Win-Win" situation for everyone. After Hludzik and Kelly left, Brozena asked John Buckley and Steve Furmanski to join the Buoys. Furmanski was playing with Eddy Day and TNT and had been with the original Buoys. He brought to the table an impressive repertoire from the John Lennon and Beatles' songbook.

Buckley had toured with Chubby Checker and later fronted Star, a popular regional band. Star was becoming "the" competition. They were starting to out-draw the Buoys with a recognizable, danceable Top 40 playlist. Buckley, whose powerful voice sounded like Springsteen, said:

> What the band lost certainly wasn't irreplaceable. When Steve and I joined the band, replacing Kelly and Hludzik, we came from different backgrounds. We brought different kinds of music into the band with us, and when that change happened, it was an updating of The Buoys' material.

Buckley immediately added another dimension to the band, belting out the vocals on the crowd-pleasing "Timothy." But, again, it was a small interconnected world. From Binghamton, New York, Buckley was a King's College

The popular band Star (L-R) Clockwise from top, Bob Chipak, John Buckley, Jerry Piel, and Paul Miele.

classmate of Bill Kelly and Brozena's former roommate. Although Buckley and Furmanski didn't know each other, Brozena said that adding them to the band worked well:

> It clicked for what we wanted to do. It was amazing how good it was. When you have a guy that can sound like Springsteen, we were at the top of the world back then. And we could do the Beatles' stuff and a lot of the other new wave stuff at the time. So we became a huge club band. That's what we were. Plus, we had the hit record.

With the new lineup, the songs became more rock and more recognizable, according to Buckley:

We're always putting new material together and trying to get commercial, salable tunes. We don't have a country-rock sound anymore. It's more versatile with different feels and musicianship.

STONE BALLOON

The Buoys played the Stone Balloon every six to eight weeks and would play an entire week. Manager Tom Fox had forged a working relationship with Stevenson and his longtime friend, Tommy Williams. Fox said:

> We still played the Stone Balloon when the split came, but with John Buckley and Steve Furmanski. Jerry-Kelly played there too. So, we would go down there and play, and then Jerry-Kelly would go down. Stevenson liked them and latched on to them.

As the band was breaking up and "beginning to develop internal problems," owner Bill Stevenson found himself caught in the middle, as recalled in *Stone Balloon: The Early Years:*

> Soon I would be in the middle of this great band splitting up, and it wasn't fun. Jerry and Bill wanted to do all originals, and Fran, Carl, and Chris (and John and Steve) wanted to continue the same path that was making the band lots of money. So the following year, they split up, and the Balloon welcomed the Jerry-Kelly Band with open arms.

The revamped Buoys forged on longer than the earlier version of the group, from 1977 to 1988. One of their accomplishments was a three-year run at The Forty Thieves Club in Hamilton, Bermuda, and arguably "the biggest band in Bermuda." Unfortunately, Brozena left in 1987 after Tom Fox sensed that it "was almost the end," and ironically, Dakota broke up in 1987, around the same time.

29

SOMEBODY'S ELSE'S DREAM

Danny Seraphine and David "Hawk" Wolinski produced *Somebody Else's Dream*. Deni King and Roy Halle, who had worked respectively with Boston and Simon and Garfunkel, were the mixers.

An impressive list of West Coast musicians participated in the project. Members of Chicago joined Hludzik and Kelly and included Seraphine (aka Cosmos Carboni), Laudir De Oliveira, Lee Loughnane, and Peter Cetera. Other musicians included Bill Dickinson, Tom Donlinger, Byron Berline, Ian Underwood, David Amaro, Don Grusin, and Earl Slick.

Slick was a giant in the industry and, at the time, as hot as molten lava. Slick had replaced Mick Ronson as lead guitarist for Bowie's 1974 Diamond Dogs tour and played lead on *Young American's* (RCA, 1975) and *Station to Station* (RCA, 1976). In addition, Slick performed on Lennon and Ono's *Double Fantasy* (Geffen, 1980).

On *Somebody Else's Dream*, the twenty-six-year-old Slick provided additional guitars on "Settle Down," "Changes," and "Magic," the initial single showcasing Kelly's superb vocals and background harmonies. "Magic" was a lively and well-crafted pop song, with punch, attitude, the requisite structural changes, and Slick's nice guitar break.

RECORD PLANT

The recording process was an arduous one, as they recorded for twelve-hour stretches, from 7:00 P.M. to 7:00 A.M. The LP was recorded in Los Angeles at the Record Plant's Studio A. The Record Plant was one of the best-known studios in the industry and where Fleetwood Mac and Stevie Wonder had cut landmark albums.

Hludzik and Kelly co-wrote all of the songs except Del Shannon's classic #1 hit "Runaway" (Big Top, 1961). Kelly claimed the monster song as his own with a powerful re-working that endures as one of the best renditions of this timeless masterpiece.

Hludzik wrote "Somebody Else's Dream," "Silly Boy," and "You Can Be," the latter stating the duo's attitude towards the constant struggles of life and a pointed musical barb aimed at The Buoys, whom Hludzik and Kelly felt had stopped striving and became complacent. "Somebody Else's Dream," written by Hludzik and realized by Kelly's vocals, begged to be on the charts. It was that good. Kelly wrote "Settle Down" and "Be My Love," a beautiful song straight out of the Eagles' songbook. Kelly's vocals and Don Grushin's acoustic piano paid homage to that group's Glen Frey and Don Henley, and on "Motel Lovers," Hludzik's vocals rode over a crest of Beach Boy's surf harmonies. Excited about their Columbia album, Kelly told *Record Whirl:*

> Everything seems to be going so well, especially the writing. Jerry and I are basically on the same wavelength, and when we write, the songs almost seem to be writing themselves.

WESTCOAST AOR

A lot of effort went into creating the *Somebody's Else's Dream* cover artwork. The front cover featured a medley of twenty photographs of the boys, Hludzik as a waiter, astronaut, conductor, Beefeater guard, soldier, physician, and Kelly as a baseball player, painter, conductor, milkman, bellhop, and laborer. The back cover featured a professional shot of the boys, Hludzik to the left, Kelly on the right. Hludzik's left arm draped across Kelly's shoulder. Hludzik was displaying his Fender Stratocaster and Kelly his Japanese Yairi.

Somebody Else's Dream was listed variously under the genres of Westcoast AOR (Album Oriented Rock), pop-rock, and yacht rock. Gerry Mullinax of the Wilmington *News Journal* described it as "a mellow sort of LA pop sound," but, however their music was defined, it represented the beginning of a tremendous musical experiment.

$250,000 PRICE TAG

Amidst high expectations and following several false starts, Epic released *Somebody's Else's Dream* during the week of September 18, 1978. According to Joe Middleton, the album racked up an estimated $250,000 price tag in production expenses:

> Epic Records pressed an initial 30,000 copies of the debut LP, and within ten days of its release, 25,000 units were sold to distributors nationally.

Because the band's contract called for the release of an album, followed by two more albums, Scranton *Times* writer Lance Evans noted the positivity:

> In the recording for the album, Seraphine and Wolinski added their highly regarded professional direction to the production, secured 'studio' musicians of stature, and saw that any rough edges The Jerry-Kelly Band might possess were quickly sanded down.

In other words, they were getting star treatment with quality musicians and state-of-the-art recording equipment. If it worked for Chicago and worked for Rufus, it should also work for The Jerry-Kelly Band. That was the plan, the promise, the expectation. Co-producer Danny Seraphine told Joe Middleton that he was high on the new album:

> It's as strong or stronger than any first album I've ever worked on, other than maybe CTA. So I put it in the category of Chicago Transit Authority. It's that strong. The tunes are that good. These guys, you can tell, are ready to happen. They're there.

After Hludzik inscribed the LP with a personal message, "You can be anything you wanna be. You just gotta give it a try, Baby," an article in the Hazleton *Standard-Speaker* raved about the LP's potential:

> Everyone at Epic and Skid Row is so ecstatic about the Jerry-Kelly album that they're talking about three or four top singles coming from it. Some even compare it as having a better-than-average shot to match or exceed in sales, another Epic act. Boston's self-titled album is said to be the largest selling debut album ever and, even to this day (4/18/78), sells about 50,000 units a week.

Using professional studio musicians, the LP had a fuller, richer sound than the earlier Scepter recordings, much of that due to technological advances over seven years. After listening to *Somebody's Else's Dream*, musician Bernie Garzio said:

> When I heard the Jerry Kelly album, it didn't sound like the other local band albums. This was polished. It sounded like the real deal. This was circa 1978. They even had the drummer from the band Chicago produce the album and play a few songs. Peter Cetera also sang some backups. They had many great musicians on that album.

Garzio said that after listening to the music of Jerry-Kelly, he was motivated to reach for the stars:

These were local guys, and they made me want to work that much harder. I have terrible recordings of me trying to play their songs from 1979. What I didn't realize at the time was how hard it is to do what they did. They made it look so easy. Jerry was always cool, calm, and singing and playing his parts perfectly, with almost no effort. At least that was how he made it look. It wasn't easy, Jerry. Same to you, Bill Kelly. It's not easy.

Epic was also home to Sly Stone, one of the wealthiest musicians. Stone's contract with Epic provided more than half a million dollars for each album, a fact that did not go unnoticed by Jerry- Kelly. Everyone was excited about the possibilities, and Hazleton Standard-Speaker reporter Joe Falatko lavished in the enthusiasm that was getting better every day:

> When Jerry-Kelly inked their initial contract with Skid Row Productions, it called for one album and two singles to be released. Since then, there has been a new written agreement calling for five albums, and an added $100,000 had been put behind their debut outing.

Corporate plans from Epic Records included a significant push for the group to have a national press week and a nationwide "Jerry-Kelly Day" on major radio stations. As a result, Jerry-Kelly would be heard nationwide, simultaneously creating a media buzz. At the onset of their Skid Row venture, Danny Seraphine energetically praised Jerry-Kelly, writing:

> These two individuals from Scranton play guitar, write, and sing all their songs. I respect them as artists and human beings. They deserve all the success and recognition that they can find. Hawk and I have done our part. Now, it's up to you after you listen to this record, and hopefully, you'll feel the same way we do about it. Go out and tell your friends about Jerry-Kelly.

The word was out about the Jerry-Kelly Band, but unfortunately, the album did not generate the anticipated sales. Hludzik explained to the Wilmington *News Journal* that *Somebody's Else's Dream* didn't sell because Epic didn't get behind it with promotion. Still, Hludzik was ever the optimist:

> That was why we went over to Columbia, Danny's label. We've heard that Columbia will concentrate on five acts next quarter and that we'll be one of them.

It was almost too good to be true, as the game plan changed from Jerry-Kelly to Dakota, from Epic to Columbia. Pink Floyd's "Money" kept playing in their heads as they marched towards the next chapter, singing, "This could be the one!"

30

THE JERRY-KELLY BAND

MOLLY HATCHET

The Jerry-Kelly Band formed around 1977, and things started impressively. They were invited in March 1979 to open for Southern rockers Molly Hatchet at The Paramount Theatre (now the FM Kirby Center for the Arts).

Formed in 1975 in Jacksonville, Florida, Molly Hatchet paid their dues on the rough-and-tumble Sunshine State club circuit. They played hard. They got good. With powerful guitars and a pounding boogie beat, they were destined for success, although their three million-selling album, Flirtin' With Disaster, wouldn't be released until 1979.

Though never as famous as Lynyrd Skynyrd, who recorded the #8 "Sweet Home Alabama" (MCA, 1974) and #13 "What's Your Name?" (MCA, 1977), Molly Hatchet nevertheless made an enormous contribution to the genre. They stood tall with other Southern rockers: The Outlaws, who scored with their #34 hit "There Goes Another Love Song" (Arista, 1975), The Marshall Tucker Band, charting with the #14 "Heard It In A Love Song" (Capricorn, 1976) and the #38 "Fire On The Mountain" (Capricorn, 1975), and .38 Special, who peaked at #10 ("Caught Up In You" (A&M, 1982) and #6 "Second Chance" (A&M, 1989).

The Kirby show offered an interesting contrast in styles. While Molly Hatchet fit squarely into the Southern rock genre, Jerry-Kelly was steeped in the intricate, multi-part harmonies of California's Laurel Canyon, represented best by Poco, the Eagles, and CSN&Y. On this satisfying night, there was something for everyone.

THE HOME GROWN MUSIC TAPES

Music production technology had evolved immeasurably in the fifty years since Sgt. Pepper with digital technology making the difference. Today's music is

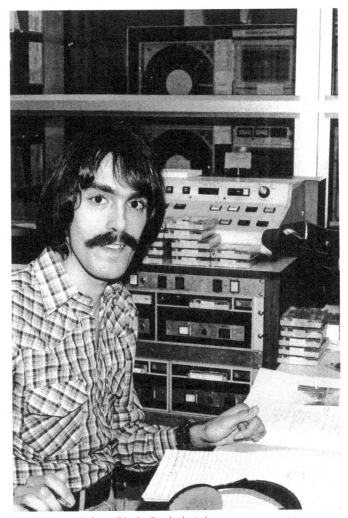

WVIA's George Graham. (Maxim Furek photo.)

either created digitally or transferred from analog to digital format. Old songs are becoming new, heard through a different spectrum. All vocals and instrumentation are recorded on their own track and then digitally manipulated and blended into the final mix. Technology has made recording a creative experiment limited only to one's vision. The Buoys were quick to capitalize on regional assets, especially 89.9 WVIA-FM.

Recording engineer George Graham created WVIA's Homegrown Music in 1976 and aired studio performances. He often spent three nights a week in a soundproof control room, bent over a sixteen-channel console. He used massive four-track recorders draped with half-inch tape reels. Along with side-kick Rick Johnson, they would endlessly set up microphones and cables, working their magic after all of the other staff had gone home.

Shadoe Steele (from 1973-1978, under the pseudonym of "Dale Michaels") did news, weather, and sports on *Mixed Bag* and *All That Jazz*, working with George Graham. Because portions of *All That Jazz* were either pre-recorded or contained extended tracks, Graham would record local artists with a twenty-four-track professional board between his on-air jazz show. Says Steele:

Radio and media professional Shadoe Steele.

> Because I knew Jerry and Bill, I stuck around after 10:00 P.M. for several nights and sat in on the 'Jerry-Kelly Band's debut release featuring the Epic/CBS Records single 'Changes.' Again, Graham was a perfectionist, and the studio was major market quality, mastering on two" audiotape @ 30 ips.

Hludzik and Kelly wanted to record the Buoys at WVIA, but producer Graham's musical experiment was only in the planning stages. Still, as far as the quality of his Pittston recording studio, Graham told *Times-Leader* staff correspondent Ron Wodaski:

> But let us not forget that *Sgt. Pepper's Lonely Hearts Club Band* was recorded in a four-track studio much like the one we have here. And that album was considered a technological marvel!

Finally, after securing funding and equipment, Graham was ready to record The Buoys for a *Homegrown Music* segment. Because most of the group was on vacation, Hludzik and Kelly decided to go it alone. Working with Graham, Hludzik and Kelly tested out original songs, polishing their precious demo tapes that had taken untold hours of writing, crafting, and recording. Demo tapes, used as a stepping-stone to secure a record contract, were their ace in the hole. They changed their name (for the demo) to the Jerry-Kelly Band, recruited a few backup members, and started recording the very demo tapes that would find their way into the hands of Danny Seraphin. Ron Wodaski observed the intricacies of Graham's production leading to the final product:

> About a week before he airs the recorded material, George will do the final remix. Special effects, such as reverb, flanging, phasing, and echo, are added at this point. Four tracks get mixed down to two in a session that can often exceed the amount of time spent on the initial recording session.

Music from the Studio proved to be WVIA's initial but short-lived venture that began and ended in 1975. However, *Citizen's Voice's* Sue Henry, writing in her "Radio Days" column, observed that Graham had more than technology to rely on:

> George Graham should also be lauded for the production of *Homegrown Music*, which he produces at the WVIA studios before a live audience. Drawing from what he calls an abundant talent pool, Graham features musicians who play anything from fusion jazz to folk. He considers this area rich in 'very good artists.'

And foremost among them were The Buoys, who had others working in their corner. KRZ's Shadoe Steele cleaned up the original Scepter and Polydor recordings, eliminating "some inherent surface noise" and re-dubbing the cartridges for pristine airplay. Steele said that this was the first time (Spring 1993) that eighteen tracks were used on CDs, resulting in the Narberth, Pennsylvania, Collectibles' CD.

Hludzik and Kelly always believed in the power of the demo tape, and writer Joe Middleton acknowledged WVIA's contribution to their eventual success:

> WVIA, with its sixteen-track recording facility, had Jerry-Kelly up at the Pittston studio shortly after they left the Buoys. They performed their new material for *Homegrown*, the program hosted by George Graham, that features the original music of area residents. They gave a tape of the show to Mike Stahl, and, as they say in show biz, the rest is history.

MICHAEL STAHL

Michael "Dad" Stahl, a native of Dalton and long-time friend, worked for Claire Brothers Audio. Stahl was at the proverbial right place and at the right time and assumed an essential role in the eventual connection with Chicago, one of the most successful bands in history. Chicago was inducted into the Rock and Roll Hall of Fame on April 8, 2016, with a legacy including eighteen

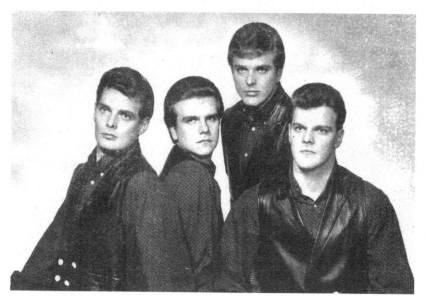

The Jordan Brothers (L-R) Bob, Lou, Joe, and Frank Jordan.

gold and thirteen platinum albums and fifty Top 40 hits, including twenty Top Ten singles and five number ones. Stahl played the Jerry-Kelly tapes during Chicago's sound checks to tune them in. When drummer Danny Seraphine heard them, he expressed interest, and Stahl hand-delivered their demo tape.

JORDAN BROTHERS

In any case, the winds of change began to swirl. In the summer of 1977, Seraphine and Rufus keyboardist David "Hawk" Wolinski traveled to the Coal Region to see Jerry-Kelly at Schuylkill Haven's The Alley. Although the LA boys didn't realize it, they were walking on hallowed ground.

The Alley, "The Home of the Jordan Brothers," was the unofficial venue for the Schuylkill County quartet. Their biggest hit was a cover of the original "Gimme Some Lovin'," heard as a raw demo by the Spencer Davis Group. Although the Jordan Brother's version of "Gimme Some Lovin'" (Phillips, 1966) never cracked the *Billboard* Top 100 and only reached # 128 on *Billboard's* 'Bubblin' Under" listing, the Jordans enjoyed a cult-like following. In addition, they were extremely popular in a five-county region surrounding their home-town of Frackville. Joe Nardone Sr. said it best. "They were big down there, and The All-Stars were big up here." They recorded on the Jamie label until payola accusations against Dick Clark robbed the Jordans of their most valuable asset.

But this night belonged to the Jerry-Kelly Band. Writing his "Linear Notes" on the Jerry-Kelly album sleeve, producer Seraphine recalled his first impressions:

> Hawk and I flew to Philadelphia and drove to Pottsville, Pennsylvania, to hear Jerry-Kelly perform. They were great. The next stop was to assemble the right players. Easier said than done. We didn't want studio players. No. Let me re-phrase that. We needed studio players, but we wanted this album to sound like a band.

After an impressive audition, Seraphine and Wolinski's Skid Row Productions agreed to take them on and produce them, studio players and all. This was the big break.

COAL REGION HOUSE PARTY

Bill Stevenson staged a huge Jerry-Kelly Band album-release party at the Stone Balloon. New York City limousines lined up in front of his bar. He later received a check from Epic records for $2,500 to offset some of the costs, the first time he "ever got paid to throw a party."

The Coal Region also knew how to throw a party. The ten-song *Somebody Else's Dream* played repeatedly. After all, it was the main attraction at a house party held at Hludzik's Japan Jeddo homestead. Over two hundred friends, relatives, and well-wishers attended the "welcome home" party. Hludzik and Kelly's parents were there. Special guest Mike Stahl flew in from the West Coast, arriving in the late evening hours. The April 15th event lasted, with considerable amounts of Yuengling Lager and Stegmaier Gold Medal beer flowing, from early Saturday evening through Sunday morning.

Things were happening rapidly on the corporate side. The CBS-owned Epic label purchased the rights to Jerry-Kelly via director Bobby Colomby, founder of Blood, Sweat, and Tears. Additionally, their association with Seraphine and Wolinski's Skid Row Productions called for another two albums. Oh, those were the days, my friend, and the best of times.

In his revealing 2011 book, *Street Player: My Chicago Story*, Seraphine related how Bobby Colomby signed him and Wolinski to a production deal at Epic Records. Colomby was the former drummer for Blood, Sweat, and Tears. Their newly-created Street Sense Productions (and some have called it Skid Row Productions) would deliver two acts a year. Epic would throw in money for studio costs. Seraphine called it "basically a budget to record demos." The Jerry-Kelly Band was their first venture:

When Chicago's soundman, Mike Stahl, caught wind that I was on the prowl for new talent, he passed on a demo tape a few of his friends had made; a group called the Jerry-Kelly Band. I immediately liked what I heard. The guys sounded like a more refined version of the Eagles. Hawk and I flew into Scranton, Pennsylvania, and signed them to a minor deal with our Street Sense Productions on the spot. Unfortunately, we never had much success taking them to the next level, but the whole experience gave me the confidence to continue to pursue my interest in producing. I wasn't going to let the fact that we didn't hit a home run out of the gate get me down. There were more than enough talented bands out there waiting to be discovered. It was only a matter of time before Hank and I found the right one.

Jerry-Kelly surrounded themselves with key players. They signed with Jeff Wald and Herb Nannas for professional management, while Jack Gaudie came aboard as their manager. Gaudie had been Chicago's manager for the previous eight years, and Wald, the husband of singer Helen Reddy, managed both Chicago and the Eagles.

Hludzik and Kelly performed as Jerry-Kelly until 1980, before renegotiating a new contract with Columbia Records, Epic's parent company. The only stipulation was that they change their name. Columbia held all the cards and didn't like the light-sounding "Jerry-Kelly Band." They said it wasn't edgy enough. Hludzik and Kelly knew that old-time feeling. It was somebody else's dream.

★ PART IX ★

THE OUTLIERS 2

31

THE BLUE OYSTER CULT RIOT

Tere was a weird cross-connection between the Buoys and the Blue Oyster Cult. Like the spinning Wheel of Fortune at the Luzerne County Fair, they went full circle, arriving at times and places each visited before, moments that enhanced their sense of purpose, meeting an impressive array of musicians in the process. Everybody knew somebody who knew somebody else, the circle continually expanding.

The Buoys had shared a bill in a Scranton college bar with Soft White Underbelly, a band from Stony Brook, New York. The band was changing its name to Blue Oyster Cult and had just signed a record contract. Their name came from manager Sandy Pearlman's 1960s poem, *Imaginos*. He had suggested the band's last name, "Soft White Underbelly," from a phrase used by Winston Churchill in describing Italy during World War II. When they asked him what he thought of it, Tom Fox, who pulled no punches, replied, "You really want to know? I think it sucks."

Fox ran into the group again when he co-promoted a Blue Oyster Cult & Humble Pie concert with Tom Makoul Productions at the Allentown Fairgrounds. The group remembered that Fox didn't like their original name, and they all had a good laugh about it.

Unfortunately, the Allentown concert was rained out and rescheduled for the next day, June 27, 1981. Technicians attempted to make the equipment and rain-soaked sound system safe to operate. Instead, a group of around a hundred rowdies screamed at the crew while throwing firecrackers and smoke bombs on the stage. When the show finally did go on, it was a bit of a letdown, according to *Call-Chronicle* reporter Len Righi:

> Two old rock warhorses—Blue Oyster Cult and Humble Pie—trotted out on
> the stage of the Allentown Fairgrounds grandstands last night. And though the

old gray mares pleased the crowd of 4,000 with their time-tested tricks, both bands seemed locked into the past, destined to repeat themselves endlessly.

Although that show may not have been their finest moment, Blue Oyster Cult had established themselves as leading proponents of heavy rock blended with cryptic lyrics. After their 1971 debut, they released fourteen studio albums, selling over twenty-four million records worldwide. "(Don't Fear) the Reaper" (Columbia, 1976) was their *Billboard* #12 biggest single with lead vocals by Buck Dharma.

A year earlier, BOC played the Kingston Armory after a successful Kansas City show. Although both Fox and Hludzik-Kelly attended the September 25, 1980 concert, tensions remained high, and the men kept their distance from each other. The Buoys' emotions were still frayed after Hludzik and Kelly left. Nobody was reaching out. There wasn't anything more to say. That was the backdrop to the Blue Oyster Cult Riot.

The disturbances erupted at about 8:15 P.M. A large group of fans had been milling around the Armory's back-door entrance. Tickets cost $8.50 each for the sold-out crowd of 2,500. Some of the backstage staff let a few of the back-door girls in for free. The impatient crowd grew angry and began to shout, and some threw rocks through the windows. More than two hundred attempted to crash their way into the BOC concert. There was shattered glass and blood on the Armory's upper floors. Unknown to the Blue Oyster Cult and the audience, there was a riot going on, Kingston style. According to the Scranton *Times-Tribune:*

> There were only four borough officers on duty. Security guards summoned police assistance, and within thirty minutes, initial units called for attack dogs and the Fire Bureau to help contain the crowd.

Kingston had turned into an ugly battle zone. The crowd clashed with the dogs, and one police officer estimated that the K-9s bit at least fourteen people. Fire units aimed high-pressure hoses on the troublemakers, and police used tear gas canisters that the rioters threw back at the police. Kingston police reported at least twenty-five smashed car windshields and windows in surrounding buildings. Gunshots were fired. Firecrackers set off. Rioters overturned a WDAU-TV news car on West Market Street. It took the police two hours to quell the disturbance.

More than twenty young people and police were taken to area hospitals to treat cuts and tear gas inhalation. Forty-one individuals, including Tour

Manager Steven L. Schenck, were arrested. Schenck, twenty-seven, was charged with disorderly conduct stemming from the riot. Arrested for swearing at police officers and smashing a beer bottle against a wall, he was freed on $25,000 bail and later placed on thirty days probation. According to *Times-Leader* Staff writer John Anderson:

> Ray Lowery, Kingston Borough administrator, testified that earlier in the night, he had asked Schenck to have the band play longer than usual to keep the peaceful crowd inside from mixing with the boisterous crowd outside.

Lowery said Schenck originally agreed to have the band play three more songs, but when he (Lowery) asked for more, he was told, 'they'll only do one.'

Enough was enough. It was a horrible evening for concertgoers and the general public. The catastrophic Who concert was still fresh in everyone's mind. Eleven fans were crushed to death at a Who performance on December 3, 1979, at Cincinnati's Riverfront Coliseum. Armory officials were concerned about safety and liability. Lt. Col. Stanley Smith, the commanding officer in charge of the 109th Field Artillery Armory, told the *Times-Tribune*, "The future looks bleak for concerts here."

But Lt. Col. Smith's bleak future soon turned sunny as rock returned to the Armory. From Switzerland, heavy metal band Krokus and Ted Nugent played a three-hour concert at the Armory on July 7, 1981. A massive security force surrounded the arena to prevent another riot. Co-promoter David Hart of Monarch Productions had budgeted $2,500 to hire security and another $800 for off-duty police. An additional eight guards patrolled backstage. Wilkes-Barre Police Capt. John Smith reported some seventy uniformed police officers and security guards inside and outside the Armory. Although the concert signaled the promise of more shows, the Motor City Madman's much-too-loud appearance drew only 3,300 ticket-buyers and a loss of $12,000 for Electric Factory and Monarch Productions.

And, as a musical side note, Soft White Underbelly made a return trip on July 11, 1985, and played at Wilkes-Barre's Station Complex. Again, it was a night of exciting music and law and order.

32

THE STONE BALLOON

The "six degrees of separation theory," as proposed by Hungarian playwright Frigyes Karinthy, affirms that we are all connected by a string of six or fewer people. For our purposes, it was sports, and not music, that provided the aforementioned six degrees. After graduating from Wilkes University, twenty-one-year-old Tom Fox went to Delaware to live, working nights at a hotel. His friend Tommy Williams lived in a Prestbury Circle apartment with Bill Stevenson. Williams was a former quarterback for the Lackawanna Trail High School football team, and Bill Stevenson had played football at Wyoming Seminary. Both earned football scholarships to the University of Delaware. They were all interconnected. Fox first met Tommy Williams when Fox worked as an assistant coach at Lackawanna Trail. Fox was a friend and "bodyguard" for Jill Jacobs, who married Bill Stevenson (1970 to 1975) and became First Lady and wife of President Joe Biden.

Stevenson purchased Merrill's Tavern and Package Store in downtown Newark, Delaware, for $250,000, renaming it the Stone Balloon. *Rolling Stone* magazine later called it "the best-kept secret in rock and roll," and, adjacent to the University of Delaware campus and thousands of students lusting for high adventure, it became an important venue for the Buoys and Dakota. So perhaps Frigyes Karinthy was on to something.

According to Stevenson, the Stone Balloon grossed almost $60,000, all cash, the first month and more than $190,000 in the first three months. He only sold draft beer, Seven and Sevens, and white wine. On February 22, 1972, Iron Hill was the first live act to play the club, and twenty-seven months later, The Buoys took to the stage. Over the years, Pat Benatar, Peter Frampton, Hall and Oates, The Pointer Sisters, Pure Prairie League with Vince Gill, Bruce Springsteen, and countless others played there.

TOM FOX

Manager Tom Fox was an expert networker. He had a Bachelor of Science in Business Administration with a minor in economics and was able to broker one of the Buoys' most lucrative deals:

> Tommy Williams asked me to bring The Buoys to the Stone Balloon. At the time we were playing concerts. We weren't playing bars at all. I said, 'I don't know if I could get the guys to play down there.' So, I said to the guys, 'Can you do me a favor and play at this bar, The Stone Balloon?' I talked the guys into doing it. I said, 'Please, do it for me.' So, we went down there and blew the place apart. The people went crazy.

The Buoys and Tom Fox had played their ace card. They were Scepter Records recording artists and had opened for some of the nation's top acts, such as Delaney and Bonnie & Friends, the Grass Roots, Nitty Gritty Dirt Band, Pure Prairie League, Sha Na Na, Frank Zappa, and a host of others. Stevenson would call them the biggest moneymakers in the history of his bar, writing that he invested over $200,000 into the Buoys' appearances and paying them $2,500 a night, the most he had ever paid a band. He cited the specific amount of $2,500 several times in his book, *Stone Balloon: The Early Days:*

> The Buoys management wanted $2500 a night, and I thought it was too much. Tommy begged me to try them once, and I did, thank God. They were booked to come in two weeks.

But, as far as the $2,500 payment, Fox's recollection, with a touch of Scranton sensibility, was not the same as Stevenson's:

> He's talking out of both sides of his mouth about what he paid us. He's just trying to sell his book. We never got that kind of money. It never happened. We were getting around $3,500 to $4,000 per week. We weren't earning $2,500 a night.

Nevertheless, the Buoys agreed to play for six straight nights, from Monday to Saturday. They had never done that before but realized that they could create a sensation on the East Coast and expand their fan base. They were scheduled to play the Balloon in May 1974 but immediately got off to a bad start. Stevenson recollected the chaos after he saw The Buoys tractor-trailer pull into his parking lot:

> I realized they were rolling a sound system into the stage area. The Buoys managed to fill it with equipment, block the emergency doors, and still have two

speakers on the new dance floor. There was so much equipment it made the new addition look small. I had just worked like a dog with everyone to get this expansion finished, and they made the place look like crap.

Fox and Williams quickly resolved that equipment snafu and The Buoys took to the stage. The Stone Balloon was one of the Northeast's top venues, packing in University of Delaware students and music enthusiasts searching for good music and theatrical performance. The Buoys and The Balloon became a winning combination, bringing in money and paying the bills on both sides. Stevenson immediately recognized The Buoys' remarkable quality:

> After the first hour, I knew this band was something. Newark had never seen a band playing the hits from Crosby Stills & Nash to the Eagles. The cool thing was when they played their material, people asked whose it was, but it was their material. During the next ten years, I invested more than $200,000 in this group. They became the biggest moneymakers in Balloon history.

The Buoys, Jerry-Kelly, and Dakota played the Stone Balloon, but other regional bands did, too, such as Hybrid Ice, Ralph, and Witness. (NOTE: According to Carl Siracuse, his wife Gail's cousin, Kristin Kwolek McGee, and her band Tin Pan Alley were a massive hit at the Stone Balloon in the post-Bill Stevenson

Dakota (L-R): Bill McHale, Bill Kelly, Jerry Hludzik, Bill Mitchell, and Tony Romano (bottom). (Richard Chizak photo.)

years. McGee's new band is Kristin and the Noise. Keyboard player Scott Babin-
ski, who had a short stint with the Buoys, worked the sound and added key-
boards/vocals from the board during Tin Pan Alley's early Balloon years.)

It was twilight's last gleaming. The Vietnam conflict was ending as Water-
gate broke into the news. There was a gas shortage, echoed in The Kinks' "A
Gallon of Gas" (Arista, 1979), and The Buoys played every three weeks on Tues-
day "concert nights." They were one of the Balloon's most popular bands. The
Stone Balloon was Chris Hanlon's favorite spot to play, observing, "It had lots
of college students, high energy and wonderful chemistry between the band and
the audience. It was my all-time favorite club, a great club." During 1974, the
Balloon promoted money-making concerts by The Buoys, Jack of Diamonds,
Supa Heat, and Moxie. In a bold and confident Bobby Fischer chess move, The
Buoys offered to play the Balloon for free as the warmup act for superstar Bruce
Springsteen's 1974 concert. There was no harm in trying, but Mother, Flag, and
Country got the call.

Stevenson knew that a hit record could bring in money for a lot of people
involved. He wanted to be among them. Recognizing their potential, the entrepreneur invested in Dakota and Jack of Diamonds over the years. Both groups
played at the Balloon's fourth-anniversary party in 1976, and Jack of Diamonds
and the Jerry-Kelly Band performed at the sixth Balloon anniversary. Witness
and Dakota played for the tenth-anniversary party in February 1982.

In the first few weeks of January 1980, Terry Powell and Don Ellis from CBS
Records visited the Stone Balloon to check out Dakota. They were impressed

with the new songs and the song-writing abilities of Hludzik and Kelly. They came back in July 1980 for a huge record release party that Stevenson organized.

For his second act, Stevenson came aboard as Dakota road manager, concert announcer, handler of Stone Balloon and Queen T-shirt monies, and jack-of-all-trades on the 1980 Dakota-Queen Tour. And then The Stone Balloon Experiment came to an end. Stevenson sold the place, claiming that he grossed over $50 million over thirty-three years and walked away debt-free, clutching a check for the sum of two hundred and forty-three dollars. Nevertheless, it remained a mind-boggling trip with a lifetime of friendships and memories for The Buoys, Jerry-Kelly, and Dakota, and everyone else connected to Frigyes Karinthy's "six degrees of separation."

33

THE EL CAMINOS

The road less traveled and the least known chapter of our saga began in Berwick, a small industrial town nestled along the Susquehanna River and home to the once-elegant West Side Ballroom.

Sixteen-year-old George Fox, a high school student, who, in the early 1960s, had moved to Berwick from upriver Kingston, was bitten by the rock and roll bug. He wanted to organize a band just like his stepfather, Phil Guinard, who played drums in a small combo at Rock's Steakhouse, a popular Bloomsburg nightclub. So piano man Fox and Berwick drummer Steve Bond

Berwick's lengendary West Side Ballroom.

The El Caminos. (L-R) Steve Bond, Tom Verano, George Fox, Jim Schrader, Carl Siracuse.

began auditioning guitar players. Fox asked Tom Varano, a childhood friend from Kingston, playing in The Bismarks to try out. Although Berwick was an hour's drive south on Route 11, Varano took a chance and joined the trio of newcomers.

Bond, Fox, and Varano began to practice at the Bond family cottage in rural Benton. First, the trio would discover old sheet music and imitate standards like "Summertime," "Stardust," and "Blue Moon." Then, during a surprise birthday party for Guinard, sixteen-year-old Varano sang lead on "My Buddy," Guinard's favorite song.

The former guitarist for the steel guitar-themed Ram Rods, Carl Siracuse, knew Verano from grade school through high school and was invited to join the band. Additionally, Siracuse owned a guitar and amplifier.

EL CAMINO REAL

Bond suggested the group's name, from the high school text, *El Camino Real*, part of his school curriculum, but something was lost in the translation. Ted Billy, Emeritus Professor of English at Saint Mary's College, Notre Dame, Indiana, was Steve Bond's high school classmate. Billy was quick to point out that his band mistranslated the Spanish title:

In choosing the name "The El Caminos," they were actually calling themselves "The The Roads," since, in Spanish, the adjective follows the noun rather than precedes it, as in English. So instead of calling themselves "The Royals," the band chose a Spanish phrase meaning "The Roads." Luckily for the band, the Chevy El Camino was quite popular at the time.

The El Caminos was consistent with naming bands after popular hot rods; Cadillacs, Cobras, Eldorados, Fleetwoods, GTOs, Hondas, Impalas, Rivieras, Ronny and the Daytonas, and many more.

WEST SIDE PARK

During the Big Band era of the 1930s and 1940s, Central and Northeastern Pennsylvania spawned a cluster of music palaces, citadels for a thriving musical subculture that attracted hordes of starry-eyed teenagers and their parents dancing to the orchestras of the day. Among them were Reading's Crystal Ballroom, Allentown's Castle Gardens, Pottstown's Sunnybrook Ballroom, Barnesville's Lakewood Ballroom, and Berwick's West Side Park. West Side was an essential part of the Big Band circuit when men and women laughed and danced and fell in love in the throes of enchantment. Strains of Harry James's "It's Been A Long, Long Time" were eternally suspended in the air. Like a butterfly from a cocoon, West Side granted a transformative shift from the mundane to the magical, a balm to take away troubles and woes — to replace heartache with music. It was not a cure, but a positive and effective distraction from, what was for many, a nightmare existence. West Side offered order, symmetry, and consistency in a world beset by chaos during the pre and post-war years.

Strategically located at 117 Raseley Street, in Berwick's lower west end section, the dance hall boasted one of the largest hardwood dance floors in the state, 10,000-square feet of ballroom flooring, surrounded by tables, benches, and fireplaces. In the artificial lighting of that bygone era, the dance floor looked like a Martian landscape, bathed in red and gold flecks of alien stardust. West Side became an important destination, conveniently intersected by New York City, Philadelphia, Harrisburg, and Pittsburgh. As many as four thousand paid attendees saw Hollywood celebrities and entertainers on a typical weekend. West Side stars included bands like Les Brown and His Band of Renown, Cab Calloway, the Dorsey Brothers, Glen Gray and his Casaloma Band, Harry James, Sammy Kaye, Glen Miller, Vaughn Monroe, Fred Waring, and Paul Whiteman step onto the dark-green stage.

After the Big Band era ended, youthful rock groups appropriated the dance halls. The bands typically dressed in blazers or matching sports jackets. Song lists involved classic instrumentals, often with saxophone accompaniment and rousing dance tunes. The bands who played at West Side circulated throughout a multi-county area. They included Angie and the Raiders, The Avantis, the Blazers, Eddie Day and the Starfires, Dee Cool and the Casuals, The Islanders, Joe Nardone, and the All-Stars, the Midnighters, The Orphans (with Jack Edwards), The Playboys, The Saints, and the local favorites, The El Caminos, who quickly became the West Side house band.

In their earliest inception, the El Caminos played a type of organic rock and roll that lent itself to the dark confines of West Side. Lead singer George Fox's arrogance and spontaneous outbursts added an unpredictable facet to their music while demanding perfection from his band. Their sound featured raw, loud vocals on classics like Ray Charles's "What'd I Say" (Atlantic, 1959), the Isley Brother's "Shout" (RCA, 1959), and Dion's "Drip Drop" (Columbia, 1963). Despite his temperament, Fox was an exceptional musician. Berwick's Playboys Inc. keyboardist, Alan Basala opined:

> I think the best rock 'n' roll piano player to come out of Berwick was George Fox. He, drummer Steven Bond, and Tom Varano, on his Gretch hollow body electric guitar, could make some great music

Fox's Market Street home became the command center and a popular hangout for the El Caminos and their fans, said Siracuse:

> We would often stay at George Fox's parents' home on the weekends. We would usually tape the West Side Park Friday night gig and listen to it later that night. Then, on Saturday afternoon, we would practice, learn new songs, or just jam in Fox's living room, often with me on George's upright bass or my guitar, George on piano, Tom on guitar and Jim Schrader on sax, and Steve Bond sometimes there with only a snare drum. Then perhaps a private gig that night or a trip to a gig in Bloomsburg.

The band consisted of George Fox, piano and lead vocals; Steve Bond, drums; Jim Shrader, saxophone and bass; Tom Varano, lead guitar; and Carl Siracuse, guitar and organ. Fox (' 64), Bond (' 65), and Shrader (' 66) were all students at Berwick High School.

BEATLEMANIA

Steve Bond's drumming style perfectly matched the band, setting a steady backbeat with his red sparkle Slingerland drum set, playing the song tight, predictable, and consistent. He was straight ahead and unpretentious, never a distraction from the lead singers or guitars. He was a team player, not a show-man, hammering tom-toms with insistent mallets and turned off snare. Berwick's Dave Eisenhower, a fellow drummer, observed:

> He was excellent and right up to snuff with the '60s music. He played for the song and didn't get crazy and improvise like today's jam bands.

Slingerlands and Ludwig drums were all the rage with bands, especially after The Beatles appeared on the Ed Sullivan Show, with Ringo perched high atop his Ludwig drum set, unique for drummers at that time. From a historical perspective, this Baby-Boomer event remains unsurpassed. At eight o'clock on February 9, 1964, seventy-three million people gathered in front of their TV sets to see The Beatles' first live performance on U.S. soil. That evening, 60% of the televisions turned on were tuned in to *The Beatles on Ed Sullivan*.

The members of the El Caminos, and the youth of the world, were under siege by an armada of jangling guitars, precision harmonies, and throbbing tambourine-laden percussion. It was an American rhythm and blues boomeranging back to us by the British Invasion, popularized by the Animals, Billy J Kramer and The Dakotas, Dave Clark Five, Gerry and The Pacemakers, Peter and Gordon, the Rolling Stones, and the indomitable Beatles.

The Beatles held the American airwaves and charts hostage. In the April 4, 1964, issue of *Billboard* magazine, the group secured the top five spots on the singles charts and the top two spots on the album charts. Another seven Beatles' singles were in the Hot 100. It represented a milestone that, in all likelihood, will never be broken.

Their uncanny success influenced generations of youthful musicians. The English Invasion followed, rip tiding across every city and town in the nation. Thunderstruck by rock's primal strains, hordes of teenagers strapped on second-hand Stratocasters and created their music.

Among them were the El Caminos, who experimented with the new sound, skillfully recreating the music. Everyone sang on harmonies and attempted to sing lead, recalled Verano:

> We figured out the three-part harmonies that John, Paul, and George did and copied everything as close as we could. People said we sounded like them, so that was a good thing. We even tried to write like Lennon and McCartney.

To emulate the Beatle's sound, Shrader switched from saxophone to bass, Siracuse brought keyboards into the mix. Bond began to play the so-called Mercy Beat while experimenting with drum breaks and microphones to enhance his drum set. They were able to imitate the Beatles' songbook admirably, leading to additional bookings. Moving away from West Side, the El Caminos began to book dances in ever-widening circles, playing Frank Milo's Rumpus Room, the Scranton Cultural Center, and The Varsity Grill. During one dance, The Bloomsburg Police, located across the street from the Varsity Grill, demanded that the band either turn down their amplifiers or be arrested for disturbing the peace.

G MAJOR

They were eager students. Driving home from Berwick, Verano and Siracuse listened to WBZ, the Boston powerhouse. "Things We Said Today," from The Beatles' *A Hard Day's Night* LP (Capitol, 1964), was playing. Although not a single release, it was one of the countless gems the Fab Four created. Awestruck, they had to pull the car over. They had never heard chord structure like that before, said Verano:

> I couldn't believe they took a song that was in G minor and, for the bridge, went to a G major. No one ever did that. I said to Carl, 'This is a miracle. How could anyone think of doing something like this?' You can feel the emotion as they go from minor to major. Just brilliant. From the day that the first Beatles album came out, it seemed that black cover with the four heads was in every record shop in the world. I picked up the album on the way to Berwick. We stayed in Berwick that weekend because we had a gig at West Side Park, and Carl and I learned every song on the album and played most of those songs in the same order on that original vinyl.

Verano's passion and dedication to his craft bordered on obsession. He was skilled and accomplished, and that did not go unnoticed. If imitation is the sincerest form of flattery, then so be it. Bob Hock, founder of Pendulum, a successful Top-40 act, was one such fan and admirer of the band:

> Tom Verano used to be my idol. I used to watch him play lead at Bloomsburg's Varsity Grill with the El Caminos. So I went out and bought a Gretsch just like his.

Gearheads like Hock and Verano were quick to embrace the advanced sound technology created by The Beatles. George Harrison played a black Gretsch Duo Jet during their Cavern Club days, and then in mid-1963, he switched to a Gretsch Country Gentleman and then a Gretsch Tennessean, both of which he played until around 1965. On the recording of "Timothy" (Scepter, 1971), Bill Kelly played a 1967 Gretsch Country Gentleman.

The new El Caminos (L-R) Top clockwise Steve Bond, Jim Schrader, Tom Verano, Carl Siracuse.

Attempting to capitalize on their popularity, the band recorded two of Varano's compositions at Bell Sound Studios in New York City. "Storm Warning" and "We Stand Alone" typified the twangy English sound, replete with lyrics screaming of teen alienation and despair. With guitars, bass, and drums, both tunes were recorded "raw," with no studio enhancements. They were among the first songs that Varano wrote.

Several obscure El Caminos' songs, "Never Change," "A Little Louie," "Because," and "327," were recorded but never released. The songs were simplistic but hinted at future potential. Most used the primitive process of cutting grooves into a metal plate, then covered in a layer of acetone. Acetates had been used in the days before tape recorders and were part of a transitional stage between the master tape and the finished vinyl record.

Siracuse, only a teenager during this exciting period, reflected on his high school days and fledgling musical career:

> The El Caminos were my first real band. Berwick's West Side Park was a lot of fun and a time when we focused on music and got the added benefit of the busy social scene like house parties and the Tastee Freeze ice cream stand. Tom Varano and I would sit in trigonometry class and plan our weekend in Berwick. How I did as well as I did in that class remains a mystery.

Things could have ended differently. George Fox, residing in New Jersey at the time, reflected on his old band in a phone interview:

> I think that if we had hung in there with the original people, we could have taken it quite far. I guess a large part of our popularity was that we knew just about everybody in Berwick Area High School, and also because the repertoire that we did at the time was very much in keeping with what was going on. We tried to do everything current.

ROCK CASUALTY

On August 16, 1966, Steve Bond died after his Chevy Impala crashed directly into a tree. He had been traveling on the winding two-lane Jonestown Road, about three miles south of Cambra, on his way to an El Caminos' concert in Scranton. *The Morning Press* reported that Bond's "late-model sedan became an instrument of death" after the impact thrust the engine block back into the passenger compartment and the steering wheel into the back of the front seat. Thrown from the car, Bond suffered multiple fractures and lacerations of the head, arms, and legs. He died on the operating table at the Berwick Hospital.

Because he was regarded as an excellent driver, Bond's death brought about much speculation. In an article titled "He Was the 6th Victim in 48 Hours," *The Morning Press* recounted the list of tragic accidents, all occurring within a short period. The drummer was leaving his father's company picnic, held at the Cole's Creek Hunting Camp, and was on his way to play a concert at South Scranton's Junior Mechanics Hall. Drummer Buddy Mecca, who was in the audience that night, filled in for Bond after he didn't arrive. Mecca, one of the best drummers in the region, later played in the famed Scranton bands Button Gwinnett and Ralph.

Bond, a 1965 Berwick High graduate, was buried in the Walnut Street Cemetery, with an outpouring of his schoolmates and fans paying their final respects. Bond was the area's first rock casualty. His untimely death signaled the inevitable end of the original band. George Fox left to pursue a musical

> # FEIFER'S BALLROOM
> ## MOUNT CARMEL
>
> They're coming to Mount Carmel . . . straight
> from their fabulous in-person appearance at the
> Rolling Stone disco in New York City . . . they
> wowed the "in-crowd" at Trude Hellers . . .
>
> ### They're the
>
> # EL CAMINOS!!
>
> And now they're gonna tear it up at Feifer's
> Ballroom, Fourth and Birch Streets, Mount Car-
> mel. Stand by . . . The El Caminos are ready
> to fill the air with their own special kind of big,
> wild, soul-beat excitement. . . .
>
> The El Caminos are just returning from an out-
> of-sight tour of the Eastern College Circuit. . . .
>
> Don't miss them . . . it's a chance to see one of
> the fastest rising "pop" groups in the nation
> . . . the date is—
>
> ## JUNE 19—8:00
>
> Remember . . . A big night . . . A top concert
> . . . FOR YOU!!
>
> ## THE
> ## EL
> ## CAMINOS

career at Berkeley School of Music, although in the 1964 Berwick High School Yearbook, he listed his future occupation as "Night Club Owner." Fox relocated to New Jersey, where he composed classical music and collected antiques.

Jim Shrader, who graduated from Berwick High School in 1966, successfully pursued a career as both musician and instructor. He holds a Bachelor of Music Education degree from Bradley University, a Master of Music in Opera Direction degree from The Cleveland Institute of Music, and a Doctor of Philosophy in Fine Arts (Conducting) degree from Texas Tech University.

Tom Verano attended Berkeley briefly, with dreams of becoming a jazz musician. He explained:

> I thought I would meet up with George Fox, and we would become great jazz
> musicians together. Then along came the Beatles. They made straightforward
> rock and roll exciting and sometimes even used jazz chords. So when I heard

what rock music could be, I had to be part of the generation of rock musicians who could be creative and artistic about their craft.

Verano left Berkley and attended Wilkes-Barre Business College. The El Caminos reigned from 1960-1968. But, as one adventure ended, another was about to begin.

Featuring
The El Caminos

DANCING
Every Friday & Saturday
8 'til 11

THE RUMPUS ROOM

34

RALPH: THE ROCK BAND
FROM SCRANTON

Charles "Buddy" Mecca III, a member of Ralph, stepped in to play at the Scranton concert after El Camino drummer, Steve Bond, was killed. Since the age of seven, Mecca played drums, influenced by greats such as Joe Morello (Dave Brubeck Quintet), Buddy Rich, and Big Band drummer Louie Bellson. He played with Button Gwinnett and The Nickel Bag, Scranton's first drug-oriented band. Mecca also briefly played with Dean Maxwell and The Druids, who released the garage rock singles "It's A Day" b/w "A Man Should Never Cry" (Columbia, 1966).

Ralph, named after a roadie who just happened to walk into the room, was a ten-piece fusion band combining rock, jazz, pop, and classical music. They incorporated complex songs in their playlist such as "MacArthur Park," "The Walrus," "Good Vibrations," and an adaptation of Tchaikovsky's "1812 Overture."

The band's impressive lineup consisted of William Cianfichi, bass; Martin Golob, trumpet; Mark "Tex" Horwitz, trombone; Bruce Keib, drums and lead vocals; William Lombardi, lead guitar and lead vocals; Buddy Mecca, drums; Martin Menichiello, trumpet, and vocals; Jeff Mitchell, keyboards, synthesizer, and vocals; Joseph Santaniello, rhythm guitar and lead vocals; and Robert Tansits, alto and tenor sax, clarinet, keyboards, and lead vocals.

Afterward, the popular group warmed up for Brian Auger, Quicksilver Messenger Company, and Tower of Power, but in April 1971, The Buoys and Ralph, two of the top acts in the region, performed at the Scranton Central Auditorium. They shared some interesting connections, as well. C. Michael Wright produced both bands. Keyboardist Jeff Mitchell later played for Dakota and co-wrote "Crazy Love," with Bill Lombardi, included on Dakota (Columbia, 1980).

Buddy Mecca, drummer extraordinaire. (Maxim Furek photo.)

Ralph's grassroots appeal quickly spread throughout New York, Massachusetts, Rhode Island, Delaware, Kentucky, Connecticut, New Jersey, and Ohio. Ralph played a wide circuit and was extremely popular at Cleveland's Agora, said club owner Hank LoConti:

> After Alice Cooper, Uriah Heap, Wishbone Ash, the Raspberries, James Gang, and Grand Funk, I'm pleased to present the next logical musical giant to appear on the national music scene.

Cleveland's Jack Cracium, president of Ralph's promotion agency, described the band's uniqueness:

> People from all over this country who have heard Ralph, fourteen million in 1976 alone, see Ralph as the other side of the coin. No drugs, no orgies. Just a musically powerful group.

Ralph performing before some 20,0000 fans at Nay Aug Park. (Times-Tribune Archives.)

NAY AUG PARK

One of the region's legendary performances was Ralph's 1974 Nay Aug Park free concert, attracting twenty thousand fans. The Scranton Tribune described the Woodstock-like scene:

> Young lovers, numbering a thousand or more and clad to the last man, or girl, in uniform faded blue denims, seated themselves directly in front of the stage. It was not possible to move in this area.

Despite the huge crowds, there was a subdued police presence, according to Tribune writer Bob McCarthy:

> Police maintained a low profile at the concert. A decision was made not to send any patrol cars into the area unless there was an emergency. The limited number of hired reserve patrolmen on hand had no significant disturbances of any kind.

While there were no accidents or episodes of violence, The Scranton *Times* reported:

> Although the crowd, with estimates running as high as 20,000, was well
> behaved, police report that the park section now looks like a garbage dump
> with beer cans, syringes, and other debris scattered around.

Mecca left the band in 1979 and later drummed with Child, Gibbs and Cullen, and the Buddy Mecca Band. He was the director of intellectual property and research for Warner Music Group Inc., New York, until his retirement. He died in 2007 at the age of fifty-eight.

Ralph's "Hang on, Be Strong" was a semi-finalist in the 1979 American Song Festival. In 1980, Ralph was featured on TV 44's *Another Roadside Attraction* simulcast over WVIA-FM (89.9). They also promoted their highly acclaimed TV special *Music is My Mother* in Ohio and New York locations.

Their press release emphasized that, despite the ups and downs, the accidents, litigations, and all the rest, that:

> Through it all, the band remained dedicated to their high standards of musical
> quality. They never succumbed to the fads, the flash, the glitter, the punk that
> have come and gone.

The original singles, "Fly by Night" b/w "Save Me" (KMA, 1980), were written by Bill Lombardi and produced by Lombardi and Mitchell. Both were impressive; however, The Steely Dan-influenced "Save Me" should have been the A-side. Nonetheless, while thumbing their noses at musical conglomerates, Ralph got the last laugh. The independent KMA label was an inside joke that stood for 'kiss my ass."

35

THE GLASS PRISM

Regrouping after Steve Bond's death, Varano and Siracuse recruited Scranton's Augie Christiano, former lead singer and bassist for The Henchmen, and drummer Rick Christian (Chojnowski) to complete the lineup. Christian's group, The Treasures (Harry Barnes, Buddy Kays, Molke Wilfong, and Christian), released a single called "I Walk with An Angel" (Crown Records, 1961) that saw some local chart action. Christian changed his name to "Richards" to avoid sounding too similar to "Christiano."

Serendipitously, the El Caminos were introduced to several key New York City power brokers through a mutual contact. Gene Weiss, vice president of Columbia Records, and Mort Lewis, manager of Simon and Garfunkel; Blood, Sweat and Tears; and jazz pianist Dave Brubeck. After forming a Marble Arch Productions partnership, Weiss and Lewis signed the El Caminos to RCA Records as their first act.

Rock acts of the era bought into the philosophy of outlandish fashion, dramatic stage presence, and psychedelic-tinged themes. The term "psychedelic" became code for anything that altered the consciousness, drugs certainly, and darker themes exploring the inner recesses of the human psyche. As the world was being *psychedelicized*, the El Caminos changed their name to the Glass Prism, suggested by Siracuse's mother Helen, during a brainstorming session at the kitchen table with Carl and his sisters. That change was in keeping with the tradition of quirky names such as Moby Grape, Pink Floyd, and the Strawberry Alarm Clock.

THE "POE CYCLE"

A big fan of horror writer Edgar Allan Poe, Augie Christiano became the catalyst blending Poe's dark pathos with psychedelia. Of the musical alchemy, Christiano said:

The Glass Prism (L-R) Carl Siracuse, Rick Richards, Augie Christiano, Tom Verano.

Yes, the idea was mine. I always liked Edgar Allan Poe and thought it would be great to put his poems to music and wanted to use his most famous poem, 'The Raven.' The music and the lyrics were a match made in heaven.

Called *Poe Through the Glass Prism* (RCA, 1969), the concept album set eleven Edgar Allan Poe compositions to a rock format, reflecting America's hypnotic fascination with the works of Poe.

Before the Beatles, there was Poe. During the early 1960s, director Roger Corman inundated America with eight Poe-derived film adaptations. Known as the "Poe Cycle," these films included *House of Usher* (1960), *The Pit and The Pendulum* (1961), *Premature Burial* (1961), *Tales of Terror* (1962), and his 1964 masterpiece, *The Mask of The Red Death*. Corman's final installment in his homage to Poe was *The Tomb of Ligeia* (1964).

These CinemaScope thrillers were extremely popular, and, as an example, *House of Usher* became one of the Top Five box office hits of 1960. Budgeted for only $270,000, it was the most money American International Pictures had ever spent for a film. Although most horror films play to a limited audience, *House of Usher* appealed to the masses. Corman had tapped into something with his mix of brilliant, stylized color sets and suspenseful themes of the macabre.

LES PAUL STUDIOS

Poe Through the Glass Prism was recorded at the Les Paul Studios in Mahwah, New Jersey. Les Paul (1915-2009) pioneered the development of the solid-body electric guitar that "made the sound of rock and roll possible." Paul developed many recording innovations, including overdubbing, delay effects such as tape pauses, and multi-track recording. He skillfully blended country with jazz. Terry Stewart, president of the Rock and Roll Hall of Fame, explained:

> Without Les Paul, we would not have rock and roll as we know it. His inventions created the infrastructure for the music, and his playing style will ripple through generations. He was truly an architect of rock and roll.

The band slept at Paul's home, adjacent to the recording studio, and Christiano remembered when Les Paul woke him up in the early morning with a cup of coffee and sent him into the studio. Christiano hammered "The Raven" in just one take in the tradition of the great early rock pioneers. Not surprisingly, the album was recorded in only three days and released just a few weeks later. Interestingly, Verano had ditched his Gretch and purchased a Les Paul guitar on April 16, 1969, just weeks before recording the Poe album.

Les Paul and his son Russ were the recording engineers for this concept LP that traded Paul's innovative overdubs and meticulous arrangement for a straightforward, stripped-down product. Varano laid down a twelve-string rhythm accompaniment, "giving it a nice midrange fill," and Siracuse added the macabre Hammond B-3 organ backdrop that added to the sparse dirge-like treatment. Weiss produced the album. A review of the album by Jason Ankeny of *Beat Ball Music* referenced the LP's "grandiose psychedelic arrangements" and praised the overall concept:

Both Tom Verano and Augie Cristiano are imaginative composers skilled at folding classical and jazz precepts into the hard rock idiom, and their nuanced arrangements (dominated by chiaroscuro shades of funeral organ) artfully convey the melancholy and macabre at the heart of Poe's verse. Equally impressive are Glass Prism's four-part harmonies, employed most effectively on songs like 'El Dorado.'

Having piqued RCA's interest, "The Raven" was selected as the first single. RCA placed full-page ads in *Billboard, Cashbox,* and *Record World.* In addition, they appeared on Jerry Blavit's nationally syndicated TV dance show, *The Discophonic Scene,* and opened for The Guess Who, Three Dog Night, and Vanilla Fudge. "The Raven" became a regional hit as it charted #3 on WARM and placed in the Top Ten on WILK, despite a lackluster promotional campaign from RCA. Still, stardom beckoned with the gravitational pull of a larger planet, and, as Verano reminisced, things were looking up:

> RCA gave us a lot of money. My contract said $16,500.00 upfront, which was a lot for 1969. We had an album deal for one or more singles. It was one of the best deals in the country at the time, along with Paul McCartney's solo album *McCartney* (Apple, 1970), where he supposedly played all of the instruments on songs like "Baby I'm Amazed."

BAD TIMING

Business was booming at RCA. After David Clayton-Thomas replaced Al Kooper as the lead singer of Blood, Sweat, and Tears, the fusion-rock band charted with "You've Made Me So Very Happy" (Columbia, 1969), "Spinning Wheel" (Columbia, 1969), and "And When I Die" (Columbia, 1969. All three peaked at *Billboard's* #2, which guaranteed visibility and sales throughout the year.

RCA planned a Glass Prism & Blood Sweat and Tears Tour. But, prophetically, just as the raven uttered "Nevermore," things came undone. Superstar Clayton-Thomas and manager Mort Lewis had a "falling out." Tempers flared. Things were said in moments of anger, and the promised tour was aborted. Recalled Verano:

> It happened at the worst time. RCA pulled the plug on the tour. They say that it is all about timing, but, in this case, it was all bad timing. Since our promised tour with Blood, Sweat, and Tears was canceled, RCA backed off on the 'push.' Our manager, Mort Lewis, and RCA broke down, and the light dimmed.

There was no light at the end of the tunnel. There was no upside. Even though Verano remained optimistic, the probability of a tour fit into a thimble:

> We thought something else would come along, or the tour would be rescheduled. Then Mort Lewis came up and disappeared. We waited for him to surface, but it just didn't happen. So at the end of that year, we were still waiting. We continued to play and book gigs just to survive.

It was a disappointment multiplied by four and an abrupt slap in the face for drummer Rick Richards. Hope and despair see-sawed between them, he said:

> When the Glass Prism & Blood, Sweat, and Tears tour fell apart, I thought, 'This could be the beginning of the end.' We never got another shot at a tour, and there went our exposure. It was all over.

Things were also unraveling for Mort Lewis, who managed Simon and Garfunkel. First, Lewis' wife, Peggy Harper, left him and married Paul Simon. Later, after Harper and Simon divorced, Simon wrote "Do It for Your Love" (Columbia, 1976) and "Train in The Distance" (Warner Brothers, 1983), describing the disappointment over his failed marriage. Then, according to rumors, Lewis silently disappeared from New York City and went off to his yacht in Florida to sulk and brood, withdrawing from the industry.

ON JOY AND SORROW

The contract with RCA called for a second album, giving the group only two weeks to prepare. As a result, *On Joy and Sorrow* (RCA, 1970) was written and recorded quickly. "She's Too Much" was intended to be the first single but was never issued, and RCA did nothing to promote the LP. Instead, it was their Descent into the Maelstrom, explained Verano:

> Next thing you know, we were doing the Poe stuff, and Mort Lewis and Gene Weiss came along and swept us off our feet. Scepter called us to do 'Timothy,' and it all was happening so fast. The RCA deal was what was happening, so nothing else seemed important. You never knew what was real and what was just people talking.

Fran Brozena overheard some of the talk. He recollected the Rhythm Aces' Bob O'Connell had invited C. Michael Wright to check out the Buoys at Pete's Place in Exeter. Brozena claims that the El Caminos—Scepter connection was only a myth and that recording "Timothy" was never a possibility:

Even if the El Caminos would have gotten that deal, there's no guarantee they would have ever met Rupert Holmes, let alone record 'Timothy.' And even if they had gotten that Scepter record deal, there was nobody in that band that could sing like Bill Kelly. There wasn't anybody in the valley, at that time, that could hit those high notes. And, in reality, Rupert liked Bill's voice on 'These Days,' our first release.

The Glass Prism's Lester T. Verano's recollection, after fifty years, was a bit different and went something like this:

Michael Wright called me and said he had a song they wanted us to do. The song, of course, was 'Timothy.' Michael may have told me the concept of the song but going through my head was the thought that for a decade, we've been trying to get on a major record label, and now that we're on RCA other labels are interested. Cool. He told me Rupert Holmes, an up-and-coming song-writer, wrote the song.

I told him we were signed to RCA and couldn't do it … I told him about The Buoys and their great lead vocalist, Bill Kelly, that I was sure Scepter would like. I gave him their phone numbers.

Along with the missed opportunities, in her final curtain call, Mistress Fate was blatantly cruel. The Glass Prism had been the first act to sign with Marble Arch Productions, but what had all the promise of rock stardom soon turned into a horror darker than The Tomb of Ligeia. Mismanaged and brokenhearted, they disbanded in 1971.

SHENANDOAH

After Carl Siracuse left to join The Buoys, the remaining members regrouped to form the three-member group, Shenandoah. A year later, Christiano left, replaced by bassist Lou Cossa, a well-traveled musician who excelled on bass, keyboards, and vocals. As a member of the blues-based power trio, he appreci-ated what his band was trying to accomplish. "Shenandoah was original," said Cossa:

We did not sound like the studio record, and we did not want to. I'm not saying that those bands that try to sound like the original artists do anything wrong, but they're just trying to make a life out of somebody else's vision. That was not for us. We wanted to get influenced and create. The artist gave us the palate; we put in different colors.

Power-trio Shenandoah (L-R) Tom Verano, Lou Cossa, Rick Richards.

That palate of colors led to Cossa, Richards, and Varano's self-titled LP, *Shenandoah* (1975). It was recorded at New York's Bell Sound Studios and produced by Seth Greenkey, who had previously worked with Screaming Jay Hawkins and David Johansen and The New York Dolls.

Shenandoah and Three Dog Night played a concert at Williamsport's Bowman Field on August 5, 1971. Both groups played for free to benefit the Muscular Dystrophy Association of America. For the next six years, Shenandoah continued to play their hard rock before disbanding in 1976.

Lou Cossa continued as a professional musician, touring with the successful road version of The Boxtops, who charted with "The Letter" #1 (Mala, 1967) and "Cry Like A Baby" #2 (Mala, 1968), and later Dakota, on their tour with Freddy Mercury and Queen. After leaving Dakota, Cossa and Richards reorganized as Public Enemy Number One.

Augie Christiano moved back to Mays Landing, New Jersey, played with a few local bands, and drove a truck. But he seemed reluctant to revisit the glory days of the Glass Prism.

After Public Enemy Number One, Rick Richards fell back on his successful electrical construction background in Dickson City, Pennsylvania, maintaining a collection of vintage sporting cars.

Carl Siracuse stayed with the Buoys (Fran Brozena, John Buckley, Steve Furmanski, Chris Hanlon, Carl Siracuse) until their breakup around 1988.

Tom Varano moved to the Binghamton, New York area, where he managed his Music Star Agency, Inc., and as Lester T. Verano, continues to promote The Glass Prism's legacy.

The *Shenandoah* LP, considered their best work, was not released for another thirty-seven years but then released as a double record on the Glass Prism *Resurrection* CD (Debra Records, 2012.) Dick Plotkin, the owner of Debra Records and former member of The Magics, was instrumental in actualizing that project.

AFTERMATH

The Velvet Underground and The Doors offered a contrary vision to the love and peace of the 1960s. As true iconoclasts, Lou Reed's band sang of sadism, addiction, and human suffering. At the same time, The Doors explored Freudian themes of patricide and incest, and Jim Morrison acted out public scenes of self-destructive behavior.

The Glass Prism belongs in that unique group as well. In *Poe Through the Glass Prism,* Edgar Allan Poe's prose immersed us in the terror and hopelessness of his macabre palette. Likewise, the musical adaptation of his poetry celebrated the beauty of Thanatos, the Greek concept of death.

The Glass Prism became forerunners of the Goth movement with their homage to Poe. "The Raven" (RCA, 1969) was the first true expression of Goth rock, predating Bauhaus' "Bela Lugosi's Dead" (Small Wonder Records, 1979) by ten years and The Alan Parsons' Project LP *Tales of Mystery and Imagination* (20th Century Fox, 1976) by seven years. Much later, Lou Reed paid homage to the tortured artist in *The Raven* (Sire, 2003).

Unlike Jefferson Airplane, also on RCA, the Glass Prism, although surrounded by a vocal counterculture that embraced psychedelic mind expansion, refused to glorify drug use. They were unique in that respect, embracing straight-edged non-conformity.

The Glass Prism were among the proponents of concept-based rock, paving the way for a new breed of progressive musicians. The Glass Prism, who began at Berwick's West Side Park as The El Caminos, were the first Northeastern Pennsylvania band to catch the gaze of the industry and net a major record label contract.

It was bitter-sweet for Lester T. Verano, who, in hindsight, viewed the events in his life in a karmic haze. He married at the time of the RCA signing, divorced after the deal ended, and then remarried after Shenandoah decided to call it quits.

In 2007, The Glass Prism performed a benefit concert for the Edgar Allan Poe National Historic Site in Philadelphia and another reunion show the following year at the Scranton Cultural Center. In 2010, the group released a fifty-six-minute documentary *On Joy and Sorrow: The Glass Prism Story.*

Although The Glass Prism were unable to sign with Scepter, the band could conceivably have recorded "Timothy," a song inspired by Sheppton and reflective of horror master Poe's dark imagery.

36

SYNCH

One of Dakota's most creative periods was during the mid-1980s when they helped produce aspiring acts. The boy-band Synch became their most successful effort, with Lou Butwin, lead singer; Dave Abraham, guitar; James A. Donnelly, bass; Chuck Yarmey, keyboards; Jimmy Harnen, drums, and vocals. Synch proved that the region could produce hit singles and a version of Beatlemania, with hordes of screaming adolescent girls.

JUMPING JEFF WALKER

KRZ's radio personality, Jumping Jeff Walker, helped launch the career of Synch after Jimmy Harnen asked him to listen to a few of his songs. Walker recalled when Harnen's group arrived with their ghetto blaster and popped in a cassette:

> He played "Play the Game" on the one side. I was honest with him. I said, 'It was OK, but it doesn't blow me away.' Then he said, here's the other one. It was 'Where Are You Now?' I said, 'This is great.'

Working a second job, twenty-three-year-old Walker played at high school dances with his mobile DJ company and began to play the song:

> Kids were calling the radio station at night. They wanted to hear it. Radio was a lot different then. Now it's all corporate control. My PD at the time said, 'Start spiking it in during your show.'
>
> The calls just kept coming in. KRZ reported our playlist weekly to the trade magazines, who are no longer in existence, and, all of a sudden, record labels are calling asking, 'What is this band called Synch and why are you playing them so much?'

At that point, Harnen's group was approached by several independent promoters who wanted to sign the band to a deal, said Walker:

Jimmy Harnan rode the charts with "Where Are You Now?"

The first time it was released, it didn't do that well. It charted, maybe at #70, and then it fell off the charts. Then a Vegas DJ starts playing it. It was always a hit here, locally, but then it exploded and worked its way to # Ten. To this day, as far as Top 40 singles, it is the biggest single in the history of NEPA.

KRZ booked Night Ranger and Bon Jovi for two separate concerts at Rocky Glen Park, and, once again, it was Walker who was instrumental in securing Synch as Bon Jovi's opening act:

My boss said, 'We need an opening act for this hot-shot rock band, Bon Jovi, that's all over MTV. I said, 'Synch is burning up our request lines. They're local. I don't even think we'll have to pay them. I don't think we paid them anything.'

They killed it that night. They were fantastic. For them, it was the thrill of a lifetime. The pavilion at Rocky Glen Park was jammed to the rafters. When Synch was in their prime, here in Northeast Pennsylvania, they were like the Back Street Boys of NEPA. Everywhere they went, the girls were just freaking out.

"WHERE ARE YOU NOW?"

Harnen and Rich Congdon co-wrote the pop ballad "Where Are You Now?" Ironically, lead vocalist Butwin sang all of Synch's songs, but Harnen's plaintive vocals pushed "Where Are You Now" (Micki, 1986) to *Billboard*'s No. 77.

The original version, recorded at Northumberland's Susquehanna Sound Studio, was engineered by Jim Garrison, while Jerry Hludzik, Bill Kelly, and Rick Manwiller later added their harmonies. Harnen was a big fan of Dakota, who crafted pop tunes with killer hooks. Harnen wanted them to get involved with the recording.

Synch later opened for Steppenwolf at Moosic's Rocky Glen Park, signed with entertainment attorneys Arthur Mann and Associates, executive producers of Bon Jovi and Cinderella, and opened for the group Expose.

COLUMBIA RECORDS

Because of solid record sales, "Where Are You Now" was picked up for national distribution by CBS. Harnen recorded an updated version of the song at The Warehouse Recording Studios in Philadelphia and the Record Plant in New York City, produced by Hludzik and Kelly and arranged by Manwiller. The piece included Manwiller's keyboards, but Hludzik's bass drove the song to another realm, giving it the needed pop. The radio play was all-important, and Harnen had several major stations on his side, according to former DJ Shadoe Steele:

> I was there in the early 1980s when powerhouse KRZ made Synch's Jimmy Harnen a local star for literally two years, first as a member of the group Synch, then when Jimmy broke away and had a solo take with 'Where Are You Now' on his own with Columbia... which set off the band when Harnen deserted the group without even a mere mention in the publicity department.

Nicole Walton, writing in Berwick High School's *Student Times*, claimed that the tune was "the biggest song by a local artist to hit the market," observing:

> It reigned as Number One on Q-102 for sixty-eight consecutive nights and was also Number One on KRZ's Top Ten, on and off, throughout the latter half of the summer.

Synch's independent album, *Get the Feeling* (Countach, 1987), "sold over 4,000 units in less than four weeks," according to manager Thom Greco, and included the re-worked version of "Where Are You Now." Harnen said that:

> We've put our all into this project, and one thing we won't do is give up. We have many loyal people out there who enjoy our music, and this is for them.

"Don't Stop Believin'" was written by Hludzik and Kelly, and "Don't Walk Away on Love" was co-written by Harnen and WKRZ disc jockey Jeff

Walker. The band was improving as Rick Manwiller explained to staff writer Joe Butkiewicz:

> Their sound is maturing a bit, and it's a little more polished. It's smoother, sort of like REO, but with a Chicago and Toto influence. Synch is becoming a band, finally.

Although the song steadily climbed the charts, Shadoe Steele explained how chart action was more clearly defined after 1998:

> A new group of Columbia studio musicians recut 'Where Are You Now?' note-for-note with Jimmy on vocals. The record went to #10 on *Billboard*, but WKRZ kept the song as the #1 request for months on end. These were the days when you simply 'called in' to industry watchdog and logistics-keeper *Radio & Records Magazine* reporting how many times the record was played, exaggerating, of course, to help the local guy.

Steele said after 1998, you couldn't get away with that type of non-exact 're-porting.' BDS (Broadcast Data Systems) encoded a digital ID within the songs themselves, which a receiver would pick up at an undisclosed location within reach of the station's signal. BDS would record precisely how many times the music played, and there were no gray areas, Steele said:

> BDS to this day doesn't lie. For example, technology put an end to the 'buddy system' in radio when Program Directors reported they played the song two hundred times a week when in reality, it was only played twenty-four times.

"Where Are You Now" received tremendous regional support from en-thused fans and radio program directors. Amid great expectations, they record-ed a second version of the song for CBS. Harnen told reporter Nicole Walton:

> Whatever we are is because of the people. The public can make or break a band. They buy the singles, the albums, and they request the songs.

THE NEW PAYOLA

Despite the good news, it came mixed with the bad, and Synch's dream shattered like glass. Miami DJ Don Cox was offered cocaine and cash to play particular records, according to a February 1986 *NBC Nightly News* report. NBC pursued the charges, alleging that independent promoters, used by record companies as a more economical means of promoting artists and records, were involved with organized crime. NBC named two independent promoters, Joe Isgro and

Freddie DiSipio, in what they called the "New payola." Synch's only crime was that they were guilty by association, and because Freddie DiSipio had signed them to Columbia, the label immediately terminated their contract.

TAYLOR AND ZAPPLEON

The only silver lining was the rights to their song reverted to the group, and Synch was free to pursue another record contract. Once again, the planets were in alignment and the moon in the Seventh House, as the song basked in the unforeseen good vibrations of a Las Vegas music director.

Jay Taylor, music director at KLUC, had actively promoted Sheriff's earlier song, "When I'm With You" (Capitol, 1982), encouraging other Nationwide Communications Radio members to play it. In Phoenix, Orlando, Columbus, San Jose, and Tucson, radio stations helped push "When I'm With You" to #1 on *Billboard's* pop singles chart. The magic happened again after Guy Zappleon, national program director for Nationwide Communications, promoted another "oldie," UB40's song, "Red, Red Wine" (A&M, 1983). The Neil Diamond composition reached #1 on *Billboard* on October 15, 1988. Taylor and Zappleon had figured out the formula that turned oldies into gold. In January 1989, *USA Today* reported that the duo was "pushing a two-year-old song by Cinch (sp), called 'Where Are You Now?' Says Taylor,' It's another No. 1.'

WTG RECORDS

Even as their hit song was getting a second chance, the band was having second thoughts. On April 27, 1988, during a concert at King's College with the Hooters and the Del-Lords, Synch announced that they were breaking up. After four years and a *Billboard*-charting song, they were calling it quits.

Although CBS never gave them any promotion, Harnen's hit spent twelve weeks on the *Billboard* charts before dying at #77. Nevertheless, it was not going away. Because of renewed airplay and a push from Nationwide Communications, "Where Are You Now" (WTG, 1989) was re-released on the new WTG label, a CBS Westcoast subsidiary founded by music executives Walter Yetnikoff, Tommy Mottola, and Jerry Greenberg. The re-issued song landed in the prestigious *Billboard* Top Ten and #3 on *Billboard's* Adult Contemporary listing.

The region celebrated Hludzik, Kelly, and Manwiller as producers of a Top Ten single that remained on the charts for thirty-eight great weeks. "Where Are You Now" became the biggest hit for any Northeastern Pennsylvania artist, eclipsing "Timothy" (Scepter, 1971), which peaked at *Billboard's* #17.

"CAN'T FIGHT THE MIDNIGHT"

Harnen's solo effort, *Can't Fight the Midnight* (WTG, 1989), was his debut album for CBS, without Synch's involvement. He recorded the album at Ocean Way Recording Studios in Hollywood and Rumbo Recorders in Canoga Park. Harnen co-produced the LP that featured guest appearances from REO Speedwagon's Kevin Cronin, Chicago's Bill Champlain, Toto's Steve Lukather, and session musician Albert Lee. One of the songs was "No Reason in the World," written by Diane Warren, who also wrote Starship's "Nothing's Gonna Stop Us Now" and Chicago's "I Don't Want to Live Without Your Love."

Former members of Secret City were recruited as Harnen's backing band and included Jerry Hludzik, Rick Manwiller, Eric Rudy, Jon Lorance, and Joe Bennish. The group played such diverse venues as Sarasota, Florida, Springfield, Massachusetts, and other locales where the song netted heavy airplay.

REPUBLIC NASHVILLE

Harnen helped promote the 1988 Kings College "Drugs Are A Deadly Game" rally. The anti-drug song, "Should Have Said No" (Countach, 1987), was written by Harnen and Mike Warner, who gave all profits to a local drug rehab. John Nasser of Holland Sound paid for the recording, mixing, and mastering of the record, while Hludzik, Manwiller, Harnen, and Warner engineered the recording, also donating their services. Additionally, in 1993, Harnen donated the rights to "Where Are You Now" to the National Center for Missing and Exploited Children, who then adopted it as their theme song.

Having moved to Nashville, Harnen worked as the national promotional director for DreamWorks Records. In 2006, he rose from vice president of national promotion to senior vice president of promotion for Capitol Records. Robert Gryziak met Harnen during his post-Synch days, playing the Woodlands with his Top 40 rock band, King Friday. Gryziac said Harnen arrived in Nashville just in time for Keith Urban and the second wave of country stars before going on to a successful career in Music City:

> Jimmy was extremely charismatic and very approachable. He would give you the shirt off his back. He was such a good-hearted soul, and he was also an excellent salesman.

Gryziac thought that Harnen connected with DreamWorks and Republic Nashville because of his varied musical aptitude:

> Jimmy had a good ear for sound and engineering and an ability to spotlight talent. He knew who was going to make it and who was not.

In 2009, Harnen became president of the new label, Republic Nashville, and in August 2016, the label was rebranded as BMLG (Big Machine Label Group) Records. The BMLG roster has included country acts Lady Antebellum, Martina McBride, and The Band Perry, the first act that Harnen signed, and a sign of things to come. It did not surprise KRZ radio personality Jumping Jeff Walker that Harnen climbed the Nashville corporate ladder so rapidly:

> Synch's success ran out right after 'Where Are You Now?' That had more to do with the changing musical landscape, and their sound was going away. But, even then, Jimmy wanted to be in the business end of the music business. He didn't want to be the singer in Synch, he was their drummer, yet he has a very unique and great voice.
>
> What made Jimmy different was Number One; he would not quit. He was tenacious. He would come up with creative ways to get the attention of these record label presidents, and he did some wild stunts. He's very talented, and he's on that list as one of the most powerful people in Nashville.

In 2019 Harnen was named president and CEO of BMLG, a label boasting thirty-one Number One singles and twenty-three records that have gotten millions in sales and billions of streams, including Florida Georgia Line's "Cruise," the most digitally downloaded single in country music history, and The Band Perry's "If I Die Young."

Synch (L-R): Bill Kossuth, Jon Lorance, Richie Kossuth, Jimmy Harnen, Charles Yarmey, and Mike Warner.

★ PART X ★

DAKOTA

37

DAKOTA

As the Jerry-Kelly Band, Hludzik and Kelly worked well together. Their stage performance was a fast-paced series of side-by-side theatrical movements learned after playing together for over a decade. The partners offered an optimal visual contrast. Kelly, the operatic clown, hamming it up with precision hand salutes and facial expressions that complemented his falsetto wailings. Hludzik, the staunch anchorman, steady, consistent, the backbone of the smooth Dakota harmony and guitar assault.

Like a million swirling grains of sand, The Dakota Sound began to take shape, blown in from faraway places. The music of Dakota is significant for at least two reasons. First, the group mastered a high harmony, Album Oriented Rock new wave sound, unique in a sea of basic hard rock. At times Dakota sounded like Asia's "In the Heat of the Moment," or Toto's "Love Isn't Always on Time" or Styx's "Sail Away," all complex and textured sonic tapestries. Second, their inspirations came from many familiar places, like Bon Jovi's "Runaway," but without the Jersey attitude. They wrote well-crafted songs with soaring guitar and Kelly's atmospheric vocals. Bob O'Connell, the former keyboardist for Mel Wynn and the Rhythm Aces, said that Kelly "could get up there. He had a wonderful soaring range and feeling. Simply put, I love Bill's voice, as well as his singing," confessed O'Connell:

> He has a remarkable range and timbre, but every bit as important, he's got, soul. I think the goal of a performing artist is to excite the listener through the instrument, and Bill does this consistently. He feels it and its genuine feeling. I've worked with a lot of musicians and heard quite a few as well. But, to me, Bill Kelly is up there with the best of them and right at the front of the pack.

There were plenty of compliments to go around, and Sound Investments engineer Tom Borthwick was equally amazed at Hludzik's abilities:

Jerry could harmonize to anything. He had a unique ability to sing harmony and also to double his voice. It was uncanny how close the second part that he sang was to the first part.

Mark Tomeo, who played with the country band Pony Express, sang high praises for Hludzik's abilities, arguing that "Jerry didn't have a country heart, he had a rock and roll heart," but also:

> Jerry was probably the best singer I ever worked with. He had such an instrument. His voice was so powerful and resonant, and he understood what to do with it too.

Kelly felt that both of them, in the spirit of teamwork, were responsible for the unique template that spotlighted their vocals:

> Our harmonies were rooted in Beatles, Hollies, Crosby-Stills, and the Eagles. It always started with the lead singer, either me or Jerry, but the next harmony above the lead was almost always me. We found that the ticket to having a fingerprint on our vocals was for me to be on the top. I was a high tenor, and my voice sounded its best when it was high. So producers used to take advantage of that and have me do some ridiculously high acrobatics just because I could. That's why they did it.

Schuylkill County's Sterling Koch had the opportunity to examine the group objectively as a fan and professional musician. He said:

> Back in 1971, when 'Timothy' was released, I was very much a hard rock fan and, in particular, a Jimi Hendrix fan. However, the single and The Buoys themselves did not interest me at the time, and I thought they were not much more than a pop, one-hit-wonder band.

That attitude soon changed after Koch developed an appreciation for the group's songwriting talents and vocal aptitude. Then, in the mid-1980s, he had the opportunity to open for Dakota with his group The Sterling Cooke Force:

> Seeing them up close like that and interacting with them brought me a newfound respect for them. They were not only performing originals from the Dakota album but also some cover tunes. At one point, they went into a Sly & The Family Stone medley that not only blew me away but that I have never forgotten to this day.

Kelly's vocals and Hludzik's harmonies were only one part of their modus operandi. The duo were innovative songwriters as well, having no interest in any cookie-cutter musical template. Dakota's songs were good. Some were great!

The second point is that Hludzik and Kelly make, time and again, is in their writing. They continued to generate the freshest, most positive lyrics and approaches to life in the revered tradition of Maurice White, Bruce Springsteen, and John Lennon. Again, Dakota's determined message is evident: Keep on trying. You can make it.

Fate presented them with an unexpected dilemma outside their control and an ominous warning of what was just around the corner. It wasn't about their music. It was all about their name. Columbia executives insisted that they change the name Jerry-Kelly, inferring that it was too light sounding, "like the Irish Rovers." Hludzik and Kelly submitted the name "Dallas," in recognition of their Northeastern Pennsylvania musical roots, but, as Hludzik recalled, Rufus drummer John Robinson suggested another geographical location, as Kelly recalled:

> He suggested 'Dakota,' and Columbia liked the name. We didn't. We hated it, but what's in a name? Call it anything. North Dakota. South Dakota. I didn't care either way.

THE DAKOTA ALBUM

Although saddled with that name change, Dakota was born amid great expectations. They had some heavy hitters in their corner after signing with Mark Hartley and Larry Fitzgerald, the management company handling Chicago, Rufus, The Brothers Johnson, Tom Jans, Toto, and Chaka Khan. High among those great expectations was a proposed tour with Steve Porcaro and Toto after Dakota's album release.

Produced by Danny Seraphine and David "Hawk" Wolinski of Skidrow Productions, the LP's cover had Hludzik and Kelly standing around a large trunk suitcase with the word "Dakota" sprayed on the surface, photographed at the 1908 era Scranton Train Station. It was light years away from the early days when Kelly started playing trumpet in the Wyoming Area Band, and Hludzik experimented with an old accordion.

They were ready for the dance. Thanks to extensive preparation, they completed the essential tracks in three days, and the Dakota album was mixed and delivered in twenty-seven days. The new LP was a departure from the Jerry-Kelly Band sound, almost to the point of being "new wave," Hludzik explained:

> The album wasn't new wave, although there are a few tracks that sound that way. The thing we have in common with new wave is that new wave is raw

and very to the point. It's not overproduced. Our new album is very live and raw and underproduced, which is how we wanted it. We haven't changed our style that much. It's just that the music is finally turning around to where we're coming from.

The songs were varied and personal. "One Step" was an intimate song about "married people who can't get it together anymore, "Crazy Love," written by Jeff Mitchell and Bill Lombardi, was an ode to teenage passion and Destiny, "a teenage pearl." "Lady" featured sassy, over-expressive vocals by Kelly, giving the song an immediate punk attitude. Their songs were all up-tempo, except for "You Can't Live Without It" being the only ballad.

Cashbox praised the album, and *Radio & Records* listed fourteen major stations supporting the LP and, years later, that album found new life after the UK's Rock Candy Records released an improved *Dakota* ('S/T' Candy 122) in Europe ($16.98 US). The album included twenty-four-bit remastering from source tapes and two bonus tracks ("The Higher You Rise" and "Give Love Another Try"). Also included was a 3,500-word essay about making the album, band involvement, and additional photos spread over a sixteen-page full-color booklet. *Rock Candy* liner notes read:

> Previously the band had operated with a more refined style, but this time around, they came out all guns blazing, sporting an AOR coat of armor and brandishing a much heavier, almost quasi pomp rock sound that invited comparison to the likes of Toto, Le Roux, Trillion and Styx. That they were great songwriters was an added bonus, making tracks such as 'If It Takes All Night,' 'Crazy Love,' and 'Restless' sound like hit singles in the making; a truly superlative slice of period-perfect AOR.

Rufus drummer John Robinson, who stepped in as the featured drummer on Dakota, had impeccable credentials, having played with Quincy Jones and Michael Jackson. As far as the name change, Rick Manwiller, in his comprehensive *A Brief History of Dakota*, recounted the resulting confusion:

> Drummer Gary Driscoll had left the band (and sadly, a few years later was murdered in an apparent case of mistaken identity). Producers Seraphine and Wolinksi had chosen John Robinson (also of Rufus and quickly became one of the world's top studio session drummers) to play drums for the now-drummer-less band. Rumor has it that John was the one who suggested the name 'Dakota,' which Columbia thought was a great name. Therefore, it stuck.

Professional musician Lou Cossa has left his imprint upon the NEPA music scene.

Hludzik and Kelly's touring version of Dakota consisted of Jeff Mitchell (keyboards), Lou Cossa (second keyboard), and Bill McHale (bass). Veteran New York studio musician Tony Romano played the drums, which was part of an ongoing problem. Dakota saw a revolving door of percussionists, including Chicago's Danny Seraphine, Rufus' John Robinson, Gary Driscoll, Syracuse-based drummer Robbie Spagnoletti, an electronic drum machine named Dexter, Jerry's son Eli M. Hludzik, and, for the tour, Tony Romano.

Lou Cossa, who had just come off the road touring with a Boxtops clone band playing supper clubs and "having fun," said although The Boxtops offered another aspect of playing music, traveling with Dakota was different and more exciting:

> I missed playing rock and roll. One of the most rewarding things about being with Dakota was playing rock and roll in front of large audiences. That was about it. It wasn't just one particular night or one particular job. It was just the whole idea of being back in rock and roll.

"IF IT TAKES ALL NIGHT"

"If It Takes All Night" was the initial single release. It was the perfect stadium song, dripping with lushly layered harmonies and guitars, with Kelly immediately taking charge, soaring, underscoring, elucidating, free-falling, and then Hludzik taking a turn, not with a bridge, but with another storyline that reclaimed the song as his own. Hludzik and Kelly's harmonies were always tight and on the money. They sang great together. Reviewed by *Time Out's* Dave Morris, the writer observed:

> It's even better than that. When Hludzik and Kelly are on, they sound very much like Richie Furay and Rusty Young in their early Poco days. That's a comparison no one can be ashamed of.

Morris also heard vestiges of Kansas and Styx in the albums' musical mix and noted that on "some cuts on this first album, the performance is electric." "If It Takes All Night" was a well-crafted and adeptly produced tour de force. It had all the ingredients to be a Top Ten hit. The song wasn't released at the same time throughout the nation but charted at #1 in Louisville, Kentucky, and Tempe, Arizona. "If It Takes All Night" was the band's first single to net regional airplay and peaked at #78 on the *Billboard* Charts in 1980. Addressing the album's release, Freeland correspondent Joe Falatko wrote:

> CBS representatives have been so impressed with advanced copies of the new Dakota album that a simultaneous release for Holland, Belgium, and France is scheduled.

Following in the wake of The Buoys and Jerry-Kelly, Dakota immediately caused a sensation performing at Newark, Delaware's Stone Balloon. Reporting for the University of Delaware's *The Review*, Donna Brown discerned:

> 'If It Takes All Night' is full of the relentless guitar, precision drumming, and urgent lyrics that characterize hit singles.

The second release from Dakota, "Crazy Love," was written by Jeff Mitchell and Bill Lombardi and, exuding raw potential, climbed to the top of the charts in St. Louis and Phoenix. The excitement began to build after *Record World* picked the album as one of the top debuts. It reached the Top Ten in San Antonio and rocketed to the #1 spot in Rochester and Syracuse, the latter being a Buoys-Dakota stronghold. Other major cities, Atlanta and Boston, placed the album on heavy rotation.

Their journey began with this triumphant first step, and, looking back, it proved to be an outstanding year of frantic applause and gratifying memories. On May 1st, 1980, The Lodge II in Chinchilla hosted Dakota, promoting their regional hit "If It Takes All Night," and weeks later, that same venue featured Ralph performing their new release "Fly by Night" b/w "Save Me" (KMA, 1980).

It would only get better. Dakota would soon be touring before thousands of fans in support of the hottest act on the planet.

38

THE DAKOTA-QUEEN TOUR

On Tuesday, August 5th, 1980, Hudzik and Kelly drove into Midtown Manhattan to secure promotional monies from Columbia Records. Instead, they met with Arma Andon and several other Columbia executives who played hardball, demanding a hit record from the band, recalled Kelly:

We handed Columbia an incredible album. Dakota was melodic and had all of the things that you wanted in an AOR record. So we pass it to them, and they respond by saying, 'I don't think so.' So they didn't like it and because of that refused to give us any promotional money.

Kelly said that seeking leverage, they mentioned the possibility of being the opening act for the Queen Tour:

We even told them there was a good chance that we might be able to get on the Queen Tour. At that point, we had no clue, and we were just throwing stuff in the air. Columbia laughed at us and said it's never going to happen because everybody wanted that tour. Queen was the most extensive tour of the year. Columbia just kind of gave us lip service, and we left there very depressed

After the non-productive meeting, driving under the Hudson River and through the Lincoln Tunnel, Hludzik called home. His wife said, "Michael Stahl just called. He left a message. He said, 'You got the gig. Be in Baton Rouge tomorrow by 5:00 P.M. You have four dates.'"

Hludzik and Kelly were ecstatic with the good news. Michael Stahl, Queen's monitor mixer, was like Heart's "Magic Man." Stahl, once again, made it happen, continuously playing Dakota tracks over the sound system every time Queen set up for their stadium concerts. So naturally, that sparked Queen's interest. Lou Cossa recollected how Dakota became the opening act for Queen:

(L-R) Bill Kelly, Mike Stahl, and Jerry Hludzik during their Glory Days. (Photo courtesy of Bill Kelly Music Productions.)

Mike Stahl played our tapes on all the Queen setups. Queen played the West Coast first and had problems with poor opening acts. So, Mike says, 'You got to try these guys.' So, Mike Stahl got Dakota on the tour. We started in Baton Rouge, Louisiana. Mike was the guy, and he came through.

Stahl single-handedly did his best to advance their career. The former Rox-Ann Records founder previously had introduced Hludzik and Kelly to Danny Seraphine, resulting in a contract and three studio albums. In addition, Dakota was guaranteed the first four dates as the coveted opening act and a "potential" thirty-five-city run of America's top concert venues because of his networking. "No pressure," Hludzik quipped, learning they had to be in Baton Rouge the next day.

NEW ORLEANS' COFFIN

The preparation for the event was overwhelming. Three of the roadies, scheduled to vacation in the Bahamas, were called back. Bill Stevenson offered to take care of the gear. He managed to get all of the instruments aboard the airplane, except for Cossa's Hammond B3 organ. Cossa borrowed the Hammond from his friend Paul Dickstein, owner of Dickstein Distributing Company, a Scranton music store and mail-order company. (Dickstein had played keyboards in a few local bands, including Mutley, and took Cossa's place in Ralph before Jeff Mitchell joined the group.) Like the incantations of a mad sorcerer, the Hammond B3 could sustain notes, change chords, and create innovative harmonic melodies, complimenting Dakota's multi-layered, textured sound.

The organ needed to get on the plane. Cossa trucked the instrument down to the Philadelphia International Airport, but as it turned out, there was a coffin scheduled for the same flight, ready to be shipped to New Orleans for burial. There was no room for the Hammond B3. As Kelly tells the story, the persuasive Bill Stevenson called the loading dock worker over to the side and slipped him a roll of bills. The Hammond B3, weighing about four hundred and fifty pounds, was lifted onto the plane's cargo bay, and the coffin shipped out on another flight.

After their redeye flight, things ramped up to warp speed. Kelly remembered when they finally arrived at the Baton Rouge Metropolitan Airport, known to the locals as Ryan Field:

> We got to the venue, and this tall, lanky guy with wild curly hair was there waiting for us. I found out later it was Brian May. I didn't know how he looked. I was not a huge Queen fan. I knew they were great, and I like some of their songs, 'Bohemian Rhapsody,' of course, was just genius, and I liked Brian's guitar sound.

Brian May saw Dakota perform for the first time. Like most Queen's fans, he had never heard of this opening group before, but relaxed and with absolute ease, Dakota blew the shows wide open. Their smooth, well-rehearsed harmonies were especially impressive, brought out in clean, superb perfection by the expertise of Michael Stahl. Everyone, except for new drummer Tony Romano, sang. Dueling guitars, keyboards, and a steady, pounding bass and drum sent a message to the crowd that this band was for real. Queen wanted to see what the band had to offer, so they were allowed to play 55 minutes during their initial performance at Baton Rouge's Centroplex.

Columbia Records never believed that Dakota would get the job as Queen's opening act, and Columbia received the news after the fact. When the band arrived at their Baton Rouge hotel, there were almost a half dozen phone messages to, "Call Columbia Records ASAP," recalled Kelly:

At least three or four nights went by, and I believe we were in Oklahoma City when we finally returned Columbia's phone calls. So, we made them wait. We were pissed at them. They had been so arrogant.

Manager Bill Stevenson and Queen's road manager Jerry Stickles took turns announcing the bands each night. On Friday, August 8th, Dakota played before 20,000 people in Oklahoma City and the next night in Dallas. However, it was after the Dallas concert that they got the good news. According to Kelly:

> Queen was wonderful. After the third date, Jerry Stickles, the road manager, came back to us and said, 'You're on the rest of the tour.' It was great. Of all of the bands we toured with, over the years, they were the most professional, the most down-to-earth, the most friendly, the most cooperative. I mean, they were just the best. And every night, two or three of them would be backstage, watching the show, throwing things at us, like ice chips, just to goof on us.

The sold-out tour took them across the continent to Montreal and Toronto, and Houston, Atlanta, and Philadelphia, with Queen rippin' it up all the way.

"CRAZY LITTLE THING CALLED LOVE"

Queen was hot. "Crazy Little Thing Called Love" went to #1 in early 1980, becoming the group's biggest-selling US single despite a sluggish record market. "Crazy Little Thing" was an uncharacteristically Presleyesque single that captivated the world along with the MTV video. Fans were almost demanding a national tour and a chance to see Freddie Mercury and what Miami Herald writer Bill Ashton called "the British band's style of grandiose show-biz rock."

Freddie Mercury started things off with "Jailhouse Rock" then kicked it up with "We Will Rock You" and a total of twenty-six tight, polished gems. The middle of the show featured Roger Taylor's drum solo, Brian May's incredible guitar wizardry, and John Deacon's trademark bass runs. Their finale consisted of back-to-back monster hits including "Crazy Little Thing Called Love," "Bohemian Rhapsody," "Another One Bites the Dust," "We Will Rock You," and "We Are the Champions." Every concert concluded with "God Save the Queen" and Mercury draped in the Union Jack.

Queen's setlist was a masterful musical assault from beginning to end. Their songs aside, Mercury could sing, and the band could rock out. They were excellent entertainers. Many of their hits, such as "We Will Rock You" and "We Are the Champions," were tailor-made for stadium-sized concerts, creating frenzied audience sing-alongs. Bill Kelly had the opportunity to hang out with Freddie Mercury and was impressed with his off-stage persona:

> My greatest compliment as a singer came from Freddie Mercury. He was the kindest, most gracious guy. For all of his pomp, he did not act like an ego-maniac. Though he certainly was, to us, he was not. He saw something in us, recognized something in us; he just wanted to—the whole band just wanted to—help us.

Bill Stevenson, familiar with live concerts and all of the requisite headaches, commandeered his way onto the tour, said, Kelly:

> He came out on tour with us immediately. He said, 'you guys need a road manager. You can't just fly by the seat of your pants.' With his personality, he became friends with everybody. And before you knew it, he was introducing the show. He would introduce us; he and Jerry Stickles would take turns intro-ducing Queen. Bill did everything a road manager needed to do. He collected our money and helped in any way he could. He was a great, great help.

Dakota didn't have a tour bus at that time, but Stevenson bought them an Oldsmobile station wagon after their vehicle broke down. In *Stone Balloon: The Early Years*, Stevenson said: "I spent over $50,000 in ninety days to support the band. It didn't work out for Dakota's taking off . . . but this was the best ninety-days of our lives." He recalled that "Freddie, Brian, John, and Roger treated us like family." Lou Cossa viewed things through a different lens. He said that Queen had a reputation for being strict and demanding, but things settled into a nice cadence after Dakota arrived. The members of Queen observed Dakota's stage show, and the group members hung out and "goofed around," except John Deacon, who seemed standoffish. Cossa elaborated:

> When we got on the tour, Queen liked Dakota's triple-guitar leads and all the live voices. They loved everything we did. Brian May made himself very personable, but he was the only one. Nobody else did. You didn't deal with the band. Queen was upper echelon. They were not around, so we dealt with all the roadies, and they loved us.

TWENTY-EIGHT SPEAKER CABINETS

The Queen tour included an assembly of thirty people. Road manager Gerry Stickells's crew handled equipment, including more than four hundred lights, totaling 63,000 watts, filling four forty-foot trucks. They carried more than twenty-eight speaker cabinets, about five tons of sound equipment alone.

Queen traveled in two tour buses while Dakota used a 1971 Mercury station wagon. Hludzik and Kelly were able to do media interviews, getting about fifty additional stations to give them airplay and boost lucrative royalties from album sales. The Dakota-Queen tour increased sales of the Dakota album (Columbia,1980) to over 500,000 copies.

Manwiller, in his *A Brief History of Dakota*, recognized the band's hardworking road crew:

> The crew was Tom Cush, road manager, drum technician; Mike Keating, house mix; and Dave "Waddy" Skaff, monitor mix and guitar and keyboard technician. Cush is now a big-time stockbroker, Skaff is out on tour with various name artists (U2, Steve Miller, etc.), and Keating (who does the main mix for Sting) took 1996 honors as *Performance Magazine's* "Live Soundman of the Year."

As Dakota (Lou Cossa, Jerry Hludzik, Bill Kelly, Bill McHale, Jeff Mitchell, Tony Romano) traveled the country as Queen's opening act, they knew that the tour could be rough. They would be at the mercy of a problematic Queen management and audiences unfamiliar with Dakota songs. Queen wanted the perfect opening act, one that would compliment them. As a result, Queen changed their opening acts frequently, and on the California leg of the tour, and for the first eight jobs, they hired a different opening act almost every night.

The Los Angeles-based group, the Blasters, an unprepared bar band, played several July dates on an earlier West Coast Queen tour. The foursome paid a high price for the $500 they made each night. As reported by Robert Hilburn:

> The week wasn't without its trouble spots. Queen fans were unruly with the Blasters' punk aura, and the San Diego audience booed the band unmercifully. The Phoenix audience pelted the musicians with ice, cups, and beer bottles, the following night.

PHILADELPHIA'S SPECTRUM

Dakota was the proverbial stranger in a strange land, with a setlist unfamiliar to the thousands of Queen fans. Nevertheless, Cossa thought they received the best response in Philadelphia:

> Philadelphia gave Dakota the warmest reception, more than anyplace else. Nobody knew Dakota's music in Baton Rouge or Oklahoma, but we received a good response on many of them. "Settle Down" and "Magic" were powerful songs and got a strong crowd reaction. "Crazy for Your Love" always went over

like gangbusters. "Lady" went over well. "If It Takes All Night" was our last song, and we always got a good response on that one.

Dakota played only twenty-eight minutes each night. The band precisely executed their playlist like a Cape Canaveral moon shot. But things changed slightly at Philadelphia's Spectrum on August 22nd, the tenth day of the tour. Faithful fans from Hludzik's Freeland-Japan Jeddo area rented two buses and drove down to see them. Queen let them use their fog machine as a special treat for the numerous Dakota fans, and they were allowed to play a little longer.

After Philly, they traveled west playing at Pittsburgh's Civic Center on the 24th. The tour concluded with three impressive sold-out Madison Square Garden shows, each with a seating capacity of 20,000. On their first night at Madison Square Garden, fans had written "WE LOVE YOU, DAKOTA" on bed sheets that hung from the balcony. Kelly and Hludzik looked at each other as their eyes welled up with emotion.

Gary Mullinax, writing in the Wilmington *Morning News*, described a solitary Bill Kelly, looking upon the immensity of Madison Square Garden, and listening as supergroup Queen went through their warming up routine:

> A solitary figure stands in front of the stage, looking up at the activity. He seems all but swallowed up in the vastness of the empty arena, maybe just another faceless fan who managed to get by security to be present at this pre-concert activity. In just three hours, though, he and the band he plays in, Dakota, will have their own time in the spotlight, on the very stage he is looking at, in front of 19,000 listeners as Queen's opening act.

MADISON SQUARE GARDEN

Even though many in the audience were unfamiliar with the band, Dakota's high-energy stage performance immediately enthralled them. The band was smooth and polished. They played with sound and fury and pulled out all the stops. The Queen Tour was the opportunity they needed.

Kelly said that Freddy Mercury loved the band. After a soundcheck, Mercury came over to him and asked, "How do you do that night after night?" Kelly explained, "That's how I make a living. I have to put leather on my vocal cords." The fellow musicians were close in age; Kelly was thirty at the time, and Mercury, thirty-four. Everyone knew that Mercury was gay, and that played out during the wild parties held after each concert. And, after all, this was sex, drugs, and rock and roll. Kelly told the *Times Leader* that the only "blatantly sexual thing he saw on tour was in the tents:

Columbia executives show up unannounced after the Madison Square Garden concert to bask in Dakota's glow. (L-R) Bill Stevenson, Jerry Hludzic, Ed Haynes, Bill Kelly, Tony Romano, Don Colbert, Arma Andon. (Photo courtesy of Bill Kelly Music Productions.)

Queen's staff set up two tents backstage. If you were straight, you went into one tent, and if you were gay, you went into the other. The heterosexual tent had beautiful topless women who acted as waitresses. They'd come over and pour you a beer or get you something to eat. And, of course, all they were wearing were tiny black leather panties. On the other side, they had these good-looking stud guys in great shape in the other tent, and they're wearing little leather short pants. And that was for the gay crowd.

'77 FORD STATION WAGON

The ending was bittersweet nectar served in a tarnished goblet. Columbia had been feuding with Chicago during the tour, and their annoyance with Danny Seraphine and Skid Row Productions left Dakota with basically no support. Cossa felt that there should have been more financial backing from Columbia Records:

> We had no budget for the Dakota-Queen tour. We had no money. We got on the tour sideways, driving eleven people across the country in a '77 Ford station wagon. It was insane.

The 1980 Dakota-Queen Tour at Madison Square Garden. (Photo courtesy of Bill Kelly Music Productions.)

This was one of the most extensive tours of 1980, where a company would put up a couple of $100,000s, take out full-page ads, have someone there selling records. Columbia did absolutely nothing. They didn't do what a responsible company should do.

Another bit of insanity was with their label. There was a lot of bad blood between Dakota and Columbia, and after the Queen tour, they decided to leave Columbia and go over to MCA. Said Kelly:

> During our last night at Madison Square Garden, Arma Andon and all of the New York Columbia executives who turned us down were there backstage, glad-handing the band, and boasting 'These are our guys. These are our guys, Dakota.'

SYRACUSE AND UTICA

Yet warming up for Queen gave them priceless momentum and national recognition. Dakota made an invaluable list of contacts and venues, auditoriums, theaters, and colleges, usually seating 2,000 or more, along the tour. They used this list to set up additional dates after the Queen tour was over. They did exceptionally well in upstate New York, playing colleges around Syracuse, Auburn, Rochester, and Elmira. Kelly commented:

> We didn't make any money on the Queen tour, but we made a lot of money after booking our Dakota shows. Queen gave us a good bounce. It didn't work out the way we hoped it would, as far as radio airplay. We did get a good response in places like Syracuse and Utica. Nationwide, it didn't help as much as we hoped it would. Columbia gave us no support for the tour. Nothing. They were worthless.

They had matured and began to see things through a different lens and, after the Queen tour, Hludzik explained the hardships of touring to *Times Leader* contributors Jim Dino and Dotty Martin:

> We're all grown men now, and it isn't easy to leave the people you love and go on the road. But you have to. You have to believe in what you're doing, and being on the road is part of it. We're not just a bunch of kids trying to impress girls anymore. We are men, and this is our profession, our career.

They were road-weary, filled with equal parts of exhaustion and exhilaration. The tour was a fantastic experience, but, in actuality, such a long road home. Still, that same year, the band performed two concerts at Scranton's West Side Theater to an estimated crowd of 1,500. And, on August 12th, Dakota appeared on Public TV Channel 44's *Another Roadside Attraction* series. The hour-long musical special, produced and directed by Allan Murphy, was simulcast on WVIA-FM (89.9), providing a celebration of Dakota's AOR compositions.

Perhaps the final word about the Dakota-Queen Tour came from Frederic Slama of AOR. Slama is one of the most prominent Westcoast / AOR music collectors globally, owning over 16,000 albums of that genre. Author of *The Westcoast Bible* and *The AOR Bible*, he listed several Dakota albums in *The Westcoast Bible: 250 Rare Westcoast / AOR albums from 1979 to 1986 — The Lost Masterpieces*, and explained:

> I knew Jerry and the rest of the band since their Jerry-Kelly album, *Somebody Else's Dream,* in 1978 and, of course, through the first Dakota album in 1980. So since a young age, I've always been a fan of Dakota, believing Dakota had the perfect mix of Westcoast Music & AOR with outstanding musicianship and fabulous vocals.

Years later, Slama played an essential role in motivating Dakota to record their final album, *Long Road Home*. As a symbolic gesture of their friendship,

Frederic Slama displays Jerry Hludzik's Dakota-Queen tour pass.
(Frederic Slama Collection.)

Hludzik presented him with one of his most prized possessions, as Slama fondly recalled:

> We had a great friendship, almost as though Jerry and I had always known each other. I think he respected me because he gave me his backstage pass for the 1980 Queen tour when he played with Dakota. He signed it on the back with some nice words.

39

RUNAWAY

*R*unaway was Dakota's AOR landmark album: animated, innovative, masterful, and recognized as the band's best album. It embraced a different sound, as well as a new technology, as Bill Kelly made clear:

There are moments on the album where the sassiness of the vocals or the raunchiness of the guitar work sounds new wave. Maybe it's timing, and the sound is right for now. The album has energy and a more sophisticated recording

Dakota

sound. I know a lot of new wave is recorded quickly and cheaply. The guitars aren't tuned properly, and a lot of the slickness is removed. We've cut the difference, possibly, by having that energetic sound but with the classiness and finesse of a 1980 recording.

They dedicated the album to the memory of Tom Jans, who co-wrote "When the Rebel Comes Home" with Danny Seraphine. Although he didn't play on the album, Eli Hludzik praised *Runaway*, noting some of the history surrounding its creation:

> The Dakota records represent two different eras of sonic integrity, but I think they stand up. They have a great sound to them, reflecting the period and the technology, especially on the *Runaway* record. The songwriting on *Runaway* is like an awesome slash-cord party. When you get into the harmonic movement of it and the static movement on top, it creates these complex upper extension triads and forms this fantastic sounding rock record.

Dakota recorded *Runaway* between February and June in 1983 at the Lighthouse and also at North Hollywood's celebrated Record Plant, where *Hotel California* (Eagles), *Load and Reload* (Metallica), *Rumours* (Fleetwood Mac), and *Appetite for Destruction* (Guns N' Roses) were recorded.

Danny Seraphine produced the album. It was engineered and mixed at Lion's Share Studios in Beverly Hills by Humberto "Hummy" Gatica, who mixed Michael Jackson's *Thriller* LP. Humberto Gatica was a Chilean-born American record producer, music mixer and audio engineer, and a sixteen-time Grammy Award-winner. Gatica had worked with dozens of the most acclaimed artists in the music industry, such as Quincy Jones, Celine Dion, Michael Bublé, Andrea Bocelli, Michael Jackson, and many other stars. As an independent engineer/producer, he won his first Grammy with Seraphine's band, Chicago.

A-LIST MUSICIANS

After the 1980 Dakota-Queen tour ended, the band began to fall apart. Lou Cossa was the first to leave. Cossa had played with The Boxtops from 1975 to 1978, and, after playing with Dakota for two years, he noted disparities between the two bands:

> When I was on the road with the Box Tops, it was more organized. Dakota was different. I didn't feel that playing with them was helping me. There's a certain amount of time you put into something, and there is a certain amount of rewards you should get. Unfortunately, the rewards were getting slimmer,

except for the fact of being a Columbia Recording Artists band. Dakota's a good band, but there was nowhere to go in that group for my advancement. So I left after our concert in Philadelphia.

McHale, Mitchell, and Romano followed Cossa's departure. The new album featured a scaled-down band with Hludzik and Kelly on guitars and vocals, Seraphine on drums, and Manwiller on keyboards. Manwiller had previously played in the progressive rock band Steph (Manwiller, Eric Rudy, Spyro Sbillis) but joined Dakota in 1982 after his group disbanded.

Seraphine brought in some of the best musicians in the business to help on the album. The A-list musicians included keyboardist Steve Porcaro (Toto), bassist Neal Steubenhouse (Blood, Sweat & Tears), singer Bill Champlin (Chicago), saxophonist Earnie Watts (Rolling Stones), guitarist Richie Zito (Mr. Big, The Motels), Thriller rhythm guitarist Paul Jackson (Michael Jackson, Elton John), and Rufus' Hawk Wolinski.

One outstanding contribution came from Wolinski, who demonstrated his expertise on the CS-80 Yamaha synthesizer, a keyboard known in recording circles as the "Dream Machine." The CS-80 can reproduce any sounds, from strings to guitars. Before the Dream Machine, only guitarists could "slide" their notes, but now, with the use of a touch ribbon, keyboardists can do the same thing, making for a sweeter, more exciting mix. Wolinski's synthesizer breathed new life into "You Can't Take It with You," with his string-like solo featured on "One Step."

"You Can't Take It with You" was the only ballad on the album and a musical card game with Hludzik dealing the hand and Kelly upping the ante. The boys share lead vocals over a jazz-infused guitar and minimalistic keyboard on this tune, another example of their splendid harmonic give and take. When they were in sync, they were simply amazing.

AS GOOD AS ANYTHING

In the single's first week after release, "Runaway" was added to the New York powerhouse WNEW-FM and other New York and Pennsylvania stations. Soon, other stations in Colorado, Connecticut, and Florida, and Illinois, Michigan, and Texas piled on, promoting the record.

It was the perfect single for radio airplay. "Runaway" kept on building, seamlessly

blending Kelly's piercing highs with Hludzik's lower registers while riding Man-willer's synthesizer into a sonic crescendo promising more. In his article, "Dakota Hoping Third Time's the Charm," *Times Focus* Editor Lance Evans reviewed the new LP:

> *Runaway*, filled with vestiges of syntho-pop gadgetry, is the two men's best effort yet. It is neatly textured music, a collection of well-crafted songs that makes for easy listening.

Interviewed decades later, Hludzik said that "*Runaway* was just as good as anything that was on the radio at that time." Lance Evans agreed and especially liked the cuts "Runaway," "When the Rebel Comes Home," and "Angry Men." He noted that Hludzik and Kelly do best when they "meld penetrating vocal work with sharp instrumentation." He went on to say:

> *Runaway* is not a gimmicky album. Instead, it is strong, assertive, pop-tinged with blues influences (ala Hall & Oates), and laced with sometimes sophisticated—but always catchy—rhythm arrangements.

ANGRY MEN

Side one tore it up with "Runaway," "Heroes," "Tonight Could Last Forever," and "When the Rebel Comes Home." On side two's sequence, the commanding "Angry Men" would have been a better first cut, while the predictable "Love Won't Last" begged for a fierce Jimmy Page or Jimi Hendrix-like solo to rip it up, should have been slotted further down.

"Angry Men," the best track on this side, showcased the sweet background vocals of Chicago's Bill Champlin building into a convincing assault. "Angry Men" was representative of the well-known Hludzik-Kelly philosophy of perseverance and that hard-fought victory. It featured Kelly snarling his delivery like a bullwhip. A live acoustic version of "Angry Men," performed at the Bartolai Winery in April 2011, showcased Kelly's lead vocals, backed by Cossa, Hludzik, and Lorance, with Kelly's searing guitar licks as further proof of his exceptionality.

The Rolling Stones' saxophone player, Ernie Watts, transformed "Over and Over" into a smooth example of yacht rock. At the same time, Manwiller's electric piano introduced the Angelo Arvonio composition "If Only I'd Known," a Christopher Cross-sounding melancholy lament. Likewise, "Into the Night" began with a majestic keyboard-driven "here comes the King" intro, followed by Kelly's soaring lead.

Runaway was scheduled for release in July 1984, and Hludzik, Kelly, and Manwiller assembled a touring band. Syracuse drummer Robbie Spagnoletti was chosen, along with Tom Navagh on bass, later replaced by Spagnoletti's friend, Jim Fricano. Unfortunately, the proposed national tour, ostensibly with Toto and essential to promoting their MCA album, never occurred. According to the website *Melodic-Hardrock.com:*

> Dakota in 1984 released their second album called *Runaway,* which was meant
> to be their best work, an AOR masterpiece, and a legendary contribution to
> what we call the Westcoast/AOR genre. Although it was released by the presti-
> gious company MCA Records, which scored big time with Night Ranger and
> other classic releases of the period (1983-1984), such as Preview, White Sister,
> The Automatix, Fortune, etc., the album suffered from poor MCA promotion,
> and it didn't become a huge hit.

EUROPEAN FANBASE

Nonetheless, an ardent European fanbase celebrated the exceptionality of the album. The UK's Rock Candy Records released an upgraded *Runaway* (CAN-DY123) in Europe and Japan ($16.98 US) in 2016. It featured twenty-four-bit remastering from source tapes, two bonus tracks ("Believin'" and "More Love"), a 3,500-word essay about the making of the album, band involvement, and additional photos spread out over a sixteen-page full-color booklet. Rock Candy filled the album notes with high praise:

> Switching labels to MCA, Dakota would record their second album, now
> regarded as one of the high points of the 1980s AOR genre. Titled *Runaway,*
> released in 1984, recorded in Los Angeles, and produced by Chicago drummer
> Danny Seraphine, the album contains nine of the most celebrated melodic
> rock tracks ever recorded. Again, the songwriting of Hludzik and Kelly makes
> an immediate impact, laced with copious melodies, huge hooks, and musical
> support from a long list of the best Westcoast session players.

Runaway marks a high point in mid-eighties melodic AOR. Radio-friendly yet aggressive enough to punch home a message, the album set the tone for years to come, laying the foundation for the likes of Survivor, Mr. Mister, Bon Jovi, and many more.

Their move from Columbia to MCA resulted in their best and most appreciated album, said Kelly:

> *Runaway* was my favorite album. *Runaway* was one of the classic AOR albums, and there are places where that album is legendary. However, it would be great if more people knew about it, and I would love my hometown to learn more about it.

"A TIMELESS CLASSIC"

Even after it was released in 1984, Runaway considerably impacted Europe, especially in France. During this period, there was no internet, and the power of the press was enormous. For example, Frederic Slama, a well-known French rock journalist, had written several reviews about *Runaway*, noting that "the album was a turning point in AOR music," calling it "a masterpiece" and declaring that every home should have a copy:

> In France, *Runaway* was quite successful, and songs like "Runaway" and "Angry Men" were well received on the radio. Every track of this album was pure harmonic perfection, and the excellent cover of Tom Jan's "When the Rebel Comes Home" was at least as good as the version on Tom's album.

An album review of *Runaway* appeared in the French magazine *il: Musique* (It's Music), and while lavishing praise upon the LP, erroneously believed Dakota to be a California group:

> It's been a long time since an American group has recorded a sudden and revealing first album, as Toto, Boston, or Foreigner have done. As one may believe, Dakota is not a group playing banjo in the most remote location of Dakota. Instead, they are a Californian band with support from the most significant recording studio musicians in Los Angeles, as Steve Porcaro, Bill Champlin, Ernie Watts, or the incredible guitar player Richie Zito and the surprising bass player Neil Stubenhaus. They are among the most requested musicians on the West Coast! With Runaway, Dakota hits a strike. It is true that the two 'leaders,' Bill Kelly and Jerry Hludzik, did not invent the genre but have enhanced and improved the kind of melodies where Christopher Cross or America are recognized, masters. *Runaway* is a very homogeneous LP where the compositions share a rare intensity but do not sound alike. Indeed, each melody has been perfectly recorded, and we feel a taste for perfectionism throughout the album.
>
> After the separation of the most prominent Californian groups such as The Eagles, The Doobie Brothers, Steely Dan, or Supertramp, and the few records

provided by the few remaining formations, it is good to know that now Dakota is launched on the rails of success and that California can expect to have one more prestigious group to its credit. A must for California music connoisseurs.

Even though there were many brilliant AOR-styled releases that year, what struck people immediately was Runaway's cover, as Slama observed:

> Many people thought this album was a Westcoast release due to the Californian style of the cover. However, fans were also excited to see that Danny Seraphine, a member of the band Chicago, produced the album. The famous Humberto Gatica, who had worked with Toto, mixed it.

Slama said that another surprise for fans of that genre was that their favorite studio musicians, like Bill Champlin, Steve Porcaro, Richie Zito, Ernie Watts, and Hawk Wolinski, provided *Runaway* with a unique sound:

> The difference from other releases of that year was that this LP was keyboard-oriented, with several synthesizers mixed with an Eagles-type of harmony and incredible musicianship.

Calling it a "timeless classic," Slama said that *Runaway* happened after the best musicians on the planet got together to record an album. So it was like taking a musical time machine back to the 1980s:

> Almost forty years later, it's surprising that *Runaway* wasn't a bigger hit and Number One on the worldwide charts. Of course, during these later years, the album was reissued several times, including great pressings on the U.S-based label, AORchives, and on the fabulous Korean Bella Terra Music with the paper sleeve. There were other reissues on various labels, and this masterpiece will live on for years to come and for future generations.

The significance of the "Runaway" single and album did not go unnoticed. In 2011, a Swedish-based group called Houston covered "Runaway" on their *Relaunch* album, maintaining the original frenetic approach but lacking Kelly's vocal versatility.

Additionally, in June 2013, Scottish street trials and mountain bike rider Danny MacAskill released Imaginate, produced by Mike Christie for Red Bull Media House and directed by Stu Thomson. Using "Runaway" as its theme song, the short film received over four million views in fewer than three weeks.

The album had all of the essential ingredients for success but lacked a financial commitment from Columbia to support a national tour or even a limited promotional campaign. Sadly, after its release, the album was ignored. However, eighteen years later, *Runaway* was re-released on compact disk (2002) and digital format and began to get noticed. Fans and websites devoted to AOR soon recognized Runaway as one of the best, yet most underrated, AOR albums of the eighties and an example of Dakota's trendsetting vision.

Although not promoted or respected stateside, the DAK album releases attracted an appreciative foreign media gaze. Japan's *Young Guitar Magazine* interviewed Jon Lorance, and Hludzik was interviewed by the Italian *Hardnheavy website*, who listed *Runaway* as one of the "Top 100 AOR Albums of All Time." *Mr. Lucky* received the "Album of the Month" designation from Great Britain's *Power Play Magazine*, while Belgium's *Rock Report* gave it a four-star review. Additionally, thanks to rock journalist Frederic Slama, Dakota gained widespread popularity and radio airplay in France.

In hindsight, not organizing a European tour was a huge mistake. Touring the UK, France, Sweden, and Italy would have netted greater international exposure and a North American rebound. Instead, it was the group's most profound missed opportunity, and we can only speculate how things might have played out if they had rolled the dice.

40

THE DAKOTA CURSE

Hludzic always claimed that a Coal Region curse, some called it the Hoodoo, hovered over them like a dark cloud. He argued that no matter how close The Buoys or the Jerry-Kelly Band or Dakota came to the gold ring, it vanished from their grasp. Something always went wrong with record labels going bankrupt or offering half-hearted support. Success was always just out of reach.

Opportunities were missed. A prime example was Rupert Holmes's appearance at the 1980 Bloomsburg Fair. A request to have Holmes and Dakota share the same stage, singing "Timothy" and "Give Up Your Guns," was ignored by the Fair Board, unaware of Hludzik and Kelly's former band. Four years later, Hybrid Ice became the first Pennsylvania-based rock band to play the Bloomsburg Fair when they opened for the Greg Kihn Band.

THE DAKOTA-QUEEN TOUR

Other prospects just didn't play out as envisioned. They received a dash of good fortune when they opened for Queen on a multi-city tour. Everyone was ecstatic at the busloads of fans who showed up at the Philadelphia Spectrum, Syracuse's Onondaga County War Memorial Coliseum, and Madison Square Garden. It was possibly the peak of their stellar career, and they came ever so close to hitting it to deep center and out of the park. Hludzik recollected the band's great expectations during a Prism TV special taped at The Warehouse in Philadelphia:

> Queen was a really fun tour. We thought everything was going to take off after that, but then the bottom fell out. It was tough to pick up the pieces, but we did. It seems like we've always found that extra energy to pull back on and pick up the pieces and continue and try it again and back to the drawing board.

It didn't help that Columbia and Danny Seraphine were feuding during the Dakota-Queen tour, culminating in the label withholding promotional support for Seraphine's Skid Row Productions. Bill Kelly tried to explain it to writer Joe Butkiewicz:

> In this industry, there is a time-lapse between the time you sign, do, and then release an album. The whole world could fall apart in the interim, and basically, that is what the Dakota Curse is all about.

It was a dollop of bad timing and incompetent teamwork, measured not in minutes but micro-seconds. Record corporations employ professionals assigned to specific groups and working to assure their success. But during their relationship with Epic, Columbia, and MCA, Dakota suffered a lack of commitment, lack of continuity, and lack of faith, the latter the bitterest pill to swallow. So much of the promotion they netted was due to their hard work, networking abilities, and nothing else. Dakota worked the phones, did the interviews, and mastered the art of promoting their product.

Former *Times-Leader* staff writer and music critic Joe Butkiewicz followed their career from the beginning. He observed:

> Their luck has been inconsistent: A little good fortune is followed by a lot of bad. And, all the while, they've tried to speed the slowly turning gears of the record trade.

The conflicted "Angry Men," Hludzik and Kelly's Runaway gem, acknowledged both the thrill and reality that "castles that we built crumble before our eyes." Eli Hludzik made clear that "Angry Men" reflected the heavy letdown the band experienced after the rush of the Queen tour had died:

> They evolved out of that. I think 'Angry Men' says, 'we just played on one of the largest tours in the world and had all of this exposure and great response, and now we're back home again.'

Was there a Dakota Curse? In retrospect, after forty years, Lou Cossa believed that the Dakota Curse was a combination of bad timing and bad luck:

> Bill and Jerry were excellent. They worked well together. But when it came to companies, when they signed with Epic for the Jerry-Kelly Band and when they signed with Columbia, before the Queen tour, they had different people at the companies saying, 'OK, we're going to take you in.'

After completing every Dakota album, Cossa said that Danny Seraphine and Hawk Wolinski had to deal with newly hired A&R men. As a result, there was no continuity and no important teambuilding to count on:

> It was the same thing with Columbia. The A&R guy was gone by the time we ended the Queen tour, and then when I left, and they signed with Mercury Records, the same damn thing happened again. The guy that they sold them to when they went to say, 'What's next. What are you going to do?' There was nothing. The guy was gone.

Eli Hludzik equated the Dakota Curse to the Paula Abdul paradox, "I take two steps forward, I take two steps back" from her "Opposites Attract" (Virgin, 1989) single on *Forever Girl*, her debut album. "It did always seem like they would do something big, and then they would hit a wall, he said, "like that dip after the Queen tour."

SOMEBODY ELSE'S DREAM

With *Somebody Else's Dream* (Epic,1978), it was the worst of times. To promote their Epic album, there was talk of The Jerry-Kelly Band opening for Chicago at the famed Greek Theatre in Los Angeles and then Detroit and Cleveland. But the familiar curse continued, and, like a funeral dirge, the promised tour died.

Jerry-Kelly had signed with Gerry Margolis, an established entertainment lawyer who handled a host of superstars and corporations, including Sony Music Entertainment, BMG Right Management, CBS, and Warner Music Group. But that relationship ended abruptly, said Kelly:

> We came up with the original deal with Danny Seraphine, and when we took it to Gerry, he said, 'This deal sucks. Danny Seraphine is taking you for a ride, and you shouldn't sign it.' So, we called Danny, and we go back and forth. We got nowhere with Danny because he's a hard-nosed Italian. So, here we are. What do you do? We have no other deal in the pot. So, we went back to Gerry, and Gerry Margolis told us, 'You're going to do what you're going to do, but I'm telling you this. If you take that deal, I don't ever want to see you guys again.' He was a great attorney, but he didn't have a deal for us. Danny did. We figured let's take the deal with Danny, and if we had some success, we would renegotiate.

Jerry-Kelly were placing their bets on Chicago, a successful and prolific band. Their "25 or 6 to 4" #4 (Columbia, 1970) and "If You Leave Me Now" #1 (Columbia, 1976) were a mere sampling of their many Top Ten hits. Hludzik concluded that *Somebody's Else's Dream* was a "sweetheart deal" between Epic and Seraphine. There were some up-front monies to appease Skid Row Productions and then nothing else. Although "Magic" received airplay on some regional stations, it was never promoted nationally and deserved a better ending.

Personnel shuffling at Epic left company president Ronald Luxenberg and six key Jerry-Kelly promoters out of jobs. Luxenberg later went over to MCA and became president of Infinity Records. He became the guiding force behind the group Orleans, and Jerry-Kelly was left out in the cold. Hludzik observed:

> There was a big political thing between the producers and the label and the label switching personnel while we were happening. We just got caught in the middle. As a result, Epic gave us no promotion on our first LP.

Without valuable airplay and corporate promotion, the album died, dumped into an unmarked grave. Kelly didn't know too much about the empty promises or a possible conflict with Seraphine. He said:

> I don't know how the conflict began. I just know that CBS was not forthcoming with any financial assistance at all. So it could well be they just didn't like the record. I don't know.

What we do know, however, is that the timing was all wrong, and even supergroup Chicago was going through a difficult period. Lead guitarist Terry Kath, 31, died January 26, 1978, when he pointed what he thought was an unloaded gun at his head and fired. After his death, the group considered disbanding. But, according to Dennis Hunt of the Los Angeles *Times:*

> Kath's death was particularly devastating because Chicago is a close-knit band. It is one of the few supergroups that has not been through many personnel changes. Before the loss of Kath, the only change in the band was the 1975 addition of percussionist Laudir de Oliveira. The others, including Peter Cetera (bass), Lee Loughnane (trumpet), Walter Parazaider (woodwinds), James Pankow (trombone), and Danny Seraphine (drums), are original members.

Kath's death threw Chicago and the Jerry-Kelly project into turmoil. It couldn't have happened at a worse time as their Epic rep was leaving, which resulted in the loss of corporate support. There were other internal issues, also. Part of the problem was producer/manager James William Guercio, known as "The Man Who Makes Chicago Tick" and considered a musical and creative genius. Guercio lost interest in the band, with Seraphine and the Jerry-Kelly project caught in the dilemma. Friction had been building before Guercio left the band, according to a Los Angeles *Times* interview with keyboardist Bobby Lamm:

Jimmy got to everybody in the band. It took him years to get to me. It was his personality and his way of doing things. It got to be impossible to work with him. Personalities were clashing everywhere, man. It was messy and very tense. We were losing confidence in our abilities. He wasn't fighting for us, but he wasn't encouraging us either.

In a page ripped from *The Twilight Zone*, The Jerry-Kelly Band's fate closely paralleled the aborted 1969 Glass Prism tour. The Glass Prism was booked as the opening act for Blood, Sweat, and Tears, the fusion band who had three of their songs, "You've Made Me So Very Happy" (Columbia, 1969), "Spinning Wheel" (Columbia, 1969), and "And When I Die" (Columbia, 1969), shoot up the charts. All three peaked at #2 on *Billboard's* Hot Singles chart, which guaranteed continual group visibility throughout the year. RCA was preparing to launch their monster Blood, Sweat, and Tears – Glass Prism Tour but pulled the plug after lead vocalist David Clayton-Thomas and manager Mort Lewis had a "falling out." The promised tour fell through just as The Glass Prism's "The Raven" (RCA, 1969) was getting airplay.

After Epic, Dakota signed with Columbia and, just like before, corporate head Don Ellis left the label. Ellis went over to Motown Records. It was another kick in the guts, and Lou Cossa said that, just like Cher's character in *Moonstruck*, "Dakota just had bad luck." He viewed "The Dakota Curse" as a fated revolving door of corporate executives, such as Don Ellis, who liked Dakota and their compositions. So he flew across the country to see them perform, Cossa recalled:

> There were only two people above him. (One was Bruce Lundvall, general manager of Columbia records.) Ellis liked the group, liked the songs. He was a sweetheart. He traveled 3,000 miles just to see us and to support us, and look what happened?

Don Ellis joined CBS Records in 1970 and was then promoted to vice president of Epic. While there, Ellis brokered the success of Edgar Winter, The Hollies, Minnie Ripperton, Dave Loggins, Labelle, Dan Fogelberg, and many others. Ellis was appointed vice president of Columbia Records in 1974, evaluating new material and signing contemporary artists like Dakota. Sadly, Dakota never realized Ellis' "Midas touch." Cossa explained:

> Suddenly, after he said, 'Yeah, sign Dakota to CBS,' he was transferred to Motown as president. His Dakota and CBS roles were now handed down to someone else, but it's not their baby. It's still Don Ellis' baby. These new people don't do as much to promote it as he certainly would have.

Everyone saw it from their perspective. Bill Kelly remembered circumstances surrounding Don Ellis and the resulting Dakota Curse:

> The Dakota Curse was everything. It would fall into place, one step after another, we'd get this, we'd get that, we'd get radio airplay, we'd get a Top Ten record, and it would all fall into place, and then what would fall apart is the record would come out to great fanfare and good reviews and then something would happen at the label.

Kelly said that before they left Epix, record executives Don Ellis and A&R man Terry Powell came to the Stone Balloon and signed them to Columbia. They were just completing the "If It Takes All Night" project in Montreal when, unfortunately, the Columbia leadership changed. Don Ellis went to Motown, and Powell left for greener pastures, said Kelly:

> Our cheerleaders were gone, and the new label people take over. They're not high on Dakota, and, at the same time, they're not real high on Chicago or Toto anymore, and we were all on Columbia. So, unfortunately, when our guys would go in and fight for some help, some money, we were at the bottom of the totem pole because they couldn't get anything for Chicago or Toto. So that's how we ended up over at MCA.

RUNAWAY

In early 1983, super-agent Irving Azoff had signed Dakota to his Full Moon label, and everyone was expecting a big promotional push. Azoff had previously signed Linda Ronstadt, Warren Zevon, Dan Fogelberg, and the Eagles but left to become president of MCA Records. After Full Moon, Dakota signed with Warner Brothers. Then, in October 1983, they were once again signed by Azoff, only this time at MCA. *Runaway* was released in the first quarter of 1984, but, as Hludzik had said, "the bottom fell out."

Rick Manwiller, recruited to become the third member of Dakota, saw the writing on the wall. Contributing his talents to the *Runaway* album, Manwiller also suffered from its unfortunate demise:

> Through the usual bad-luck-bad politics syndrome that followed, the *Runaway* album never got the proper promotion, and it 'withered on the vine.' It has since been re-dubbed 'The Dakota Curse.'

Hludzik, Kelly, and Manwiller assembled a touring band before *Runaway's* release. Syracuse drummer Robbie Spagnoletti was chosen, along with Tom

Navagh on bass, later replaced with Jim Fricano. That tour was over before it started, as Dakota decided they could only afford to maintain the band's nucleus. They recruited "Dexter," Manwiller's drum machine, as part of the group, and Manwiller quipped, "Dexter went on to become the most used drummer in Northeast Pennsylvania, playing at hundreds of studio sessions, by dozens of artists."

Runaway was a great album that had a not-so-great promotion. The Dakota Curse may be a matter of the glass being half full or half empty, wearing rose-colored glasses, or any of those symbolic arguments. Fran Festa, the former bass player for the Great Rock Scare and Glass Prism, examined the Dakota Curse from another angle:

> One might agree! As always, it's timing, and man, were they close? I tend to
> look at it like, 'hey, they did at least get to record on major labels, be on the
> charts, work in the big studios, record good songs by good writers, and tour
> with Queen in some fine venues. Most of us can't claim that. So that's a certain
> kind of success.

There was a lot of psychic energy invested in the Buoys-Jerry-Kelly and Dakota. The entire region was pulling for them, waiting for them to break out nationally, and in a macabre endnote, the "Record Whirl's" Richard Chisak opined:

> Granted, Dakota never became the stars we hoped they'd become, but for
> ten years, they were one of the area's most popular attractions and Wyoming
> Valley's only real brush with the national recording scene. They will be missed
> greatly.

Missed, but not forgotten. We will always have Dakota's incredible music catalog, including their independently produced DAK Enterprises albums, as timeless gifts and remembrances of their creativity and perseverance.

GARY DRISCOLL

The most extreme example of the Dakota Curse centered around one of their band members. The body of former Jerry-Kelly Band rock drummer, John Gary Driscoll (1946–1987), was discovered in the basement of a two-story wooden duplex, his hands and feet bound with soldering wire, and shot twice in the head. Police charged John J. Shillingford with the killing and speculated that robbery was the motive. Driscoll had been a tenant at the Ithaca, New York

The Jerry Kelly band (L-R) Bill Mitchell, Lou Cossa, Bill Kelly, Jerry Hludzik, Bill McHale, Gary Driscoll. (Maxim Furek photo.)

residence for only five days. In August 1988, the jury deliberated for nine hours, finding Shillingford not guilty of the murder.

Driscoll began his career in 1965 with the Ithaca, New York band, Ronnie James Dio (Ronnie Padavona), and The Prophets. The band transformed into The Electric Elves, The Elves, and finally, in 1969, Elf. Deep Purple bassist Roger Glover produced several of Elf's Epic studio albums. Elf was a legendary group, setting themselves apart from the other area bands with their "impact, look, and sheer decibel force," according to Hybrid Ice's Jeff Willoughby:

> Elf was a visual and musical power that was unmatched by anyone at the time. They would roll into town several times in a season. They wore studded denim jackets, hair to the waist, walls of Marshall and Sunn amplifiers, and a sound that would shake the embroidery from your torn bell-bottomed pants, part your shoulder-length hair down the middle, and leave your ears ringing for days afterward. It was magical. Their effect on the crowd was mesmerizing.

Elf disbanded in 1975, forming the rock act Rainbow, consisting of Driscoll, Ronnie James Dio, former Elf keyboardist Micky Lee Soule, bassist Craig Gruber, and former Deep Purple guitarist Ritchie Blackmore. After Rainbow's debut album, titled *Ritchie Blackmore's Rainbow*, Driscoll was replaced by

Gary Driscoll (second from left) with his group, The Elves.

British rocker Cozy Powell, ostensibly because Blackmore did not like Driscoll's R&B drumming style and wanted someone who played harder. After he departed from Rainbow, Driscoll joined the Jerry-Kelly band from 1978 to1980, but, once again, ran into issues concerning his drumming, recalled Bill Kelly:

> When Danny and Hawk came to see us, the feeling was that Gary would not cut it in the studio. He was a fine live drummer, but he did not have the timing to make the solid studio record we all wanted to make. So, of course, he was very disappointed and ended up quitting, and that's when we recruited Tony Romano.

Driscoll immediately returned to work, forming Bible Black and releasing the LPs *Ground Zero* and *Thrasher*, but with an inadequate public response. Driscoll made a little extra money as a session musician and carpet installer before his tragic death.

41

AD: AFTER DAKOTA

T o everything, there is a season, and, as the Dakota algorithms twisted and turned, it was ordained that some doors would close while others would open. So now, they walked towards an opportunity to embrace change and try something different.

That fated opportunity prompted them to try their hand at record production as another adventure began. Magnum, an Allentown-based group (Mike DeFrank, Butch Samolewicz, Lonnie Warner, Dave Werkhiser, Tommy Zito), released "Public Memory No. 1" b/w "Your Way," the former a 1983 *Billboard* magazine pick hit. Hludzik and Kelly produced the band's independent five-song mini-LP, recorded at Grandslam Studios in West Orange, New Jersey, and digitally mixed and remastered in New York and Quebec.

DAKOTA'S RUN FOR RUNAWAYS

The duo were eager promoters looking for any advantage to promote their name and products. On August 26, 1984, they sponsored "Dakota's Run for Runaways" to benefit the National Runaway Child Hotline Foundation. Hludzik told *The Scranton Tribune* that Meg Polak, director of the Austin, Texas Runaway hotline, endorsed his race. Hludzik also expected a letter of support from President Ronald Reagan.

Initially, the idea was to locally promote their new album, Runaway, with the title song about the teenage runaway problem, but MCA decided to take the race nationally. The idea was to stage a 5K race in every city as a run-up to a Dakota concert.

In the inaugural event, sponsored by Rock 107 and MCA Records, Scranton's Bill King (15:09) and Michelle Pinger (18:36) were the overall winners of the Dakota 5K run that raised over $3,300 for the charity. Three members of

Dakota finished the race, with Hludzik (23:42), Kelly (24:14), and Manwiller (31:16) competing.

"GIVE A LITTLE LOVE FOR CHRISTMAS"

They found other ways to give back. In 1986, Dakota recorded Hludzik's "Give a Little Love for Christmas" at John Nasser's Holland Sound Studios, a region version of Bob Gandalf's 1985 "We Are the World." Ten groups each donated a recorded song for the compilation album *Holland Sound's Best of 1986*, raising $25,000 to aid the area's hungry and homeless. The compositions included

Included on the LP was "Diamonds Away" (Alpha,1986) by Rudi and the Living Dolls (Butch Rao, Charles Phillips, Joe Tocket, Vic Williams). Rudi and the Living Dolls, in the mode of David Bowie, espoused their message that "Beauty Isn't Everything, Love Is." "Diamonds Away" was recorded at Holland Sound and produced by Hludzik and Kelly, with Manwiller mastering the project, playing keyboards, and programming Dexter, his drum machine.

Synch's "Something We Already Had," Dakota's "Give a Little Love For Christmas," TNT's "The Chance You Take," The Remains' "Run To Me," and Quest's "All I Need." Others were John Nasser and the Don't Walk Band's "Dear John," Asylum Blues' "Goodbye," Mark Wanko's "Miles Away," Rudi and The Living Dolls' "Diamonds Away," and Bobby Ross' "Halley's Comment."

The good vibes continued into the following year, when John Nasser released *Open Your Heart for Christmas,* a ten-track compilation of music recorded by local bands and performers. Nasser distributed over 2,000 albums and cassettes for this benefit.

Another side project was finalized towards the end of the year when WNEP-TV debuted a new "Hatchy Milatchy" children's song. *Hatchy Milatchy,* a popular regional children's TV program, first aired in 1959 with hostess Miss Judy and featured Rosemary Clooney singing the signature tune, "Hatchy Milatchy." The new song, "All of Your Dreams Come True," was composed by Hludzik and Manwiller after WNEP's Bill Christian requested they update the original piece. In addition, three Dakota offspring appeared in a video showcasing the song. Bill Kelly, who provided additional vocals for the music, acknowledged his long-time partner's compassion and generosity:

> Jerry had a great heart. He loved kids and participating in the new makeover for the Scranton-based children's show, "Hatchy Milatchy." In addition, he had a heart for the homeless. He encouraged several bands and musicians from the area to produce the record "Give A Little Love for Christmas" to raise money for and awareness of Scranton's homeless.

That same year, riding one of their creative peaks, Hludzik and Kelly produced TNT's "Chance You Take," written by Ray K. and Dewey Styles and Joe Lemongelli (aka Joe Cella), a group later evolving into Twice Shy. The industrious Hludzik also recorded jingles for the Scranton/Wilkes-Barre Red Barons and the Steamtown Mall.

THE BREAKUP

In February 1987, Dakota opened for the Rascals at the FM Kirby Center. Blending R&B and the British Invasion sound, The Rascals evolved as major proponents of "blue-eyed soul." Frontman Felix Cavaliere, fascinated with the Hammond B3 organ, was a trained musician who defined their energetic sound and inspirational messages. But for Dakota, the energy and inspiration had died, and their fantastic journey was ending.

Four months later, at Scranton's Montage Mountain Pavilion, Dakota played their final performance at the Lackawanna County Independence Weekend Festival, held over several days. It was public knowledge and widely publicized that they were breaking up. WEZX-FM, Rock 107, would broadcast Dakota's concert in its entirety, while four other radio stations broadcast live at various times.

Gary Puckett and the Union Gap and the Northeastern Pennsylvania Philharmonic played on the Fourth of July. Then, on July 5, 1987, Dakota performed along with The Pulse, the Great Rock Scare, AKA, and Tommy Conwell and the Young Rumblers. Despite all of that talent, the majority of roughly seventeen thousand loyal fans were there to say goodbye to their hometown heroes, Dakota.

The worst darkness was right before, and they would share in that gloom soon enough. Montage was the official end of a seventeen-year association. Hludzik, 35, and Kelly, 36, felt that they had said it all and that their music had become too predictable. There was a constant repetition of a theme, a well-crafted formula that some found comforting but others tedious. *Time Out's* Dave Morris made that point seven years earlier after reviewing their first Dakota album:

> The only problem, and it seems to be a trend with high harmony groups, is predictability. About halfway through the second side, listeners feel like they know what's coming up next. Usually, too, the listeners are right.

Thirteen years later, reviewing *Little Victories*, AOR specialists *Odayrox* observed similar themes:

> Still retaining their classic '80s AOR, *Little Victories* showcased a more modern Melodic Rock sound and emphasized stronger guitar lines, punchy arrangements, and multiple vocal harmonies. And, although the songs have a similar musical theme throughout, there is enough difference to make each one unique.

Eli Hludzik

Jon Lorance

Rick Manwiller

Jerry G. Hludzik

42

GOING UP THE COUNTRY

OAK RIDGE BOYS

The personal and musical differences began to pile up, and both Hludzik and Kelly felt that they needed a change, thinking that solo careers might lead to tremendous success. Even though their partnership had dissolved, the promise of the opportunity presented itself after a local musician, Great Rock Scare keyboardist Dave Murray opened the heavenly doors to Nashville. Murray had written "Lookin' For Love," which the Oak Ridge Boys recorded for their LP *Where the Fast Lane Ends* (MCA, 1987).

Country Jerry Hludzik

Like a Hollywood understudy ready for a leading role, Hludzik never stopped learning new techniques and styles, country being just the next part of the equation. Teaming up with Manwiller, they hitched their wagon to the profitable strains of country music, the popular sounds of Garth Brooks, Little Big Town, and Florida Georgia Line.

It was at this juncture that, once again, sound technician Michael Stahl lent a helping hand. Stahl's mediation resulted in the Oak Ridge Boys recording two of their songs and a contract to write for MCA Nashville. Duane Allen, the lead singer of the Oaks, approved the signing of Hludzik and Manwiller to a publishing contract and underwrote some session expenses to speculate on a recording deal. He said:

> I have always believed in the men who came from the 'Dakota' group of musicians and writers. There is a gold mine of talent there. I have recorded their work, and there are many more songs in their catalog that I love.

Eli Hludzik explained that Hludzik's Ha Daddy Productions was developed between the last Dakota record and their foray into country music and may have played a part in their MCA writer's contract:

> He and Rick signed a writer's contract with MCA to develop a country catalog for about twenty-five songs, and out of that was born the two cuts that they got on the Oak Ridge Boys records.

The wheels were set in motion with their Nashville success. Hludzik met Stonebridge bass guitarist Mark Wanko at Holland Sound, where Wanko recorded "Miles Away," produced by Hludzik and Kelly. Almost immediately, Hludzik and Wanko began to collaborate, writing "Too Many Heartaches," included on the Oaks' *Monongahela* (MCA, 1988) and performed live at the 1988 Bloomsburg Fair. Hludzik and Wanko also joined forces on what they called their "country project," recording "All-American Boy," "Velvet Elvis," and "Your Place or Mine?"

Hludzik and Manwiller wrote "Don't Give Up," included on Oak's *American Dreams* (MCA, 1989), considered one of their best albums. The gospel-flavored "Don't Give Up" spoke of "the promised land" and was tailor-made for the Oak Ridge Boys' tight up-tempo harmonies. Duane Allen, who worked closely with Hludzik, Kelly, and Manwiller, told this writer:

> Over the years, we have become dear friends. So I put together a group of people to listen to the catalog of these men. I feel that they are some of the best

writers in our business, and I have always felt that if they could 'get inside' The Nashville Scene, their music could happen.

PONY EXPRESS

Hludzic and Manwiller decided to try something new, forming Secret City. The band played covers of Bruce Hornsby, Police, INXS, and Toto and included Manwiller's friend, guitarist Eric Rudy, drummer Robbie Spagnoletti, and later Jon Lorance. After Spagnoletti left, they began to use Manwiller's drum machine, Dexter. Secret City played as the backing band for Jimmy Harnen and lasted, as a group, until around 1992. Then it was on to their next project, Pony Express.

With ex-Dakota member Lou Cossa, Hludzik and Lorance formed the country band Pony Express. Hludzik looked for a steel guitar player and reached out to Scott Fritz at Danville's Schoolhouse Music. Mark Tomeo, the former member of the *Billboard*-charting Rubber Rodeo, played an MSA single neck twelve-string pedal steel. He auditioned for the band in Scranton, adding to the harmonies of Cossa, Hludzik, and Nancy Graziano. Tomeo:

> I was blown away after that audition. I couldn't believe what good musicians they were. I wanted to be in that band so bad. They were all friends and had worked together before in various capacities. They were all from the Scranton area.

Pony Express featuring vocals by Nancy Graziano.

Good things come to those who wait, and after a few weeks, Tomeo, "the stranger in the band," got the nod:

> The whole idea of Pony Express was fairly mercenary. It was right at that time when Garth Brooks and Billy Ray Cyrus, those 90s guys, kind of redefined country music from the '70s outlaw music to more of that '80s Garth arena-pop country kind of thing.

And why not emulate Billy Ray? Billy Ray Cyrus's "Achy, Breaky Heart" (Mercury, 1992) was huge. It was the first country single to be certified Platinum since 1983's "Islands in the Stream" by Kenny Rogers and Dolly Parton, but more importantly, Cyrus helped kick off the urban cowboy line dancing craze of that era. "Easy Mark" Tomeo said that Pony Express wanted to be a part of that enthusiasm:

> My impression was that they just wanted to get a piece of the action. At the time, bars were looking for those types of bands. I didn't know it, but part of their rationale for being a cover band was that they wanted to play for line dancers.

Back in 1992, Tomeo had never heard of line dancing, but his first gig with Pony Express was at a place called Ecklers, in Scranton, that featured line dancing, he recalled:

Bandmates Hludzik and Lorance

Pony Express was very much a way to cash in on that kind of reinterest in country music that came about with people like Garth Brooks and Clint Black and George Strait, and those people.

Still, none of the guys were country guys, especially Jon Lorance, who Tomeo described as a "blistering, blasting rock guitar player, who was really, really good." Tomeo said:

Jon Lorance was an outstanding guitar player with a beautiful ear. He could cop the solos to any of those country records we were covering without even thinking about it. His ear was that good.

Pony Express did mostly cover material in bars and clubs around Scranton. They carried on from about 1992 till 1995, with Eli Hludzik playing drums during their final ten months. After breaking up, Tomeo joined Neon Cactus, a country band from the Williamsport area, who opened for Merle Haggard in 1996. He said:

I talked my way into a gig with them in the summer of 1995 after I saw them playing at Knoebels, not long after Pony Express called it quits. They all had true country hearts. Between the drummer and I, we built it up from a local bar band to playing at Jamboree in the Hills for 175,000 people in the summer of 2000.

Hludzik and Manwiller formed a rock band called Little Big in their evolving musical landscape, with rock singer Josette Miles. Her album on Escape Music, LTD, "a compilation of music recorded over the years with various musicians," was produced by Hludzik and engineered by Manwiller. No matter the band, Hludzik brought tight, layered harmonies to the mix, and like Brian Wilson, instinctively knew what textures he wanted on the record, said Tomeo:

Pony Express had such good singers. It was just incredible how strong they were. Jerry would be working out a part and would say, 'The harmonies here, Nancy's got the lead, Louie's got the third, I'd have the fifth, whatever. Bring the beef.' That's what Jerry always said about the harmonies. 'Let's bring the beef, guys.' And boy, did they ever?

Hludzik relocated to West Chester and reformed Dakota with his son Eli on drums. Eli had a bachelor's degree in jazz and Music percussion from the University of Cincinnati, which he attended on a full scholarship. One of his initial projects was to help out with the recording of *The Last Standing Man*.

COUNTRY ROADS

It was time for a dramatic change, and, in 1991, Bill Kelly closed his eyes and tossed the dice. Nashville was waiting, so, with country roads taking him home, he headed south.

Almost immediately, he found success, or perhaps, more accurately, success found him. Within the first year, he scored his longest-running Nashville gig. Kelly had been in Nashville for about a year, often strolling (playing out) around Opryland Park with other musicians:

> It was a fabulous place for musicians to work and still make a living until their break came through. It was a lot of fun, and everyone in that group had played with people like Tim McGraw or Vince Gill. There were no slouches, and you had to be up on your chops.

Kelly's breakthrough came when he received a phone call from drummer friend Harry Stinson, who asked if he was "ready to go on the road." Stinson (now the drummer for Marty Stuart) had just finished working on an album with Canadian singer Charlie Major. After setting up a meeting, Major came over to Kelly's apartment:

> We sat around and talked, and then he played me the CD, and it was terrific. We threw a little harmony around to see what our voices sounded like together. Charlie was a mix of Bruce Springsteen and John Mellencamp, and he had a great guitar player, Steward Smith, who went on to play with the Eagles.

After that, Kelly received a call from Major's business office saying he needed to stop by the office to pick up his tickets to Toronto:

> It was amazing because I never auditioned for the job. It was all word-of-mouth and on the strength of Harry Stinson's recommendation. My first gig with Charlie was the Canadian Country Music Award Show, where he won everything; New Artist of the Year, Album of the Year, Single of the Year, and Singer-Songwriter of the Year.

One of their opening acts was Shania Twain, another Canadian, just starting in the business.

Major moved to Nashville in 1994, about two years after Kelly. In 1993 he tied Michael Jackson for having six consecutive number one hits off his debut album, *The Other Side*, which sold over 200,000 copies. Over the past twenty-five years, Major accumulated three Juno awards for Country Male Vocalist of the Year, multiple Canadian Country Music Association awards, a SOCAN

Songwriters Honor, a BMI Award, and ten number-one hits. Kelly played with Major, across Canada and the States, for about six years.

CHARLIE LOUVIN

Kelly was getting a reputation in Music City as a skilled picker. After taking a two-year break, he received a phone call from seventy-four-year-old Grand Ole Opry star Charlie Louvin, a country music singer and songwriter known as one of the Louvin Brothers. A member of the Grand Ole Opry since 1955, Louvin had over twenty singles that placed on the country charts. The rich harmonies of the Louvin Brothers, Ira's high tenor, and Charlie's lower-pitched, blanket-warm voice, called "the third voice," had a singular sound. They would later influence country rock artists such as Emmylou Harris, Gram Parsons, and The Byrds.

Around 2002 Kelly began playing with Charlie Louvin, but he had been familiar with the country star since Kelly's early youth:

> When I was a kid playing my Beatle 45s, my uncle and Dad would knock me away from the record player to play their Charlie Louvin and Louvin Brothers' records. Of course, I would be so mad, but that was how I first heard of Charlie Louvin.

Once again, Kelly never auditioned. Louvin just called him and said, "we're going to rehearse, and these are the songs you need to know." So Kelly played, off and on, with him, for seven or eight years, until Louvin's death:

> I went down to see him about two weeks before he died, and I was very honored because before he passed, he asked me to be a pallbearer. He used to pick on me because I was the only Yankee in the band.

Louvin underwent surgery for pancreatic cancer in 2010 and died of complications on the early morning of January 26, 2011. He was eighty-three. Kelly played with the country superstar "right up until he passed away." Kelly served as a pallbearer, along with Louvin's three sons, Sonny, Glenn, and Kenneth, and Grand Ol' Opry guitar player Jimmy Capps, at Nashville's Memory Gardens. Charlie Louvin offered a profound message during an earlier interview, suggesting:

> If you have any roses that you would like to lay in front of somebody or put in their hand, do it while they can still smell 'em. This deal of saying how great a guy was after he's gone doesn't mean squat.

KANE AND KELLY

Kelly's Nashville experience was part country and part contemporary Christian. He speaks proudly of his religious conversion, something that profoundly changed his life:

> In 1993 I met my wife, Annie. She was a Christian who dragged me down to the church in Belmont. The word hit me between the eyes, and I couldn't hide it anymore.

At that point, he moved in the direction of his truth, his true north. Kelly had met Jennifer Kane at The Bridge Fellowship Church in Lebanon, Tennessee,

Kane and Kelly, contemporary Christian musicians. (Photo courtesy of Bill Kelly Music Productions.)

and had known her for about fifteen years. Still, while rehearsing with a church worship band in Mt. Juliet, Kelly heard a pleasing feminine voice that sent shivers through his musical soul. Both shared a strong faith, and, being musically talented, they formed "Kane and Kelly," a contemporary Christian duo:

> We are not chasing the brass ring. We are doing what God puts on our hearts to write. We've had two singles now that have gone into the Top Ten. One of them, "The Storm," went to number one for a month.

"The Storm" was out for a year and a half, reentering the charts at #32 and going up to #27. The CDX Traction Southern Gospel and Positive Country charts added it to their listing. Another successful single, "Written in Red," went to #37 in August 2020 on PowerSource's Top 100 Christian Country chart. The mournful Gospel hymn, "His Eye Is On the Sparrow," also charted on the inspirational country music charts.

ANGEL ARMIES

Today, Kelly and Jennifer Kane blend harmonies in the duet Angel Armies. This unique yet straightforward Christian ministry combines song and prayer to give hope and comfort to people confronting such crises as cancer, death, divorce, and bankruptcy. They took their name from Christian singer-songwriter Chris Tomlin's song, "Whom Shall I Fear (God of Angel Armies)," which takes its chorus from Psalm 27: "The Lord is my light and my salvation; Whom shall I fear?" They describe their sound as just voices and guitar, being "very intimate" and "incredibly healing, with words expressed as prayer.

In 2021, the Inspirational Country Music Association recognized Kane & Kelly as Vocal Duo/Duo Performance of the year and New Artist of the Year, and in August Kelly and Kane performed live at the Pittston Tomato Festival, with a meet and greet at Joe Nardone's Gallery of Sound.

43

MAKING PEACE

Much like the alienation of Oasis's Noel and Liam Gallagher, or the Beach Boys' Mike Love and Brian Wilson, or the firing of Lindsey Buckingham from Fleetwood Mac, Kelly could relate to the animosity between himself and his former partner, as told to reporter Caitlin Heaney West:

Bill Kelly on stage. (Maxim Furek photo.)

We wanted nothing to do with each other at that point, and it was okay
because we did need a break.

What had kept them together for so long, the mutual respect and the joy
of spontaneity and improvisation were replaced with a stark animosity, said
Hludzik:

> We had our ups and downs, but eventually, the downs got to be too much,
> and, in 1987, we decided to go our separate ways. We both were just tired of
> each other and needed a musical change. I was the one to pull the plug, and,
> unfortunately, there were many hard feelings over many years. Sadly, we didn't
> even speak for about eight years.

Around the time that Melody Blvd/ Aorchives remastered and reissued
Runaway on CD, Hludzik recalled his scheduled business trip to Nashville:

> Scott Sosebee and my sweetheart Annie convinced me to call Kelly, so I did. It
> could have been another short call, but it turned into almost an hour, mostly
> filled with family conversation, as all the lost years had never happened.

Then, thanks to an intervention by Jim Della Croce, that phone call led to
a surprise dinner in Nashville. Hludzik and Kelly came together, face to face,
for the first time in years and reconciled. As Kelly put it:

> We mended our fences and formed new plans. Where I was cautious, Jerry was
> ready to jump back in, with both feet, just like always. Jerry didn't know the
> meaning of the words 'I give up,' maybe to a fault. He was truly unstoppable.

Eli Hludzik agreed with that assessment of his father:

> My Dad was always trying to push forward and be positive, even during those
> days that were super dark. You couldn't stop him. Kelly said that 'There's some
> kind of IV drip or pacemaker that's attached to my father's heart.' As soon as
> he's pointed in a direction, it's over. If you tried to stop him, he'd just run you
> over.

Although Hludzik could be dogmatic and obstinate, Kelly regretted what
he called "such wasted time" and lost years of bitterness. Nevertheless, they were
still able to mend fences and start all over again. Hludzik recalled when the
emotional burden lifted:

> It was a great feeling of relief, talking, laughing, and even making some
> tentative plans with a dear friend and musical brother. So we got together

downstairs that morning and started singing some of the old Jerry-Kelly stuff, and it was terrific. We just looked at each other, and I know I got tears in my eyes because it was an emotional experience and because it was us 18 years later. It was like we never split up.

On November 14, 2005, it came full circle after Hludzik and Kelly returned to WVIA's *Homegrown Music* to perform some of their best-known songs in an acoustic duo setting. Homegrown music was where they first laid down the "Jerry-Kelly" tracks that would become the all-important demo tapes that Mike Stahl delivered to Danny Seraphine, which led to a record contract.

DAKOTA AND THE BEACH BOYS

A host of events were planned to commemorate the Bicentennial Celebration over the Fourth of July. Unfortunately, a free concert with Dakota and the Beach Boys (minus Brian Wilson), scheduled for Kirby Park, was canceled. Due to extremely heavy rains, the mighty Susquehanna crested, forcing the evacuation of most of the city on June 28, 2006. The rescheduled Beach Boys concert was held in Kirby Park on Labor Day weekend, Sunday, September 3, 2006. Dakota was the opening act, with Lou Cossa, Jerry G. Hludzik, Eli M. Hludzik, Bill Kelly, Jon Lorance, and Jeff Mitchell. Pennsylvania Governor Ed Randell attended the free Labor Day concert.

Bill Kelly, Rick Manwiller, and Jerry Hludzik leaving their celebrity imprints at 1984 MCA Dakota album release party. (Photo courtesy of Bill Kelly Music Productions.)

Despite the breakup, Dakota had a massive following in Europe and was regarded as a progressive Album Oriented Rock band. Hludzik discussed the band's style and success in a 2008 interview and didn't hold back about the lack of corporate support and publicity. He told Vincenzo Ferrara, of the Italian *Hardnheavy* site:

> Yes, I agree that Dakota's sound is Album Oriented Rock and Westcoast sound-ing. We were produced in that vein. That was our sound from the beginning. I feel that if we had received more of a push from our record labels, Dakota would have been a household word. Despite this, we still have a large world-wide fan base.

44

DAK ENTERPRISES

THE LOST TRACKS (1987)

Their final hurrah, and perhaps their most fitting legacy, was DAK Enterprises. It all started with a collection of almost forgotten tracks recorded between 1984 and 1987. Dakota's remaining members, Hludzik, Kelly, and Manwiller, knew they were sitting on a gold mine. The odd collection, which would be called *Lost Tracks*, represented an archive of previously unreleased materials, scattered out-takes, and unfinished songs that could be cleaned up, jazzed up, and marketed. They recorded the majority of songs at Dunmore's Holland Sound Studios and Manwiller's Closet Studios. Since the early days at Scepter, recording technology had changed from analog to digital, and everyone seemed to have a studio. Closet Productions, Manwiller's high-quality sixteen-track unit, was built inside a walk-in closet in his bedroom. Eli Hludzik remarked that "Rich was a complete genius. He was completely running the spaceship." The independently financed album was what Jerry Hludzik described as "a songwriter's record."

Lost Tracks was filled with hidden gems denoting future promise. The optimistic "The Tables Are Turning for Mr. Lucky," "Don't Count Me Out," and "Don't Stop Believing" were examples of the band's trademark positivity and optimism. One of the outstanding cuts was "Believing," featuring a searing guitar solo and Kelly's banshee-like scream as the song fades. Dave London of WEZX-Rock 107 told *Record Whirl* that countless listeners were awaiting the LP's release:

> We're inundated with questions about the album every time we play a track from it. I've heard the entire album, and I think it's a shame Dakota broke up because this is so good that I think it could've been their big break.

Several tracks received enthusiastic airplay on local radio, notably the pop ballad "All Through the Night," which spent seven solid weeks on the Top Five request list along with "Believin'" and "Mr. Lucky."

MR. LUCKY (1996)

Around March 1994, Hludzik started to get positive feedback from overseas. The good news was that, despite the passage of years and spotty support in the States, Dakota was a well-known and respected AOR band in Europe with an impressive fan base. As a result, Hludzik negotiated a distribution deal with the Sweden-based Escape Music to re-release a slightly modified *Lost Tracks* as the newly christened *Mr. Lucky* (ESM-005) to capitalize on this sudden good fortune.

The *Mr. Lucky* LP was the same as *Lost Tracks*, with a few notable exceptions. Included on the European album were "These Eyes" and the re-worked "Mr. Lucky," a rockier version of the original. Two years later, *Mr. Lucky* was spotlighted as the "Album of the Month" in Great Britain's *Power Play* Magazine as, around the same time, it began to climb the Japanese charts.

Liking what they heard, Escape Records asked Hludzik to record a new album for them. After some deep soul-searching, he realized that this was an opportunity knocking at his door. And he didn't have to be asked twice.

THE LAST STANDING MAN (1997)

The success of *Mr. Lucky* led to Hludzik contacting Manwiller to start writing again, paving the way for *The Last Standing Man*, a cryptic reference to Hludzik, the only remaining original member of Dakota. The album, produced by Hludzik and Manwiller, was recorded at SI. Studios, Scranton, Pennsylvania, signaling a new beginning. Jerry and Eli Hludzik, Jon Lorance, and Rick

Rick Manwiller.

Manwiller contributed to the album, but Bill Kelly did not. Although *Last Standing Man* was the first Dakota project without Kelly's participation, Kelly told *Citizen's Voice* reporter Caitlin Heaney West that he gave Hludzik all the credit for carrying on the name and legacy of Dakota:

> All of Jerry's album efforts sound like they're reconnected to Dakota. Even though I wasn't involved in them, there's still that connection because that's where his heart is. So the new stuff is going to sound like a logical outgrowth of the *Runaway* album.

Escape Records released *The Last Standing Man* for the European market in September 1997, while Barebuckle Records released the album in Japan in February 1998.

SAVING THE BEST FOR LAST

In a sense, they were saving the best for last. After disappointing promotion and halfhearted commitments from Epic, Columbia, and MCA, Hludzik, Kelly, and Manwiller formed DAK Enterprises, their own management company. The unit also included sound engineer Mike Stahl and former Stone Balloon owner, and Dakota manager, Bill Stevenson.

The timing was perfect. Audio production had evolved, and everyone, like Rick Manwiller, recorded out of their private studio, taking advantage of technological innovations. Musicians were more cautious about major record corporations and restrictive contracts, and, for Dakota, a sense of independence and freedom defined their latest incarnation.

The plan was to record their self-composed music in the hope of securing national distribution and promotion, sidestepping any middlemen. Over the years, C. Michael Wright, Rupert Holmes, George Graham, Danny Seraphine, and Humberto Gatica mentored them. They learned the art of recording, double-tracking, reverb, overdubs, synthesizer sweeps, and intricate studio techniques required to create their layered sound. Last *Standing Man* (1997), *Little Victories* (2000), *Deep 6* (2003), and *Long Road Home* (2015) were recorded at Sound Investments Recording Studios in Old Forge, Pennsylvania. Owner and Mastering Engineer Tom Borthwick, a graduate of Wilkes University, observed that Hludzik and Manwiller felt at home at his studio:

> Jerry Hludzik had worked with us on a couple of different things. He liked the studio, and we had the necessary equipment to get the sounds he and Rick Manwiller needed. We had a good working relationship for all those albums over all those years. We just clicked together.

SI Studios represented a new chapter in their career, according to Eli Hludzik:

> *The Last Standing Man* is when we started this whole new cycle of Dakota records. It was the first revamp of the brand with Escape Records as the record label. So The *Last Standing Man, Little Victories, Deep 6, Long Road Home* were all part of that.

But for Jerry Hludzik, *The Last Standing Man* was personal. He confessed that he had to make another Dakota record to "exorcise a lot of demons." *The Last Standing Man* contained no love songs, only songs about family and real-life challenges. The song "Mama Teach" was about Hludzik's son Eli leaving the nest to go off to college, while the title song, "The Last Standing Man," intoned, "Believe in the power of your convictions, believe in the power of love." Their redundant and persistent message came from the very marrow of Dakota's soul. "The Last Standing Man" philosophy resounded throughout every album Hludzik crafted, reminding his listeners of his indefatigable resilience.

On "Hot Nights," he sang about being on the road and the celebrity status of being in the spotlight, testifying what a "Long crazy road it's been, and I've had my fun."

Kelly always said they complimented each other, sounding great with the vocals and guitars, but the songwriting efforts were equally productive. Hludzik was great with writing songs with clever hooks, such as on "Possession," "Restless," and "If It Takes All Night," and Kelly as well with "Settle Down," "One Step," and "Be My Love."

Making the most of the band's popularity, Escape released The Last Standing Man in Europe in September 1997, while Barebuckle Records did the same in Japan in February 1998. Tom Borthwick was witness to that international attention:

> Dakota had several European distribution deals, and there was money put forward to release them. I don't know the details, but Dakota had a couple of different international labels licensed to distribute their records. In the back of Jerry's mind, he was probably hoping something big would happen, but I think he just created music because he loved doing it.
>
> He would take the extra time and effort. He loved writing; he loved being in the studio; he loved putting out music. But, Jerry was more concerned about finishing something up so he could start the next one.

"Hot Nights" and "The Last Standing Man" were cerebral rockers blending Dakota's long-established rhythms with personal and philosophical insight, something they never stopped promoting. Additionally, another considerable musician was Mountain Top's Jon Lorance, who was "an amazing guitar player and a total sleeper," according to Eli Hludzik:

> Jon would be playing the most ripping grooves, ever, just killing it, but just standing there, kind of like watching golf. He was never putting his foot on the monitor or doing any of that headbanging that other rock guitarists would do. He was all business, just a regular dude. A lot of the solo ideas on the later Dakota albums came from Jon. He was a big part of the band and of how those songs sounded.

The Dakota sound was bright, clean AOR, and free of distortion. It introduced excellent harmonies combined with Lorance's adrenalized guitar improvisations that were nothing short of brilliant by anyone's standards. Lorance upped the ante, playing faster, cleaner, and with more harmonic solos. He was a demon, evidenced by gems like "Hot Nights" and "Believin'," helping define their sound.

LITTLE VICTORIES (2000)

Encouraged by the success of *The Last Standing Man* in Europe and Japan, Dakota went to work on their next studio project, *Little Victories*.

Released in 2000, Dakota once again found success overseas. *Little Victories*, boasting layered melodic rock and harmonic ingenuity, was released in Japan on Nexus KICP-734. 2000. Included on the Japanese album was the bonus track, "Mr. Lucky." Another exciting selection was a fierce yet controlled cover of "Friday on My Mind" (United Artists, 1966), originally recorded by the Australian rock group, The Easybeats. The up-tempo rocker had reached #16 on the American *Billboard* Hot 100.

Standout cuts included "Little Victories," "Go Easy (On My Heart)," "IOU," "The Deep," "Hearts on Fire," "Wish," and the reworked "Workin' Hot" and "Brother to Brother." "Brother to Brother," with backing vocals by Chicago's Bill Champlain, was a song Hludzik co-wrote with Manwiller and Champlain about his estranged brother, explained Eli Hludzik:

> I understand that he was trying to make up with his younger brother, my Uncle Bob. But, unfortunately, their relationship was messed up for quite a while.

In "Brother to Brother," Hludzik pleas, "Life's too short, and there's no time to waste," fading away with the insistent refrain, "it's time to talk about it, it's time to talk about it." Then, in the spirit of public absolution, Hludzik dedicated the song to his brother when they debuted it at Pittston's Staircase Lounge and gave "extra special thanks" to his brother on the *Little Victories* CD. Bobby D. "Cowboy" Hludzik lived in Colorado for a while before relocating back to Freeland, and sadly, within two years, Jerry, Bobby, and their mother, Irene, had passed.

MELODIC ROCK / AOR

Most of the Dakota discography had been out of print, but, in 2016, a treasure trove of their albums was reissued, including *Mr. Lucky, Little Victories, Deep 6, Dakota*, and *Runaway*. *Odayrox* affirmed that the album "kicked up the resurgence of the Melodic Rock / AOR scene fifteen years ago, and still sounds relevant today." The magazine's 2006 review of the "wonderfully crafted melodies" on the reissued *Little Victories* was glowing:

> Still retaining their classic '80s AOR sound, *Little Victories*, originally released in 2000, showcased a more modern Melodic Rock sound and emphasized stronger guitar lines, punchy arrangements, and multiple vocal harmonies. As a result, we have some truly fantastic choruses here.

Hludzik played a significant role in those "fantastic choruses" and possessed an uncanny sixth sense for harmony, as observed by "Easy" Mark Tomeo, a former Rhode Island musician. Tomeo, who charted on *Billboard* with his group Rubber Rodeo's "Anywhere with You" # 86 (Mercury, 1984), played pedal steel from 1993-95 with Dakota and Pony Express. He said:

> Jerry was by far the best singer I ever worked with. His voice was an enormous instrument, his range and control were impeccable, and his ears frighteningly infallible. He was a good guy and good bandmate, and he played hard all the way through.

LINNDRUM MACHINE

The band was viewed respectfully by other musicians. Bernie Garzio had the pleasure of playing with Kelly for about two years, on and off, calling it "an amazing experience to listen to him sing like that night after night." Garzio also acknowledged singer, composer, keyboardist Manwiller as an exceptional one-man-army:

> These guys were not human, and they had a non-human keyboard player named Rick Manweller. This guy would play drum fills on a LinnDrum

Machine while playing left-hand bass on the keyboard and still play the piano and sing.

Manwiller's LinnDrum was the first drum machine to use samples of acoustic drums and one of the first programmable drum machines. It was prevalent in the 1980s and was used on many successful recordings, including Frankie Goes to Hollywood's "Relax," #10 (ZTT, 1983), Tears for Fears' "Shout" #1 (Mercury, 1984), and Madonna's "Lucky Star" #4 (Sire, 1983).

Little Victories continued with Hludzik's unremitting positivity, and as a gracious epitaph on the album, he wrote:

> In order to believe in yourself, you first need a few other human beings to honestly and unconditionally believe in you and your quest. I have been blessed, for, without question, I have my strong beliefs because of all of you. You know who you are. Thank you once again for my strength.

DEEP 6 (2003)

In August 2003, Hludzik and Manwiller, with a guest appearance from Kelly, entered a recording studio for the first time since 1984 to record several tracks for the *Deep 6* album. They took almost two years to prepare the material for the studio album released in 2003 and reissued in 2016. The album is inventive and captivating, with crystal-clear vocals, harmonies, and majestic surges of instrumentation. The album received lavish praise, rightfully so, from *Odayrox:*

> *Deep 6* is one of the best albums in Dakota's history and easily among the best Album Oriented Rock albums to have appeared in the past decade. Hludzik and keyboardist Rick Manwiller took almost two years to prepare the material, and the result is nothing else but stunning.

Comparing *Deep 6* to previous Dakota efforts, Hludzik told Vincenzo Ferrara of the Italian *Hardnheavy* site:

> We chose to get back to the '80s style with this project, which meant that *Deep 6* could easily be compared to *Runaway*. The new songs are as good or better than what we had on *Runaway,* including the performance and the production. It could have been the obvious follow-up to that record.

"Deep 6," the title track, was an ambitious acapella mix of all twelve songs on the album, highlighting Dakota's perfect harmonies and studio experimentation. Eli Hludzik said that "Dakota was always known for their strong vocals, and with *Deep 6*, they were saying, 'This is what we sound like. So we're confirming it.'

But, despite his continued creative output, Hludzik's true purpose was to outdo any previous efforts, using past accomplishments as a launchpad for future projects. He was driven, relentless, and consumed. He simply could not stop and would draw everyone close to him into the spinning vortex. Eli Hludzik understood that part of his father's personality:

> He was always trying to get people to do things, and he was a talker. I remember when he and Rick Manwiller were on the outs, and Rick said, 'I don't want to talk to you on the phone because you always talk me into something I don't want to do. So we're going to do this by e-mail.'

Deep 6 was one of Hludzik's favorites, as he related to *Hardnheavy*:

> I just love the creative process of writing, arranging, and recording. Being in a recording studio with my bandmates is magic time and where I want to be. My favorite studio project was *Deep 6*. It was a labor of love, lasting over a year and a half, and it had me possessed. I was happy with the outcome.

SI's Borthwick worked hand-in-hand with Hludzik on the DAK album projects and observed his old school methods:

> Jerry didn't utilize technology very much. He just had things written down on paper and would come in with a satchel that looked like something you would put on the back of a horse. It was filled with papers, CDs, and all kinds of information. Jerry would dig through it and pull out whatever it was that we would be working on.
>
> Jerry would usually have the chord structure down on acoustic guitar and ideas of how he wanted to put it together, and Jon Lorance would add his guitar stylings to it, and his son Eli would put drums to it. Jerry played bass, or sometimes we'd sub other bass players out. The songs just kind of came together.

Borthwick said that Jon Lorance's stamp was all over the DAK albums, pushing them into loftier realms, "Jon was a phenomenal guitar player. There's no doubt in my mind that he's world-class, and he's a nice guy too, which helps."

Some of the *Deep 6* songs contained a .38 Special feel, while, in the spirit of Toto, the masterful "Back to Me" introduced Hludzik's authentic delivery and Chicago's Bill Champlin's backing vocals. Hludzik painfully asks, "What will I do if I give love to you and you don't give it back to me?"

Among the best cuts were "Eye of The Storm," "Back to Me," "Deep 6," "Luck, Mind, and Time," and "Brothers in Arms," another personal song from Hludzik. Co-written with Scott Sosebee, it was a message to Kelly about the "senseless time" that had passed, urging that "it's never too late to mend fences."

LONG ROAD HOME (2015)

After a hiatus of eleven years, Dakota reunited in 2014 with Eli M. Hludzik, Jerry J. Hludzik, Bill Kelly, and Jon Lorance to record a brand-new album titled *Long Road Home*. They spent months at SI. Studios and released the LP on October 30, 2015.

To complete the album, Hludzik and Kelly traded MP3 files and tentative lyrics back and forth. Kelly could not go up to Pennsylvania, so he recorded his parts in Nashville and sent them up to Hludzik to be placed on the master track. Kelly told *Times-Tribune* staff writer Caitlin Heaney West that *Long Road Home* had a "little more of a rock edge." A lot of that "rock edge" came from the brilliant playing of Mountain Top's Jon Lorance, whom Kelly felt added another dimension to their sound, something they couldn't do on their own, as Kelly told me:

> We could do these solos on the first two albums, but there were things we heard in our heads that we just couldn't play. We had our niche, but if we wanted an Eddie van Halen rift, I couldn't play it, and Jerry couldn't play it. So Jon Lorance was the man and, to this day, is one of the best-undiscovered guitar players I've ever worked with. He's silly good.

FRÉDÉRIC SLAMA

Long Road Home included several collaborations with French rock journalist and AOR musician Frédéric Slama, recognized for bringing AOR/Westcoast

Hludzik, Slama, and Chasing Violets. (Frederic Slama collection.)

(Frederic Slama collection.)   (Frederic Slama collection.)

music to his native country. While residing in Los Angeles, Slama worked with an impressive lineup of Westcoast musicians. In 2011 he asked Hludzik to sing two songs on his new album, *The Colors of LA* (AOR Blvd, 2012), and in March 2012, Hludzik provided lead vocals on "Dreams from Silver Lake" and "Benedict Canyon," both from the album. *Myglobalmind.com*, an online magazine for hard rock and heavy metal, reviewed Slama's LP:

> The trademark Westcoast sound is clearly visible with its production, which is superb and handled by Tommy Denander. Pure AOR staples like "Benedict Canyon" are great examples of the style that Slama portrays best, with an excellent job on vocals by Jerry Hludzik.

Hludzik also lent vocals on Slama's song, "Hold Back the Dawn," featured on Chasing Violet's first album, *Outside Heaven*, produced by Slama. "As usual, with Jerry, the results were fantastic," he said. Chasing Violets were French sisters Sarah and Mélissa Fontaine, who, along with Slama, visited with Hludzik's family in New York and at his West Chester home:

> We talked many times on the phone, and Jerry invited the girls and me to sing and play with him in West Chester. We met in New York City, where we had an epic lunch with Jerry and his daughter, Abby. Jerry and his wife, Annie, invited us to their home, and so we played, rehearsed, and had fun for a few days.

Hludzik's friendship with the AOR proponent became a motivating force behind Dakota's final LP, Long Road Home, as Slama explained:

Jerry harmonizing with French duo, Chasing Violets. (Frederic Slama collection.)

At that time, Jerry was not doing anything with Dakota, so I motivated him to record a new album with his band day after day. I offered three of my songs (which were already released in my AOR albums) to cover on his new Dakota album, *Long Road Home.*

These songs were "Secrets in Her Heart," re-named "Secrets," "Jenny at Midnight," and "Web of Lies," re-named "You Threw it All Away." On the latter song, Hludzik rewrote some lyrics for Slama's original music.

Long Road Home may have had some great music, including Slama's three songs. Still, the songwriting credits were sloppy and unprofessional, and even his name was misspelled as "Frederik" according to Frederic Slama:

> Unfortunately, there was considerable confusion with the album credits where my name was misspelled. People like Tommy Denander were credited as a writer (Tommy had nothing to do with it) and other mistakes. Jerry was sorry about these mistakes and apologized for months. But it was a confusing time, and Jerry was starting to get ill, so his health was more important to me. We couldn't change the credits after the album was printed.

Note: Slama wrote "Jenny at Midnight" and "Secrets in Her Heart" (re-named "Secrets"); "Web of Lies" (re-named "You Threw It All Away") was a collaboration between Slama and Hludzik, "where Jerry rewrote some lyrics on my original song."

HUMBERTO GATICA

With traces of Night Ranger and Survivor, outstanding cuts included: "Long Way Home," "Heaven or Hell," "You Threw It All Away," "1-2-3 Baby Baby," and "One From The Heart." Hludzik's "Remember When" took a nostalgic look back to when we were "young and wild and out of control," on roads "that would last forever," and living the days and nights "that would never end."

Besides *The Lost Tracks* and *Long Road Home*, Bill Kelly didn't participate in Hludzik and Manwiller's DAK productions. However, in a 2020 interview, he explained that there was no comparison between the production work of the DAK recordings and their *Runaway* masterpiece:

> You don't get any better than Humberto Gatica, the guy who engineered Michael Jackson's *Thriller*. I don't care who you have behind the console. When you have the number one guy working on your last album (*Runaway*), the bar is set so high.
>
> We were producing ourselves as best as possible but fell short of what we had done at Columbia and MCA. Still, the DAK Enterprises LPs were good-sounding records, and the signature harmony was undoubtedly there. In addition, those recordings had some of our best guitar work ever, and a lot of that had to do with bringing Jon Lorance into the picture.

The well-regarded website *Odayrox* was high on Dakota's final CD:

> Let me put this straight: *Long Road Home* is AWESOME. Dakota has crafted in 2015 the album all fans of the 'true' American '80s AOR wanted: the sound, the arrangements, all is pure gold here. Just check the pulsating mid-tempo 'Push,' the keyboard-driven 'Secrets,' or the melodic rock heaven of "Remember When," a duet with Bill Champlin. These cuts alone are worth the purchase.

Their six independently produced albums represented a fantastic collection of inspired songwriting and studio creativity. Still, because most of the Dakota discography was out of circulation, in 2016, *Mr. Lucky, Little Victories, Deep 6, Dakota,* and *Runaway* were reissued overseas to an enthusiastic and younger audience, regarding Dakota as leading proponents and innovators of Westcoast/AOR.

★ PART XI ★

COAL REGION HOODOO

45

SHEPPTON

Many have alleged that "Timothy" was based on the Sheppton mining disaster and its cannibalistic urban legend. Yet, despite that gruesome undertone, the song shares a connection with other paranormal elements.

Although not documented in any academic books of science or medicine, the arcane Coal Region Hoodoo is that incomprehensible curse that affects both the good and the not-so-good. The fear of being cursed by demonic forces was common to Eastern European superstitions in the Coal Region. In Polish, it was called *przeklenstow, prakeikimas* in Lithuanian, and *proklyattya* in Ukrainian.

Many stories abound about unfortunates caught up in the curse, and Sheppton is a prime example. After being trapped for two horrible weeks, the rescue team extricated two miners. Cheers celebrating the miners' rescue then took a dark turn when skeptical villagers demanded to know what happened to the third miner.

DANTE'S NINE CIRCLES OF HELL

It's no surprise that eating human flesh in a Pennsylvania coal mine has become part of the backwater hoodoo. Weird things have always transpired in the woods, abandoned coal mines, and nearby Centralia "— a cursed ghost town. "Timothy" dwells in realms far removed from rock and roll and is more entwined with unnatural elements, such as those involving Father Daniel Ignatius McDermott, the conjurer who damned a town, breathing life into the Coal Region Hoodoo.

Father McDermott, assigned to Centralia's Catholic church around 1868, was beaten by Molly Maguire thugs. The legend purports that McDermott cursed the community and prophesied that a day would come when the St. Ignatius Roman Catholic Church would be the town's last remaining structure.

In the early 1960s, Ignatius' prophesy came to pass after a dump fire ignited an underground coal seam, clandestinely spreading like cancer. The cache of anthracite smoldered and burned beneath the surface, over an eight-mile stretch of over 3,7000 acres, the Coal Region's version of Dante's Nine Circles of Hell. The asphalt surface of Rt. 61, popularly referred to as the Graffiti Highway, melted, grotesquely buckling upwards as spouts of hot sulfur and toxic gases spewed into the air. Called the "Devil's Fire," the hidden coal seam burned under Centralia's cursed town for more than 50 years and has been the theme of countless books, horror films, and documentaries. For example, director Christopher Gans created a series of Silent Hill horror films, using Centralia as inspiration for the fictitious Silent Hill.

Centralia personified the Coal Region Hoodoo, an ecological disaster of toxic carbon monoxide fumes, massive sinkholes, and government buy-outs, forcing residents to evacuate like Oakies fleeing the Dust Bowl. The smoldering fire continues today, an ongoing terror that began with a seemingly harmless trash fire and a curse from an angry Catholic priest. Perhaps.

W.A. "TONY" BOYLE

The Coal Region Hoodoo did not end there. W.A. "Tony" Boyle, President of the United Mine Workers of America, was cursed with the Hoodoo and would pay with his life. Strutting about with a red rose in his lapel, Boyle took full credit for the Sheppton rescue operations. Although he expected a heroes' parade through downtown Pottsville and the key to the city, a jury convicted Boyle of murdering United Mine Workers' Jock A. Yablonski, his wife Margaret, and their daughter Charlotte. Boyle was sentenced to three consecutive life terms in one of the most bitter internal struggles of the Anthracite labor movement.

DARK MYTHOLOGY

After the rescue of two miners, the world celebrated the innovative rescue technique that would later save countless lives. But in local patch towns, church bells pealed as black-clad women clutched rosary beads and sobbed for the departed while their men hung out at Dado's Bar on the corner of Pine and Shepp Streets, seeking companionship and asking the most difficult of questions. "What happened to the missing miner?" Did they eat him? "Could it have happened?" These words echoed in an endless barrage, a tormenting narrative that morphed into a dark urban legend. Where it started didn't matter, but, like a foul-smelling breath, it spread from one to another. Soon voices were muttering the same accusation, pointing fingers and wagging tongues, and telling tales heard over clotheslines and in dark recesses of musty-smelling bar rooms.

With the monster unleashed, there would be no escape. Accusations of cannibalism resounded from sources like the Chicago *Daily News* and J. Ronnie Sando's book, *The Famous Sheppton Mine Rescue,* asking, "What happened in the coalmine?" And then, almost a decade later, "Timothy" resurrected those terrible memories. As more listeners began to understand the disturbing lyrics, the song assumed a life that went beyond the scope of a mere 45 rpm recording, and as a graveyard specter, dark mythology took shape and form. "Timothy," intertwined snakelike with Sheppton, remains the Coal Region's forbidden urban legend.

Vintage Joey Reynolds concert poster.

JOEY REYNOLDS

An interesting footnote to The Coal Region Hoodoo has been attributed to a legendary disc jockey. A&R man Jim Drucker, whose Drucker Publishing Co. owned "It Feels Good," the flip side of "Timothy," claimed that DJ Joey Reynolds singly broke "Timothy" on Buffalo's WKBW, introducing the song to the world in his unique, unorthodox manner:

> I was informed by Florence Greenburg's son, Stanley, that Joey Reynolds played 'Timothy' incessantly at WKBW 1520 AM. He played it over and over, just like when he played Randy and the Raindrops' "The Kind of Boy You Can't Forget" (Jubilee, 1963), for a solid hour and a half. Ninety minutes of the same song.

Reynolds was constantly burning down the house during a time when disc jockeys ruled over an adolescent world. Reynolds organized bizarre fan clubs, encouraging members to burn candles and chant sophomoric incantations, and with fellow DJ Danny Neaverth recorded the novelty hit, "Rats in My Room" (Swan,1963). Reynolds pioneered the garish style of 1990s shock rock, later championed by KRZ's Jumping Jeff Walker. An *Encyclopedia Britannica* article credited to Ben Fong-Torres read:

> In 1963, he returned to Buffalo, New York, where he worked at WKBW, the powerhouse station whose signal reached two-thirds of North America. Mixing traditional Top 40 histrionics with rants and raves about anyone who had upset him—be it his boss or his listeners—he became a sensation and moved on to stations in Cleveland and Detroit.

Reynolds was a Pied Piper who swayed rebellious teenagers listening on their transistor radios. According to David Hinckley, New York *Daily News* "On the Radio" columnist:

> Reynolds was one of the great personality jocks of that age, herding listeners into his "Royal Order of the Night People." He helped boost significant artists like the Four Seasons. He helped make a Top-10 hit out of "Wild Weekend" (Swan, 1962), an instrumental by a Buffalo band called The Rockin' Rebels, the theme song for his pal and fellow Buffalo DJ Tom Shannon before Reynolds picked it up.

Musicologist LinDee Rochelle, exploring the myth that Reynolds broke "Timothy" while at WKBW, said:

You got me curious on this one. I looked all through my notes for my interview with Joey and could not find that (1) he was at WKBW in 1971 and (2) that he broke the record. So, I did what any curious cat would do—I went straight to the source. Joey confirmed that he was at Philadelphia's WIBG in April 1971, and he does not recall breaking 'Timothy' but loves telling the story of breaking The Four Seasons' 'Sherry' (Vee-Jay, 1962).

After Reynolds left WKBW, he celebrated a spectacular fourteen-year run (1996-2010) on New York's WOR-710 AM. Sadly, April 2, 2010, signaled the end and the final song Reynolds played was Lou Christie's "Beyond the Blue Horizon" (Three Brothers, 1973). George Noory's *Coast to Coast*, an enormously popular show dabbling in UFOs and paranormal themes like Sheppton, replaced him.

Others helped open doors for "Timothy," and, according to researcher Davie Gordon, "Timothy" was first issued in early 1970, got played in a few markets, but didn't take off nationally:

In late 1970, a Scepter promo man who believed in the record 'pitched it to WKBW in Buffalo in preference to the new B. J. Thomas single he was supposed to be plugging.' So Scepter re-serviced the record, which started being picked up by stations in major markets, including WCFL in Chicago, who had it as their 'Pick Hit of The Week.' At that point, the song had yet to take off nationally, but AM radio stations, quick to spot a poppy and novel tune, began placing the piece into regular rotation.

Scepter A&R man Glen Robbins frequently visited the offices of WKBW, promoting Scepter artists through free records and promotional giveaways. At the time, his specific assignment was to promote BJ Thomas's "No Love at All" (Scepter,1971) but, surprisingly, began to hype "Timothy," believing that it was the more commercial of the two. Robbins' success combined savvy marketing skills, inside contacts, and a hard-to-define sixth sense.

CULTURAL ANOMALY

"Timothy's" premise was about creating controversy. It wasn't about the inevitability of death or the meaning of life, but about implied flesh-eating, stirring a graphic visual in the minds of millions of teenagers, ears glued to their transistor radios. "Timothy" was rhythmic, cryptic, and slathered with the requisite "yuk factor," the fetid domain of Chaucer's tales and adolescence, what became the Bevis and Butthead crowd. What began as an inside joke morphed into a robust, compelling yarn. Although it wasn't Rupert Holmes's magnum opus, it provoked over a million teens to reach into their wallets and purses, handing over crisp dollar bills for a copy of "Timothy."

WABC-AM

Success was a two-edged sword. After deciphering the juicy lyrics, big stations, like New York City powerhouse WABC-AM, refused to play the record. Scepter Records started a rumor that "Timothy" was a mule to get the stench of cannibalism out and jumpstarted the song into the Top 20. That was a lie. "Timothy" wasn't a mule; he was a man of flesh and bone, but Scepter thought that if you repeat something enough times, people will start to believe. Think of George Orwell's 1984.

"Timothy" was a cultural anomaly belonging to another era. It was a retro period existing before the Internet, Twitter, Facebook, iPods, cell phones, and other technological devices redefined the teenage wasteland. "Timothy's" word-of-mouth pseudo-controversy would not be possible in today's cyber optic and the digitized world of instantaneous communications.

SHEPPTON-ONEIDA

The 1963 mining disaster occurred at the Oneida #2 mine shaft and not in nearby Sheppton. Somebody got the name of what the Associated Press called "one of the top stories of the year" wrong, and "Timothy," to this very day, has become forever associated with Sheppton. One can argue about whether Holmes knew about Sheppton. Holmes said that he knew nothing about the mine disaster and learned about Sheppton only after "Timothy" was on the charts. He maintains that his song was purely an experiment in musical fantasy:

> If I had known about that at the time, I probably never would have written the song because I don't want to make fun of something tragic. I sadly found out that there was a parallel in reality, but only after the fact. It never occurred to me that there could be anything quite like that. It's one of those things that I wish would go away, but I have to live with it.

Although Holmes has consistently stated that he did not know about the Sheppton mining disaster, in an article titled "The Truth About 'Timothy,'" conducted in 2013 on the 50th anniversary of the mining disaster, he told Hazleton Standard-Speaker reporter Kelly Monitz:

> It is possible that the (Sheppton) incident was filed away somewhere in my subconscious and popped up subliminally during the writing of the tune,

unbeknownst to my conscious mind. But my suspicion is that this is just an uncanny and unearthly coincidence.

The connection to Sheppton was an ambiguous, murky corridor of half-truths and conjecture. And, as often happens, three groups emerged: the first believed there was a connection, the second did not, and the third could care less either way. Jerry Hludzik belonged to the first group and told Hazleton's *Standard-Speaker* writer Ed Socha:

> Rupert Holmes always said it doesn't have anything to do with the Sheppton disaster, but I think it does.

The Buoy's ode to cannibalism is connected to Sheppton's urban legend, pronounced a "continuous, collective hallucination," an out-of-body experience, a miracle by Pope John XXIII, and proof of life after death. Sheppton has become a popular topic on paranormal programs, including *Midnight in the Desert, Exploring the Bizarre,* and *Australia's Mysterious Universe. Fate Magazine* described Sheppton as "unmatched in the annals of psychic research," and the old-timers, who are still alive, simply call it the Coal Region Hoodoo.

46

LONG ROAD HOME

Like Huntington Beach surfers, they rode the waves of expectation, hanging ten, wiping out, and suffering the crash of unfulfilled promise. And then they paddled back, screaming against the foaming tide. They were young and ambitious downtown singers, dancing at the palace of Scepter, Polydor, and Ransom, Epic, Columbia, and MCA. The Buoys, Jerry-Kelly and Dakota, were survivors. Their journey, one of sunny days and rainy days, too, ringing loud with Longfellow's warning, "that into each life some rain must fall."

As we listened to their music and followed their careers, we all asked the same questions. Could a local band break out and make it nationally, and, if so, how would that success look?

School is now in session.

Success begins with ideas and dreams. Everything builds upon a foundation, and everything builds upon everything else. One must be ready, willing, and able to forge ahead, with the required competence and confidence, wearing the armor of resilience.

It is a dangerous pathway, wrought with unexpected pitfalls and anticipated detours: a road not for those lacking strength or patience. Very few travel as solitary horsemen, as we need help from others. We cannot do it on our own. Bill Baughman, Bob O'Connell, C. Michael Wright, and Julian Gill helped The Buoys during the early days. And other essential individuals serendipitously happened to be at the right place and at the right time. George Graham and Shadoe Steele helped with demos, Tom Fox got them gigs, and Michael Stahl, a vagabond traveling in Dakota's circle of empathy, hooked them up with Seraphine and Queen. The highly accomplished Stahl had worked as the sound engineer for Michael Jackson, Chicago, Queen, and Kenny Rogers, but exemplified so much more, said Bill Kelly:

Everything good that ever came to my career before moving to Nashville was because of Michael. He was our best friend, and he was our most prominent cheerleader. Behind the counsel, he was brilliant, and Claire Brothers used him like crazy. Because Michael was our sound man, Dakota sounded great every night on the Queen Tour.

During those first four dates when Dakota auditioned for the Game Tour, Stahl mastered the soundboard, bringing out Dakota's best sound quality, and making them technically as good as Queen. He was good to them, but they were good to others, as well. Through their interpretation of his song "Timothy," The Buoys advanced the career of Rupert Holmes through the gift of notoriety, as explained by The Glass Prism's Lester T. Verano:

> The Buoys helped Rupert have a successful career in the music world. Rupert's idea of doing a song that's controversial worked; however, I firmly believe that it was Bill Kelly's voice that made all the difference in the world.

A community of musicians recognizes Bill Kelly's vocal prowess. "Bill Kelly had an amazing voice, period," offered Bob Gryziac in the ultimate acknowledgment to a former bandmate. Sterling Koch only required one descriptive word, "Awesome! Bill had a fantastic voice, and he and Jerry could harmonize like Stills and Nash. As I got better as a musician myself, I came to appreciate their abilities all the more." Bill Kelly's vocals were high-pitched and soaring, reaching peaks of rock elegance that others could only dream of—"one of the greatest lead vocalists of all time," according to Rupert Holmes. An Internet blogger and huge fan, Souldeep 69, remarked:

> Once in a while in life, two things come fortuitously together to make magic. I've always thought that the marriage of the song "Timothy" with the voice and style of lead singer Bill Kelly was one of those magical combinations. I think Bill's a great singer, but to this very day, he never sounds better than when he sings "Timothy." That magic is still there after almost fifty years. And he can still hit and hold those notes. Thanks to Rupert Holmes and Billy Kelly for creating one of my favorite things ever in pop music.

SONGWRITER'S VULNERABILITY

Leo Tolstoy wrote in War and Peace, "The strongest of all warriors are these two, Time and Patience." Tolstoy was correct. The universe has a way of unfolding, revealing its truth in a sacred timetable that can never be altered or perverted.

It was always about patience and timing. Steve Fermanski, along with Robert "Shadow" Shumbres, Bob Hammond, Mike Paradise, and Jim Dietz was a member of Bicycle, one of the region's first rock acts. Frustrated with unfulfilled promises, Furmanski quit The Buoys to play with Eddie Day and TNT. He then rejoined The Buoys in 1977 and said:

> I didn't tour with the Buoys. After I did 'Timothy,' being young and dumb, I
> left the band. To this day, I regret that move. That was my biggest mistake. I
> should have stayed there with the Buoys.

Nothing ever happens until it's time. Chris Hanlon came to that conclusion, as well, when he said that if "Timothy" had been released in the major markets simultaneously, it would have been a Top Ten million-seller. Some twenty years later, after the release of their masterpiece album, and with the gift of hindsight, Jerry Hludzik broke it all down:

> I feel that *Runaway* was just as good as anything that was on the radio. I
> believe that, but it's all about politics and timing. It's about how much money,
> promotional dollars your label will throw in, and how far they're going to go to
> bat for you. And if they don't, you're just a tax write-off. So you can't take that
> personally.

Success takes timing as much as it takes courage, and make no mistake, being a creative songwriter requires the courage and fortitude to protect oneself from the distant storm of criticism. It brings inner strength to battle the tentacles of self-doubt. Although viewed as a successful musician, when interviewed by the *Baltimore Evening Sun*'s Michael Wentzel, Los Angeles' songwriter Tom Jans, pondered, "I wonder if I'll ever make it." He had already written his classic "Loving Arms," covered by countless artists including Elvis, while Dakota recorded "When the Rebel Comes Home" and "Workin' Hot," two of Jan's compositions.

Songwriters explore the pain and contradictions of everyday life, making symmetry out of disorder, discovering the music within the chaos. They give meaning to a world that sometimes punishes those worthy of forgiveness and rewards those who least deserve it. Hludzik and Kelly wrote songs advocating perseverance and survival. Tom Borthwick said that "All of Jerry's songs had messages. The lyrics were all pretty personal for him." Hludzik penned songs like "Last Standing Man," "Somebody's Else's Dream," and "You Can Be." You can make it if you try became Dakota's mantra, repeated in songs like "If It Takes All Night," "Heaven or Hell," and "Angry Men," inspired words of determination, similar to the Grateful Dead's, "I will get by, I will survive," on "Touch of Gray" #9 (Arista, 1987).

The Hludzik and Kelly compositions were rich and multi-layered. They were not basic three-chord progressions regurgitating the A-E-D, D-C-G, or C-F-G chords that every garage band learns. Hludzik and Kelly could have stayed with the CSN&Y format, claiming it as their own, but they opted to venture into newer frontiers. They could have jumped on the drug bandwagon and wrote pro- or anti-drug songs but chose to craft their unique sound, and that took courage.

Dakota's songs flowed with lyrics defining their essence. It was central to their philosophy, reflected in phrases like "Ride into battle," "Rewrite history," and "No time for indecision." In addition, they verbalized upbeat messages, shared by their Cleveland pal, Frank Zappa, who said:

> None of us have the promise of tomorrow. God forbid, if this is my last day on this beautiful earth, it won't be spent listening to some news person telling me how rotten we are or how rotten life is. I'm going out and seeing how beautiful life is.

Life is good when we dare to live it, and Kelly acknowledged the fortitude that defined his partnership with Hludzic when interviewed by Alan K. Stout on *Music on the Menu:*

> Jerry and I were, if nothing else, tenacious. I've never been one to give up on a goal that I had and have never given up on anything. So the best partner I could have had would be somebody like Jerry, who not only did not understand the concept of giving up but was a pit bull about it. When he had something in his head that he wanted to get or had to have, get out of the way, he was that relentless.

Revealing their inner truths, songwriters visit universal themes of sorrow and heartbreak, emotions at the core of popular music. Pain has always torn at the heart of the tortured artist, punishing individuals like Charles Baudelaire, Vincent van Gogh, and Sylvia Plath and inflicting suffering upon musicians like Judy Garland, Billie Holiday, and Tim Harden. Dylan's "Idiot Wind" expressed his contempt for ex-wife Sarah, while Eric Clapton's "Layla" proclaimed his love for Patty Boyd, begging her to leave her husband, George Harrison. John Lennon's primal scream was painfully heard on "Mother," while songwriters like Brian Wilson, Lucinda Williams, and Melissa Etheridge revealed the hurt at the core of their songs. "Timothy" writer, Rupert Holmes, explained his songwriting style while addressing his vulnerability:

> My songs are dangerous for me; they are very specific; I'm out of a limb because I can't hide behind any kind of obscurity. I take a chance when I write these songs because I say exactly what I mean.

Arguing that it's too easy to hide behind symbolism, he defended his lyrical specificity when interviewed by *The Charlotte Observer*'s David Earl:

> I'm not a symbolic writer; I don't write stream of consciousness. I don't write about the shadows in the corners of the smoke rings of the echoes of the distant visions of my past.

UNIQUE SOUND

Years later, in the land of waxing moons and Joshua trees, Dakota created music with melodic grooves and secondary rhythms, a blend of AOR power and balance, assault and retreat. Unknown to many American fans, the band attracted an impressive following in Europe, thanks partly to the reviews of French rock journalist Frederic Slama. During the 1970s and 1980s, Slama wrote for some of the most prominent European magazines:

> I grew up listening to Dakota, and they were one of my favorite bands during my youth. Over the years, I bought every Dakota album, including their solo ones. We were, in fact, label mates on Escape Music, where they released *Mr. Lucky* and *The Last Standing Man*, and I released several of my AOR CDs as well.

The lead vocals and harmonies and the dual guitars and keyboard sweeps comprised their sound. Kelly said, "We like to think that our harmonies are like a knife's edge, a one-two punch that took fifteen years to develop." But what got everyone's rapt attention was their uniqueness, something they claimed as their own and not somebody else's. Explained Hludzik:

> We try to write songs that relate to many people, and we're trying to keep away from sounding like any other group. If we're going to establish a name for ourselves, I want to do it with our unique type of music. I don't want to cash in on disco or whatever, just to break in.

But, not to digress (or argue with Mr. Hludzik), note many bands successfully cashed in on the disco craze. The list includes The Rolling Stones' "Miss

You" (Rolling Stones, 1978), Rod Steward's "Da Ya Think I'm Sexy?" (Warner Bros, 1978) and "Passion" (Warner Bros, 1980), Paul McCartney and Wings' "Goodnight Tonight" (Columbia, 1979), David Bowie's "Let's Dance" (EMI America, 1983), and Blondie's "Heart of Glass" (Chrysalis, 1979) and "Rapture" (Chrysalis,1981).

Not everyone agreed, and the opposing opinions were as stormy as Plato debating Aristotle. Tom Fox, a business-minded pragmatist, believed the duo could have performed originals while throwing in danceable cover songs. On the other hand, the idealistic Hludzik and Kelly thought they had the drive and imagination to write their songs, which was what they did, despite an unexpected offer from the Pure Prairie League.

PURE PRAIRIE LEAGUE

Sharing the Stone Balloon stage with Pure Prairie League (PPL), Dakota was the perfect fit. As the Buoys, they had amassed an impressive repertoire of high harmony country-rock songs, including those sung by PPL. Moreover, the two bands had a relationship. The Buoys shared a bill for a Harrisburg, Virginia, country-rock show at James Madison College in the early days of their career, featuring PPL and The Nitty Gritty Dirt Band. Years later, on that night in Newark, Delaware, PPL played a two-hour set with celebrated lead singer and multi-instrumentalist Vince Gill (vocals, guitars, mandolin, banjo, fiddle). The twenty-one-year-old Gill was hired in September 1978 and performed the lead vocals on "Let Me Love You Tonight" (Casablanca, 1980). Gill intended to leave PPL and start a solo career, which presented an exciting business proposition for Dakota. Bill Stevenson recounted the incident in his Stone Balloon book:

> The day after the concert, Bill Kelly and Jerry Hludzik met Pure Prairie League and their management for lunch in Newark. Bill and Jerry were offered the chance to replace Vince Gill in Pure Prairie League, as Vince was about to embark on a solo career.

Replacing Vince Gill would be challenging; however, being offered the chance was one of their proudest moments. Gill's career was stellar, a superstar in every way, from his guitar licks to his honeyed voice. Gill came up through the bluegrass scene and joined Pure Prairie League in the late 1970s before launching his Grammy-winning solo career in the mid-1980s. He turned down an invitation to join Dire Straits but in 2017 agreed to join the reformed Eagles after Glenn Frey passed.

They would meet up again when Dakota played as the opening act for Pure Prairie League's "Something in the Night Tour 1981." The bands played in front of 2,200 country-rock fans assembled in the King's College gymnasium. The now 24-year-old Vince Gill provided the lead vocals with harmonies by keyboardist Mike Connors and bassist Mike Reilly. According to former *Citizen's Voice* music critic Jerry Kishbaugh, it was "the first concert in Wilkes-Barre since the infamous Blue Oyster Cult riot at the 109th Armory in September 1980." In his review of the concert, Kishbaugh observed:

> Dakota showed it is more than an opening act by delivering mesmerizing harmonies complemented with solid instrumental backing. Jerry Hludzik and Bill Kelly alternated on singing leads and did the same when dishing out guitar licks. Bill McHale joined with Hludzik and Kelly for precision three-part harmonies, while the boys (no pun intended) produced a fine synchronization with guitars and keyboards.

The Buoys embraced the country-rock sounds of CSN&Y, Poco, Firefall, and similar groups. With perfect three-part harmonies, their rendition of "Judy Blue Eyes" was always a crowd favorite, but, while evolving, they stood at the crossroads, sharing in the Clash dilemma, "Should I stay, or should I go?" They could have easily stayed with country rock and expanded upon it, or they could have joined the Pure Prairie League and rode their commercial coattails. Dakota's decision to take their chances and create their original sound purposely. Bill Stevenson said that Hludzik told him that if the Pure Prairie League offer had come a month sooner, he and Kelly might have jumped at it but decided, instead, to go in another direction and write and perform their songs.

After many years of reflection, former Buoys manager Tom Fox believed that Hludzik and Kelly could have gone further if they had compromised on their dream:

> After Bill and Jerry left, they had a lot of opportunities to make it. I think they blew it because they were so hard-nosed about writing their music. That was the whole argument with the band. We would still do our music and the cover songs and make $1,500 to $2,000 a night. We had a formula, and we were successful.

Professional musician and former Boxtops-Dakota member Lou Cossa argued that their song selection should have been less highbrow and more recognizably commercial:

There was never a 'Brown Eyed Girl' in there. There was never a 'Mustang Sally.' The songs and lyrics were sometimes a tad too cerebral, and they went on too long.

Nonetheless, Dakota's over-extended cerebral musicality was one of choice. Hludzik and Kelly believed in themselves and, wanting to be true to themselves, were unwilling to accept "somebody else's dream." As a result, they have always worn the cloak of the iconoclastic rebel, marching to the beat of their drummer, making their own way.

ONLY FOUR ACTS

The Stone Balloon's Bill Stevenson boasted that he possessed the ability to identify a band with future potential, quipping, "if a band has talent, that hungry look in their eyes, and an attitude that drives them to seek perfection, they will be great." Inscribed upon his list were four acts that he endorsed, The Hooters, Jack of Diamonds, the A's, and Dakota.

Bursting with confidence, The Buoys and Dakota rode the carousel, reaching for the brass ring. They bewitched our Gypsy souls with songs laughing in our heads, with voices that knew us better than we knew ourselves. *Get Back* film director, Peter Jackson, reflecting on the works of The Beatles, spoke of the timeless and significant joy their music gave us:

> The Beatles are only the icons they are because the music was so majestically good. I'm not a musicologist. That's not where I come from. But all I would say is, no matter if it's two tracks or four tracks or eight tracks, there's a joy in the songs that they sang. In decades and decades to come, it will never be dulled. It will never be suppressed. That joy, that infectious joy, is part of the human psyche now.

INFECTIOUS JOY

Those words could have easily been written by Brad Patton, Allen K. Stout, or Jack Smiles addressing The Buoys, Jerry-Kelly, and Dakota. Those hometown bands spoke to us in a way that only music can, with infectious joy, now ingrained into our regional psyche. It was a great ride, and what a ride it was. One of their biggest fans, Judi Orgie-Hoffer, saw The Buoys perform countless times and said:

> I thought that for a band from Northeastern Pennsylvania, like the Buoys, success was good for this area. I don't think any other group ever duplicated their

success from this area. I was a bit young when 'Timothy' and 'Give Up Your Guns' came out because I didn't start going to dances until 1972. The first time I ever heard them play was at a dance at the West Pittston Armory. I was fourteen. We would see the Buoys play two or three times a month, sometimes more.

Observing their musical odyssey, Musician Bernie Garzio, who played with Hybrid Ice as well as with Bill Kelly, said:

Knowing these guys were local musicians and watching them become the local legends they became was awesome. It made many local musicians realize if you worked your butt off, you could also do it. It didn't matter that small coal patch towns surrounded us. Jerry Hludzik was from Jeddo, Pennsylvania, and Bill Kelly, with the amazing voice, was from the Wilkes-Barre area.

Drummer Eli Hludzik realized that what they did was about as probable as a long shot coming from behind to win at the Pocono Downs racetrack. He said:

Everybody respected Dakota, The Buoys, and Jerry-Kelly because they broke out of this area. They're like hometown heroes, and they influenced many different groups and a lot of other people. But, unfortunately, the statistics of being able to do that are super small because there is so much crap that can derail you at any moment, whether it's the marketing department or a record executive being an asshole. The whole record industry game is super nefarious.

THE DAKOTA LEGACY

The Buoys, Jerry-Kelly, and Dakota released eleven albums and charted several times on *Billboard*. In addition, they were significant proponents of Westcoast/ AOR music; their *Runaway* album is one of the best representations of that genre. The matter of a proper legacy will continue to be discussed and evaluated, but for Eli Hludzik, it touches on altruism:

What does an artist want their legacy to be? You're either in it for the fame, and the booze and all that, or you're in it because it's the only thing you know how to do. It's the one thing that you can use to serve the universe.

When asked about the Dakota Legacy, Kelly, who has reaped his share of varied success, refused to accept any accolades:

It's difficult for me to talk about having a significant impact on our profession or our fans. We had our impact, yes, but we weren't the Beatles. I understand

Drummer Eli Hludzik.

that. Our fans cared about our music and were special to us. I only hope that we were also something special to them.

And they were something special. Our lads had accepted the dare, rolled the dice, and watched as their numbers came up. There's was a lesson in physics that Brian May could have calculated. They had been betrayed and knocked down so many times, the only place to go was up. "You take the rough with the smooth," as Eric Clapton once said. It was euphoria, and it was madness, the most exciting, most eventful time of their lives. It was as much art as it was pain, the type of pain that nobody escapes, suffered by every one of us.

Like ol' blue eyes, they did it their way. It was their story, never to be dupli-cated or replicated by Clove, The Badlees, Breaking Benjamin, The Glass Prism,

Hybrid Ice, Lenore O'Malley, Ralph, Synch, or anyone else. It was never about the destination. It was always about the incredible journey that took them to places never known before. In the brilliant songs that become markers for our lives, we saw a landscape of deserts and seas magically bringing us closer to the stars. And then, as all things must come to an end, linking arms, stepping to the center of the stage, taking their bows for one final curtain call, and with their music still ringing in our ears, we said farewell to The Buoys, Jerry-Kelly, and Dakota.

They have now left the building . . .

47

JAMMIN' FOR JERRY

Jerry Hludzik was diagnosed with Frontotemporal dementia (FTD) around 2015. FTD is an uncommon brain disorder that affects the areas of the brain controlling social skills, decision-making, and language. Some experience dramatic personality changes and become socially inappropriate, impulsive, or emotionally indifferent. The disease is often misdiagnosed as a psychiatric problem or as Alzheimer's disease. Still, FTD tends to occur at a younger age than Alzheimer's, usually beginning

Jerry G. Hludzik, the last standing man.

between 45 and 65. Despite his sickness, Hludzik did not know the meaning of "quit," and courageously forged on, as Kelly explained:

> Even as Jerry was beginning to show the early signs of his illness, he would call me, and we would talk for hours about the 'next record.'

Eli Hludzik and Bill Kelly organized an event to honor Hludzik's legacy and raise money for medical treatments. Genetti's Hotel and Conference Center in Wilkes-Barre hosted Jammin' For Jerry on April 26, 2018. Writing about the event, Eli said:

> Sadly, this will most likely be the last time Jerry will be performing, so let's give him a proper send-off; while he still can remember the feeling of joy he brought to you, come back to him.

Bands performing included Archangel, Bill Kelly and Jerry Hludzik, Dakota, Danny Seraphine, Flaxy Morgan, Idol Kings, Stonebridge, and Strawberry Jam. In addition, Dakota and Pony Express guitarist, Jon Lorance, was there to pay respects to his friend and to offer thanks:

> Thirty-two years ago, I played on my first Dakota song, 'Give love for Christmas.' Since then, we've made all kinds of music, and I'm proud of it all. We've played in the trenches of clubs to make a buck, doing a duo with country, classic rock, and in the studio. You saw something in me which you nurtured. You're my hero. Thank you, partner. I love you, and let's do it some more. I loved hearing your voice with Kelly again.

There were an estimated one thousand people in attendance. Kelly, who flew in from Nashville, addressed the event and his "brother in arms" in a Facebook post:

> The dust has finally started to settle after the most amazing week in Pennsylvania. To everyone who could attend the 'Jammin for Jerry' event, there are no words to express how grateful we all feel. My best friend is going thru an incredible challenge, and my heart aches for him and his wonderful wife, Annie. But the 'Valley with a Heart' came through so far beyond what any of us could have imagined and made me so proud to say this is where I came from. Jerry is an amazing talent and a wonderful man, and there's no telling what is in store for him next, both health-wise and music-wise. Time will tell.

Almost two years later, to the day, Jerry Hludzik died. It was Easter Sunday, April 12, 2020. When word exploded across the internet about his death, there was an outpouring of love and celebration, honoring the legacy of this great musician and hometown hero. AOR specialist Frederic Slama highly regarded Hludzik as an influential musician, saying:

> Jerry was one of the most talented men in music, a kind soul, and a great family man. He has influenced thousands of musicians, and his legacy will live on forever. A great man I'm honored to have met is gone but never will be forgotten. Rest in peace, my friend.

Jerry G. Hludzik, the last standing man, was an individual whose personality exuded determination, perseverance, and survival. Eli Hludzik offered:

> I hope that people will continue to listen to his music, be moved by it and that his message will still prevail through the decades.

Jerry's music touched many of us, and his optimism gave us hope. His tombstone reads Musician. Singer. Songwriter. Loving Family Man and Friend.

Jerry Hludzik's tombstone.

ACKNOWLEDGMENTS

Portions of the chapter "The Buoys" and "Rupert Holmes" have appeared in *Timothy: Northeastern Pennsylvania's First Music Publication* (1981).

Copyright information follows for the lyrics quoted in this volume and is gratefully acknowledged.

"Back to Me," written by Rick Manwiller and Jerry G. Hludzik. Copyright 2003 by Hahdaddy Productions. All rights reserved.

"Bring the Boys Home," written by Angelo Bond, Greg Perry, and General Johnson. Copyright 1971 by Gold Forever Music, Inc. (BMI). All rights reserved.

"Give Up Your Guns," written by Rupert Holmes and Danny Jordan. Copyright 1971 by Moonbeam Publishing Corp. (ASCAP). All rights reserved.

"Mama Ubangi-Bangi," written by Charles E. Calhoun. Copyright 1962 by Massa Music. (BMI). All rights reserved.

"Opposites Attract" was written by Oliver Leiber. Copyright 1989 by Virgin Music, Inc. (ACAP). Ollie Lieber Music (ASCAP). All rights reserved.

"The Battle Hymn of Lt. Calley," written by Julian Wilson and James M. Smith. Copyright 1971 by Shelby Singleton Music, Inc. (BMI). All rights reserved.

"The Last Standing Man," written by Rick Manwiller and Jerry G. Hludzik. Copyright 1997 by Escape Music Ltd. All rights reserved.

Timothy," written by Rupert Holmes. Copyright 1971 by Plus Two Music (ASCAP). All rights reserved.

"Timothy," written by Rupert Holmes. Copyright 1971 by Jordan-Herman-Holmes Publishing Inc., and Universal Music Corporation (ASCAP). All rights reserved.

"Touch of Gray," written by Jerry Garcia and Robert Hunter. Copyright 1987 by Ice Nine Publishing Company, Inc. (ASCAP). All rights reserved.

"Stranded in The Jungle," written by Ernestine Smith, James Escar Johnson, and Al Curry. Copyright 1956 by Shag Music Publishing Co. All Rights

Owned and Controlled Exclusively by Peer International Corporation. (BMI). All rights Reserved.

All photos of The Buoys, Jerry-Kelly, and Dakota courtesy of Bill Kelly Music Productions.

All Satsop River Fair and Tin Cup Races Festival photos courtesy of John Caldbick.

Cover design Danielle Crockett Design Co.

Thanks to Ted Billy, Emeritus Professor of English, and Christine Curley, Director of the McBride Memorial Library, for their command of the English language and proofreading expertise.

I am indebted to the collective memories of the following individuals, without whom this project would have lacked those fantastic shades of gray and to the musicians who offered their shared expertise: Alan Basala, Mike Boback, Jim Broyles, Jim Cullen, Dave Eisenhower, Rusty Foulke, George Fox, John Gonska (aka Sonny California), Bob Hock, David Allen Karchner, Sterling Koch, Richie Kossuth, Paul Metzer, Joe Nardone Sr., Bob O'Connell, Charles "Rudi" Phillips, Rick Richards, Barry Rogers, Ronnie Sando, Robert Shumbres, Jay Smar, Billy Angelo Stella, Mike Vale, Lester T. Verano, and Jeff Willoughby.

Many thanks to fans Robert Gryziac, Irven Lorance, Judi Orgie-Hoffer, Leann Paul, Patty Phillips, J. Michael Reagan, Fred Takacs, Michael Slavich, Avaline Stees, and Bob Welby, as well as, organizations including Fred Beldin's All Music Guide, Classic Bubblegum Music, www.Historylink.org, The Keystone Record Collectors, The Olympia Historical Society, The Pennsylvania Museum of Music and Broadcast History, and The Pennsylvania Music Society.

Much appreciation to Casey Kasem's *American Top 40* for introducing "Timothy" and The Buoys to America with his radio countdown.

I owe much to Shadoe Steele, who walked me through a Ph.D.'s worth of information on recording techniques, radio broadcast journalism, payola, and the inside scoop on Media Sound, WABC, and WVIA.

I am grateful to all of the Rock Journalists and Disc Jockeys who preserved our musical legacy, including Rich Appell, Gene Axton, Andy Bergey, Joe Butkiewicz, Richard Chisak, Roc Crumless, Jim Dino, Jim Drucker, Frank Dutton, Lance Evans, Joe Falatko, Brian Fulton, George Graham, Sue Henry, David Juncos, Jerry Kishbaugh, Michael Kuzmin, Jay Levan, Matt Mattei, Joe Middleton, Banana Joe Montione, Mike Naydock, Bill O'Boyle, Cary D. Pall, LinDee Rochelle, Ron Schacht, B. Derek Shaw, Jack Smiles, Allen K. Stout, L.A. Tarone, Bill Trousdale, Harry West, Bobby Vanderheyden, Jumpin' Jeff Walker, and Rod Wodaski.

And much appreciation to The Buoy's and Dakota "Inner Circle" for sharing their recollections: Duane Allen, Bill Bachman, Tom Borthwick, Fran Brozena, John Buckley, Lou Cossa, Jim Della Croce, Tom Fox, Steve Furmanski, Bernie Garzio, Bob Gryziac, Chris Hanlon, Eli M. Hludzik, Jerry J. Hludzic, Rupert Holmes, Bill Kelly, Carl Siracuse, Frederic Slama, and "Easy" Mark Tomeo.

Lastly, my apologies for any names I may have omitted. Profound gratitude to everyone who helped me navigate the fundamental changes and tempo shifts of this songbook. I hope I got at least some of it right!

Peace out.

REFERENCES

BLUE OYSTER CULT RIOT

41 Arrested, 20 Injured at riot During Rock Concert in Luzerne. 3. *Scranton Times-Tribune*

Anderson, J. (October 4, 1980). Tour boss to face more legal action. *Times Leader*, 3.

Biederman, H. (July 8, 1981). Rock Concert—Cops Alert, Crowd Behaves. *Citizen's Voice*, 15.

Furek, M.W. (October 4-5, 1980). The Blue Oyster Cult creates music for riot. *Time Out*, D-3.

Gruson, L. (August 9, 1986). 12 Are Charged With Smuggling tons of Cocaine. New York *Times*. Retrieved from https://www.nytimes.com/1986/08/09/us/12-are -charged-with-smuggling-tons-of-cocaine.html

Hart, J.M. (September 26, 1980). W-B Rock Concert Explodes Into Riot. *Scranton Tribune*, 1.

Hitchcock, J. (July 1, 1981). Rock returning to armory. *Times Leader*, 3.

Kishbaugh, J. (July 10, 1981). Off the Record: Motor City Madman Attracts 2,800 in Loud Show. *Citizen's Voice*, 36.

Reinhard, K. (August 17, 1986). Authorities Had their Eye on Cocaine Ring Suspect. *The Morning Call*. Retrieved from https://www.mcall.com/news/mc-xpm-1986 -08-17-2538181-story.html

Righi, L. (June 26, 1981). Fans irked as storm halts concert. *The Morning Call*, 9.

Rock group manager put on probation. (April 16, 1981). *Times Leader*, 7.

THE BUOYS

Beatles Hold Top 5 Chart Spots. Best Classic Bands. Retrieved from https://bestclas- sicbands.com/beatles-billboard-april-1964-4-4-18/

Beck, K. (February 28, 2015). Singer-picker Bill Kelly rocks across the decades. Leba- non, Tennessee The Wilson Post. Retrieved from https://www.wilsonpost.com /community/singer-picker-bill-kelly-rocks-across-the-decades/article_26a9fb3c -b336-51c9-bd33-b7c2ef8fc719.html

Beldin, F. (1971). The Buoys. All Music Guide. Retrieved from http://www.answers. com/topic/the-buoys-1971-album-by-buoys

'Buoys' set CSI concert. (September 9, 1971). *Twin Falls Times-News*, 6.

Butkiewicz, J. (January 31, 1993). Coming Home. *Times Leader*, D43.

Butkiewicz, J. (January 10, 1987). Local talent polishes up their acts. *Times Leader*, 38.

Butkiewicz, J. (November 29, 1991). Where the Buoys Are. *Times Leader*, 15.

Callaio, T. (April 15, 2018). Mark your calendar for special event honoring former area musician April 26. The Dallas Post. Retrieved from https://www.mydallaspost.com/uncategorized/33013/mark-your-calendar-for-special-event-honoring-former-area-musician-april-26

Chintala, J. (1996). The Buoys. DISCoveries. Retrieved from http://www.dakota jerrykelly.com/The%20Last%20Standing%20Man/the_buoys_by_j__chin.htm

Diana, M. (June 27, 1971). Today's Youth: Miles Questions Popularity of Rock Groups. *Newport News Daily Press*, 23.

Dino, J. (July 6, 1987). Hludzik, Kelly end 17-year relationship. *Hazleton Standard-Speaker*, 16.

Dino, J. (July 24, 2005). Hludzik-Kelly'spartnership began in the '70s with Buoys. *Hazleton Standard-Speaker*, 52.

Donnelly, D. (May 17, 1971). Dave Donnelly's Hawaii. *Honolulu Star-Bulletin*, 4.

Doughty, R. (January 5, 1971). Youth Beat: The National Report on What's Happening. *Wilkes-Barre Times Leader*, 13.

Evans, L. (November 20, 1980). 'Buoys' Continue to Show Quality Rises to the Surface. *The Times-Tribune*, 25.

Evans, L. (December 16, 1983). Record Artists Follow Various Routes in Quest of a Hit. *The Scranton Times*, 19.

Furek, M.W. (December 22-23, 1979). Disaster meant success for Buoys. *Time Out*, C-3

Furek, M.W. (August 1991). Rock N' Roll: The Buoys Twenty Years Later. *Metro*, 17.

Furek, M.W. (October 27-28, 1979). 'Toyz' strictly a fast, metallic '60s group. *Time Out*, D-10.

Harada, W. (July 15, 1971). Wayne Harada's On the Record. *Honolulu Advertiser*, 33.

Homecoming for Jerry-Kelly; Duo poised for record smash. (April 18, 1978). *Hazleton Standard-Speaker* 24.

Kishbaugh, J. (February 12, 1993). Off the Record: After a 15- year absence, Buoys return to the Valley. *Citizen's Voice*, 35.

Kishbaugh, J. (March 11, 1984). Off the Record: Bill Kelly toughing it out on the Nashville music scene, *Citizen's Voice*, 29.

Kishbaugh, J. (November 20, 1992). Off the Record: Kelly now a good ole' buoy. *Citizen's Voice*, 27.

Kishbaugh, J. (June 19, 1981). Off the Record: Musical Odyssey of Bassist Bob Gryziec. *Citizen's Voice*,23.

Lackawanna County Races: Commissioner: (May 5, 2011). The Triboro Banner. Retrieved from http://triborobanner.com/news/1.1141147

Loftus, B.S. (November 4, 1973). The Younger Set. *Times Leader*, 15.

McAuliffe, J. (January 21, 2016). Lifestyles: Manwiller remembered as a 'brilliant' musician. *The Times-Tribune*, C1.

Middleton, J. (December 31, 1970). The Buoys have a National Hit. *The Wyoming Valley Observer*, 1.

Banana Joe Montione. (November 13, 2020). RE: *Dinner Music* LP. Personal e-mail correspondence.

Rock Concert Will Feature 'Bloodrock.' (November 19, 1971). *Hazleton Standard-Speaker*, 22.

Rubin, N. (February 19, 1989). The 'Hall of Shame' elevates the common to infamy. *Times Leader*, 85.

Smiles, J. (November 29, 1992). Bill Kelly. Where on Earth Did You Go. *The Sunday Dispatch*, P2.

Smiles, J. (August 15, 2014). Former Buoys guitarist passes away at 63. *The Citizens Voice*. Retrieved from https://www.citizensvoice.com/news/former-buoys-guitarist -passes-away-at-63-1.1736272

Smiles, J. (August 12, 2018). Musician Bill Kelly returns to perform at Tomato Festival. *The Citizens Voice*, P9.

Stout, A.K. (April 18, 2020). Music on the Menu podcast interview with Bill Kelly.

Stout, A.K. (September 10, 2004). Nightlife: From the Buoys to Benjamin. *Times Leader*, 64.

Strubeck, D. (July 29, 1979). Sounds: The Buoys Are Back in Town. *Pittston Sunday Dispatch*, 49.

The Buoys—"Timothy." (September 1, 2020). Mental Itch. Retrieved from https:// mentalitch.com/the-buoys-timothy/

WOLF biography spotlights The Buoys. (November 22, 1999). *The Times Leader*, 27.

Wozniak, B.A. (November 12, 1967). Saint John's HS News: Halloween Dance. *Pittston Sunday Dispatch*, 43.

Yonki, D. (May 9, 1971) Teen Record Review. *Pittston Sunday Dispatch*, 30.

CENSORSHIP

A timeline of TV censorship. (August 1, 2007). CNN. Retrieved from http://edition. cnn.com/2007/LIVING/wayoflife/07/31/censorship/

Bozeka, J. (February 1, 2019). The Day "Louie, Louie" Was Deemed Pornographic. WHBC.com. Retrieved from https://www.whbc.com/the-day-louie-louie-was -deemed-pornographic/

Calley apologizes for role in My Lai massacre. (August 21, 2009). NBC News.com. Retrieved from http://www.nbcnews.com/id/32514139/ns/us_news-military/t /calley-apologizes-role-my-lai-massacre/#.Xm-w6i3MxBw

Drug Songs Banned on Airwaves. (March 7, 1971). *Brownsville Herald*, 12.

Campbell, S. (April 19, 1970). Sound All Editions from the underground. Phoenix, Arizona Republic, 191.

Eveleth, R. (May 23, 2013). The FBI Investigated the Song 'Louie Louie' for Two Years. Smithsonian Magazine. Retrieved from https://www.smithsonianmag.com /smart-news/the-fbi-investigated-the-song-louie-louie-for-two-years-78752777/

Furek, M.W. (October 2020). The Drug War's Censorship Weapon. *The Sober World*, 9 (10), 8 &10.

Publishers Say Tune Not Dirty at All. (February 8, 1964). *Billboard*, p. 4, & 57.

Shuster, A. (May 1, 1971). US Army Radio Bans Calley 'Battle Hymn.' *Arizona Daily Star*, 45.

The FBI Laboratory weighs in on the "dirty lyrics of "Louie Louie." (February 24, 2020). History.com. Retrieved from https://www.history.com/this-day-in-history/the-fbi-laboratory-weighs-in-on-the-dirty-lyrics-of-louie-louie

Turner, T., and Loder, K. I, Tina: My Life Story. New York: William Morrow and Company, 1986.

US Command Bans Song from Network. (July 18, 1971). *Lafayette Daily Advisor*, 26.

US Song Banned from Viet Radio. Piqua, *Ohio Daily Call*, 10.

Welch, D. (April 3, 2018). Why Jesus Christ Superstar is No Longer controversial. *World Religion News*. Retrieved from https://www.worldreligionnews.com/religion-news/jesus-christ-superstar-no-longer-controversial

Westheider, J.E. *Fighting on Two Fronts: African Americans and the Vietnam War*. New York City: New York University Press, 1997.

Wilcox, B. (November 21, 1970). 'Jesus Christ Superstar,' Rock-opera selling fast, banned on AM, played on FM. *The Miami News*, 9.

DAKOTA

AOR-The Colors of LA Review. (October 24, 2020). Myglobalmind.com. Retrieved from https://myglobalmind.com/2012/02/29/aor-the-colors-of-l-a-review/

Beck, K. (September 28, 2017) Singer-picker Bill Kelly rocks across the decades. *The Wilson Post*, 13.

Brown, D. (March 21, 1980). Dakota arrives with a vengeance. The University of Delaware Review, 1.

Boyanoski, J. (June 26, 1998). Dakota gets another bite at the apple. *Scranton Tribune*, 29.

Butkiewicz, J. (July 27, 1984). A new LP for rock's most unsung heroes. Can 'Runaway' undo the Dakota Curse? *Times Leader*, 35.

Butkiewicz, J. (December 1987). Banding together. For John Nasser, helping the needy is what 'Christmas' is all about. *Times Leader*.

Butkiewicz, J. (October 25, 1987). Extinct rock band Dakota dusts off some old tracks for a new album. *Times Leader*, 103.

Butkiewicz, J. (November 16, 1983). From bars to big-time: Magnum takes the step. *Times Leader*, 29.

Chisak, R. (July 5, 1987). 'Dakota' Makes Final Bow in Concert at Montage Mt. *Citizen's Voice*.

Chisak, R. (March 1981). Is There Life After the Garden? The Dakota-Queen Tour. Timothy: Northeastern Pennsylvania's First Music Publication.

Col Names Ellis Coast A&R VP. (December 7, 1974). *Record World*, 3.

Dakota—Deep 6 [2016 reissue]. (October 26, 2016.) Odayrox. Retrieved from https://0dayrox.org/2016/10/dakota-deep-6-reissue-2016.html

Dakota—Little Victories [2016 reissue]. (October 26, 2016.) Odayrox. Retrieved from https://0dayrox.org/2016/10/dakota-little-victories-2016-reissue.html

Dakota Runaway, 1984. (November 7, 2020). Melodic Hardrock.com. Retrieved from https://melodic-hardrock.com/reviews/dakota-runaway-1984/

Dino, J. (December 24, 2006). Hludzik hoping that Dakota can ride again in 2007. *Hazleton Standard-Speaker*, 47.

Dino, J. (May 3, 1998). It's Dakota, all grown up. *Hazleton Standard-Speaker*, 41.

Evans, L. (October 10, 1980). 'Dakota' Hits Rock 'n' Roll Heights in Hom3coming. *The Scranton Times*, 4.

Falatko, J. (April 7, 1980) Jerry Hludzik, Bill Kelly now lead 'Dakota.' *Hazleton Standard Speaker*, 17.

Furek, M.W. (March 22-23, 1980). Dakota: A chance for musical fame. *Time Out Magazine*, C-8 & 9.

Furek, M.W. (1981). Public Enemy Number One: Over the Wall. Timothy: Northeastern Pennsylvania's First Music Publication, 11.

Furek, M.W. (May 17-18, 1980). What's going to happen to music? *Time Out Magazine*, C-3.

Goodwin, D. (May 10, 1988). DA: Never heard of Driscoll until slaying. *The Ithaca Journal*, 1.

Hambrose, J. (November 23, 1986). Local Band's Album to Aid Area Homeless. *The Times-Tribune*, 28.

Hludzik, J.G. (November 4, 2020). *Sunny Days and Memories: The Jerry Hludzik and Bill Kelly Story*.

King, Pinger. (August 29, 1984). Cop Run Event. *The Times-Tribune*, 27.

Kishbaugh, J. (September 2, 1988). Off the Record: Hludzik-Wanko land tune on Oak Ridge Boys' album. *Citizen's Voice*, 28.

Kishbaugh, J. (April 10, 1981). Off the Record: League Concert: More Country Rock Than Bluegrass. *Citizen's Voice*, 39.

Kishbaugh, J. (January 9, 1981). Off the Record: Dakota Gets Losing Hand as Columbia Stacks Deck. *Citizen's Voice*, 28.

Kishbaugh, J. (August 1, 1980). Off the Record: 'Dakota' Waiting for its Turn in National Limelight. *Citizen's Voice*, 20.

Marcus, L. (August 23, 1984). Dakota's Run for Runaways May Become National Event. *Scranton Tribune*, 11.

Mattei, M. (April 24, 2018). Concert to benefit member of The Buoys, Dakota living with dementia. *Times Leader*. Retrieved from https://www.times leader.com/features/701156/concert-to-benefit-member-of-the-buoys-dakota -living-with-dementia

Morris, D. (July 26-27, 1980). Turntable: Dakota electric. *Time Out*, C-5.

Morse, S. (December 15, 1980). Roadie supreme rock shows now call for caravan. *The Paducah Sun*, 22.

Mullinax, G. (October 5, 1980). Ahhh, realizing the ultimate joy in rock 'n' roll. *Wilmington Morning News*, 53.

Mullinax, G. (March 23, 1980). Jerry-Kelly, now Dakota. *Wilmington News Journal*, E-3.

Sheffield, R. (September 2020). And in the End. *Rolling Stone*, 33.

Frederic Slama. (October 26, 2020). RE: Album Oriented Rock. Personal e-mail correspondence.

Socha, E. (July 23, 1980). Hludzik, 'Dakota' still seek success. *Hazleton Standard-Speaker*, 43.

Stout, A.K. (April 19, 1998). Back with raves. Dakota. Former Regional favorites and national recording artists release new album. *Times Leader*, 95.

Stout, A.K. (October 26, 2018). Memories of Mercury. *Times Leader*.

Stout, A.K. (April 18, 2020). Music on the Menu podcast interview with Bill Kelly.

Strubeck, D. (August 10, 1980). Sounds: Dakota Concert on 44. *Pittston Sunday Dispatch*, 24.

Ferrara, V. (January 20, 2008). Interview with Dakota (Jerry G. Hludzik). Hardnheavy. it. Retrieved from http://www.hardnheavy.it/sito/Interviste/Dakota/01Dakota_eng.html

West, CH (August 14, 2014). Distinctive Voices Blend Again. Reunited Dakota to release new album 'The Long Road Home' in September. *Citizen's Voice*, J14.

EL CAMINOS/ GLASS PRISM

Ankeny, J. (May 22, 2020) Glass Prism: Poe through the Glass Prism. AllMusic. Retrieved from https://www.allmusic.com/album/poe-through-the-glass-prism-mw0000842718

Fran Brozena. (May 24, 2020). Scepter Records. Personal phone interview.

Frank's Vinyl Museum presents. Poe Through the Glass Prism: Quote the Raven, "Oh My God!" Retrieved from http://franklarosa.com/vinyl/Exhibit.jsp?AlbumID=79&page=23

Furek, M.W. (1981). Back to the Roots with the El Caminos. Timothy: Northeastern Pennsylvania's First Music Publication.

Furek, M.W. (August 18-19, 1979). El Caminos starred at West Side. *Time Out*, C-12.

Glass Prism: An Interview with Tom Varano. (2008). '60s garagebands.com. Retrieved from http://www.60sgaragebands.com/glassprism.html

Les Paul. (2007) Rock and Roll Hall of Fame + Museum. Retrieved from http://www.rockhall.com/inductee/les-paul"'Louie'

Mc Cauliffe, J. (October 19, 2007). Reflections of Poe. *The Scranton Times-Tribune*.

Patton, B. (April 25, 2010). Glass Prism Shines Again. *Times Leader*, F1.

Shadoe Steele. (May 22, 2020). Broadcast Data Systems. Personal e-mail correspondence.

Shamanski, R. (June 5, 2008) The Glass Prism Through the Time Continuum. Electric City. Retrieved from http://www.ecweekend.com/features/story.asp?id=47018

The Open Paul Simon Biography. (2010). Retrieved from http://www.paul-simon.info/

Tom Varano. (February 8, 2010). RE: El Caminos and Glass Prism. Personal e-mail interview.

Varano, T. (2010). The Story of the El Caminos – Glass Prism. Retrieved from http://www.glassprismband.com/

"GIVE UP YOUR GUNS"

Dakota. (July 1984). MCA album liner notes.

Fallwell, M. (February 22, 1975). Country Music. Watch This Face: Tom Jans. The Indiana, Pennsylvania Gazette, 26.

Tom Fox. (July 2, 2020). RE: Holland visit. Personal phone interview.

Hosie, E. (February 6, 1976). Rompin' at the Savoy: A folksy evening. *The Berkeley Gazette*, 15.

Lakeyta M. Bonnette-Bailey. (September 9, 2020). RE: "Give Up Your Guns." Personal e-mail communications.

Leyde, T. (November 30, 1974). Tom Jans: Music Tender, Poignant. *Santa Maria Times*, 21.

Record Reviews. (November 20, 1971). Give Me Your Guns: The Buoys. *The Carlisle Sentinel*, 24.

Wentzel, M. (December 11, 1975). Tom Jans: Songs Filling His Childhood Like Toys. *Baltimore Evening Sun*, 25.

RUPERT HOLMES

Earl, D. (May 23, 1980). Small, Tangible Ideas. Rupert Holmes Vs. His Critics. *The Charlotte Observer*, 51.

Erlewine, S.T. Rupert Holmes: Artist Biography. AllMusic. Retrieved from https://www.allmusic.com/artist/rupert-holmes-mn0000364445/biography

Furek, M.W. (August 1991). Rock N' Roll: The Buoys Twenty Years Later. Rupert Holmes and the Story of Timothy. Metro, 17.

Furek, M.W. (October 11, 1980). Rupert Holmes remembers The Buoys. *Time Out*, D-4.

Furek, M.W. (March 1981). Rupert Holmes—The Pina Colada Man. Northeastern Penna's Adopted Son Comes Home to Crow. Timothy: Northeastern Pennsylvania's First Music Publication.

Lloyd, J. (October 27, 1974). This Is a Holmes Masterpiece. *The Philadelphia Inquirer*,118.

Rupert Holmes. (September 26, 1980). Bloomsburg Fair. Personal interview.

HYBRID ICE

Autry, P. (October 5, 2000). Danville's Hybrid Ice still a force. *Sunbury Daily Item*, 31.

Blackledge, K. (March 1, 2013). Former Journey lead man to sing with Hybrid Ice. *Danville News*, A4.

Blackledge, K. (June 28, 2012). Rusty Foulke still follows a dream. *Danville News*, A6.

Blackledge, K. (February 24, 2012). Survivor frontman to rock with Hybrid Ice. *Danville News*, B5.

Creasy, M. (September 29, 1983). Local band no overnight success. *Danville News*, 6.

Rusty Foulke. (July 17, 2021). RE: Hybrid Ice. Personal phone interview.

Furek, M. (May 24-25, 1980). Hybrid Ice returns from the south. *Time Out Magazine*, C-16.

Furek, M. (February 1989). "No Rules" Now for Hybrid Ice. *Pennsylvania Musician Magazine*, 9.

Hawkins, D. (February 6, 1987). Hybrid Ice playing hot on covers, works on LP. *Carlisle Sentinel*, C6.

Tomeo, M. (May 15, 1987). Hybrid Ice cuts hot album. *The Danville News*, 9.

Jeff Willoughby. (April 20, 2020). RE: Hybrid Ice. Personal interview.

THE JERRY-KELLY BAND

Chisak, R. (October 8, 1978). Record Whirl: Area Musicians Excited on Release of First Album. *Sunday Independent*, H-4.

Evans, L. (September 18, 1978). Going in Circles: Will History Repeat Itself? These Two Musicians Hope Not. *The Times-Tribune*, 17.

Falatko, J. (April 18, 1978) Homecoming for Jerry Kelly; Duo poised for record smash. *Hazleton Standard-Speaker*, 23.

Fessier, B. (March 11, 2016). Drummer Danny Seraphine seeking peace. *Palm Springs Desert Sun*, WE14.

Furek, M.W. (May 5-6, 1980). Jerry-Kelly to release second LP. *Time Out Magazine*, C-10.

Henry, S. (May 7, 1994). Radio Days: A mainstay celebrates 20 years. *Citizen's Voice*, 4.

Jerry J. Hludzik. (May 1980). "Future of music" personal interview.

Hunt, D. (November 24, 1978). Death Forces Chicago to Play A Different Tune. *Charlotte Observer*, 62.

Bill Kelly. (May 1980). RE: "Future of music" personal interview.

Martin, D., and Dino, J. (November 12, 1980). They're not kids anymore. *The Times Leader*, 19.

Middleton, J. (September 10, 1978). Jerry-Kelly's 'Magic.' *Wyoming Valley Observer*, 15.

Middleton, J. (October 1, 1978). Jerry-Kelly selling big in NE Pa. *Wyoming Valley Observer*, 15.

Seraphine, D. and Mitchell, A. *Street Player: My Chicago Story*. Hoboken, NJ: John Wiley & Sons, 2011.

Schumacher, M. Crossroads: *The Life and Music of Eric Clapton*. New York: Hyperion, 1995.

Wodaski, R. (March 8, 1979). At 'Homegrown' studio, you can record for a song. *Times Leader*, 11.

THE PIONEERS

Axton, G. (November 21, 2015). Doo-wop returns to the Kirby. *The Times Leader*, 25.

Barrett, M. (May 11, 1972). 'Heavy rock' Entrepreneur Learned Trade by Listening. *Springfield News-Leader*, 7.

Butkiewicz, J. (December 15, 1995). Fill your dance card with video memories. *The Times Leader*, 45.

Chisak, R. (February 19, 2003). Delightful doo-wop. *The Citizens Voice*, 32.

Conmy, J. (April 20, 2003). For Joe Nardone, the beat goes on. *Citizen's Voice*, 105.

Furek, M.W. (July 9, 1989). Lost in 'Fifties' (Again). *Citizens Voice*, 7.

Furek, M.W. (October 20, 1987). "No Chemise Please." The Gerry Granahan School of Music. *The Merchant*, 8.

Furek, M.W. (October 21, 1986). Randy "A"—The Doo-Wop Man. *The Merchant*, 5.

Furek, M.W. (May 19, 1987). Shootout on Doo-Wop Avenue. (The Resurrection of an Art Form.) *The Merchant*, 2.

Gaydos, K. (May 16, 2013). Same Old Songs. Doo Wop Vol. 6 brings nostalgic acts to Kirby Center stage. *The Citizens Voice*, C6.

Bob Gryziec. (August 13, 2020). RE: Joe Nardone's All Stars. Personal interview.

Kashatus, W.C. (August 9, 2015). It was only rock 'n' roll & they loved it. *Citizens Voice*, C1.

Kishbaugh, J. (March 26, 1993). Take a nostalgic journey with Mel Wynn & the Rhythm Aces. *Voice*, 23.

Kishbaugh, J. (July 22, 1988). Eddie Day will light up the night as part of Hanson's Dance Party II. *Citizens Voice*, 3.

Kishbaugh, J. (March 6, 1992). Joe Nardone and the All-Stars get together for 'The Reunion.' *Citizens Voice*, 25.

Kishbaugh, J. (March 4, 1992). Joe Nardone & the All-Stars set to bring you 'Reunion III.' *Citizens Voice*, 27.

Kishbaugh, J. (August 9, 1991). Shake a tail feather at Hanson's 'Quake at the Lake—Part III.' *Citizens Voice*, 27.

Kishbaugh, J. (February 26, 1993). Take a nostalgic journey with Joe Nardone and the All-Stars. *Citizens Voice*, 23.

Lewis, B. (August 20, 1994). Utall Credited with Sowing Seeds of Cassidy's Success. *Scrantonian Tribune*, 80.

Joe Nardone, Sr. (August 17, 2020). RE: Musical career. Personal phone interview.

Nothing 'Square' About Festival Here on Sunday. (September 29, 1969). *The Scranton Tribune*, 3.

Pro Audio Veteran Michael Stahl Passes Away at 68. (September 24, 2014). Lighting & Sound America. Retrieved from http://www.lightingandsoundamerica.com/news /story.asp?ID=NCGRBD

Rhythm Aces Reunion Dance July 31. (July 23, 1993). *Hazleton Standard-Speaker*, 10.

Stout, A.K. (April 20, 1997). A well-timed Tune. *Times Leader*, 21.

Styklunas, D. (July 1981). TNT: No More Trials and Tribulations. Timothy: Northeastern Pennsylvania's First Music Publication,9.

Bobby Vanderheyden, "The Duke of Doo-Wop." (August 4, 2020). RE: Doo-wop revival. Personal phone interview.

Wellock, B. (September 6, 2019). Mel Wynn, popular Rhythm Aces frontman, remembered. *Citizens' Voice*, A1.

Yonke, D. (July 31, 1994). Age of hanging out and harmonizing captured on new definitive collection. *The Citizens, Voice*, 59.

POLYDOR RECORDS

15 Individuals, 6 Corporations Indicted for Alleged 'Payola' in Record Industry. (June 25, 1975.) *Scranton Tribune*, 1.

Alan Freed. (August 11, 2020). Ohio History Central. Retrieved from https://ohio historycentral.org/w/Alan_Freed

Alan Freed Fired Over Payola. (November 20, 1959). The Daily Doo-Wop. Retrieved from https://www.dailydoowop.com/alan-freed-fired-over-payola/

Bank, B. (October 1, 2005). Media Sound Studios. MIX. Retrieved from https://www.mixonline.com/recording/mediasound-studios-375356

Davis, R. (August 3, 1972). Musical Notes. Arcadia, *California Tribune*, 19.

DeLuca, D. (July 29, 2012). Joe 'Butterball' Tamburro, 70, longtime DJ on WDAS. *Philadelphia Inquirer*, B10.

Dick Clark. (July 19, 2019). Biography. Retrieved from https://www.biography.com/media-figure/dick-clark

Dominguez, R. (October 3, 1993). The Good, the Super Baaad, and the Ugly. *New York Daily News*, 1113.

Furek, M.W. *The Jordan Brothers: A Musical Biography of Rock's Fortunate Sons*. Kimberly Press: Berwick, Pennsylvania, 1986.

Goldfarb, K. (March 27, 2018). The Dramatic Rise and Fall of Alan Freed—"Father of Rock and Roll." Allthatsinteresting.com. Retrieved from https://allthatsinteresting.com/alan-freed

Hogan, E. (August 12, 2020). MFSB. TSOP (The Sound of Philadelphia). AllMusic. Retrieved at https://www.allmusic.com/song/tsop-the-sound-of-philadelphia-mt0004018553

Klein, A. (September 3, 2020). How Record Labels Work. howstuffworks.com. Retrieved from https://entertainment.howstuffworks.com/record-label1.htm

Nelson, V. J. (September 28, 2008) LA Attorney counseled Rolling Stones, R. Kelly. *Los Angeles Times*. Retrieved from https://www.latimes.com/archives/la-xpm-2008-sep-25-me-margolis25-story.html

Payola-Indictments Revive the Term. (June 25, 1975). *The Miami Herald*, 111.

Sharbutt, J. (July 9, 1975). FCC out of payola probes. *Hackensack Record*, 33.

Singleton, R.G. *The Untold Story: Berry, Me, and Motown*. Chicago: Contemporary Books, 1990.

Speers, W. (September 8, 1981). By the time that Woodstock ended, they were heavily in debt. *Baltimore Sun*, 13.

Shadoe Steele. (June 7, 2020). RE: Media Sound. Personal e-mail correspondence.

Siracuse, Carl. (June 5, 2020). Scepter and Polydor Records. Personal phone interview.

Takiff, J. (March 19, 1976). Pop Music: Press That Reject Button—Please. *Philadelphia Daily News*, 34.

Takiff, J. (June 27, 1975). Pop Music: Turn Table on Under- the Table 'Turntablers.' *Philadelphia Daily News*, 48.

Bobby Vanderheyden, "The Duke of Doo-Wop." (August 4, 2020). Payola. Personal phone interview.

Wechsler, P. (June 25, 1975). 19 Indicted in Music Payola Probe. *New York Daily News*, 468.

QUEEN TOUR

Ashton, B. (September 14, 1980). Hard Times or No, Queen's Hot Again. *The Miami Herald*, 206.

Louis James Cossa. (June 27, 2020). RE: Dakota-Queen tour. Personal phone interview.
Hilburn, R. (August 10, 1980). LA's Blasters: A Cinderella Tour. *The Los Angeles Times*, 381.
Bill Kelly. (September 14, 2020). RE: Dakota-Queen tour. Personal phone interview.
Stevenson, W. *The Stone Balloon: The Early Years*. Wilmington, DE: Cedar Tree Books, 2005.

RALPH
Bornino, R. (February 8, 1974). Ralph is at top 10 at Agora. *The Cleveland Press*, 1.
Garcia-Pons, M. (April 17, 1977.) Famed Sasson Hair Designer in City to Style 'Ralph.' *Scrantonian Tribune*, 52.
McCarthy, B. (1974). 20,000 at rock Concert. *Scranton Tribune*.
Originals on Ralph Show. (February 9, 1980). *The Scranton Tribune*, 25.
Ralph Concert Monday at Park. (August 11, 1974). *The Scrantonian*, 1.
Ralph returns to Scranton. (August 12, 1974). *Binghamton Press*, 3-B.

JOEY REYNOLDS
Jim Drucker. (May 7, 1979). RE: Joey Reynolds. Personal interview.
Hinckley, D. (April 6, 2010). On the Radio: Farewell to variety show era. *New York Daily News*, 62.
Hinckley, D. (July 6, 2009). On the Radio: Reynolds' rap: He's up for Hall of Fame. *New York Daily News*, 60.
Hinckley, D. (April 6, 1986). On the Radio: The New Kid in Town. Imitating Howard Stern? Don't be stupid. WNBC's latest afternoon deejay Joey Reynolds is an original. *New York Daily News*, 254.
Phillips, B. (February 6, 1964). Off the Record. *Angola Evans Journal*, 6.
Reynolds, J. *Let a Smile Be Your Umbrella, But Don't Get a Mouthful of Rain: The Joey Reynolds Story*. Hobart, NY: Hatherleigh Press, 2000

SATSOP RIVER FAIR AND TIN CUP RACES
ACLU To Challenge Festival Police Acts. (June 23, 1971). *Spokane Spokesman-Review*, 7.
Caldbick, J. (April 17, 2019). Satsop River Fair and the Tin Cup Races (1971). HistoryLink.com. Retrieved from https://www.historylink.org/File/20757
John Caldbick. (July 4, 2020). Satsop Rock Festival. Personal e-mail correspondence.
Cross, A. (June 24, 1971). At Sun Lakes Park: Youths, Officers Differ on Dispersal. *Spokane Spokesman-Review*, 34.
Dembosky, A. (March 23, 2016). Drug Company Jacks Up Cost of Aid-In-Dying Medication. NPR. Retrieved from https://www.npr.org/sections/health-shots/2016/03/23/471595323/drug-company-jacks-up-cost-of-aid-in-dying-medication
Dougherty, S. (April 13, 1992). A 70s Burnout Lights Up Roseanne. People. Retrieved from https://people.com/archive/a-70s-burnout-lights-up-roseanne-vol-37-no-14/

Festival Losses Set at $300,000. *Spokane Spokesman-Review*, 6.

Furek, M.W. (November 2020). The Public Anguish of Eric Clapton. *The Sober World*, 9 (11), 8 &10.

Quest Comes to End. (June 21, 1971). *Spokane Chronicle*, 9.

Grant County Group, Evans Talk Festival. (June 3, 1971) *Spokane Chronicle*, 23.

Nelson, D., and Castillo, E. (September 6, 1971). Rains, shootings, bus crash plague Satsop's festival. Longview, *Washington Daily News*, 16.

Rock festival attracts 18,000 opening night. (September 4, 1971) Longview, *Washington Daily News*, 1.

Rock Festival Controls for Study by Officials. (September 1, 1971). *Spokane Spokesman-Review*, 9.

Rock Fete Promoters Win Case. (August 25, 1971). *Centralia Daily Chronicle*, 4.

Deborah Ross. (July 1, 2020). Olympia Historical Society. Personal e-mail correspondence.

Smith, J.M. (Summer 2000). Bonnie Bramlett: Don't You Remember You Told Me You Loved Me, Baby? A Conversation with Bonnie Bramlett. Swampland.com. Retrieved from http://swampland.com/articles/view/title:bonnie_bramlett

Stiffer Law on Festivals Is Aim of Rep. Bledsoe. (June 22, 1971). *Spokane Spokesman-Review*, 5.

Turner, T., and Loder, K. I, Tina. *My Life Story*. New York: William Morrow and Company, 1986.

Wyatt, J. (March 21, 2016). Eric Clapton's Battle with Overcoming Drug Addiction. Royal Life Centers. Retrieved from https://royallifecenters.com/eric-claptons-battle-with-overcoming-drug-addiction/

SCEPTER RECORDS

Bacharach, B., and Greenfield, R. *My Life and Music: Anyone Who Had a Heart*. New York, NY: Harper Collins Publishers, 2013.

Fran Brozena. (May 24, 2020). Scepter Records. Personal phone interview.

Cartwright, G. (November 11, 2009). Luther Dixon obituary. He wrote dozens of hits in the '50s and '60s. *The Guardian*. Retrieved from https://www.theguardian.com/music/2009/nov/11/luther-dixon-obituary

Friedman, R. (April 28, 2011). "Baby It's You" New Broadway Musical: Carol King Says No. *Showbiz* 411.

Gensler, A. (October 28, 2013). Lou Reed RIP: What If Everyone Who Bought the First Velvet Underground Album Did Start A Band? Billboard.com Retrieved from https://www.billboard.com/articles//5770584/lou-reed-rip-what-if-everyone-who-bought-the-first

'Gram' Makes Scepter Discs. (July 28, 1970). *Dayton Daily News*, 21.

Hilburn, R. (June 19, 1992). Housewife Gets Out of the House, Into the Record Biz. *Los Angeles Times*, 251.

Lardine, B. (October 5, 1969). Personalities in the News: A Record Achievement. *New York Daily News*, 254.

Layne, J. (March 28, 2020). Luther Dixon artist biography. *AllMusic*. Retrieved from https://www.allmusic.com/artist/luther-dixon-mn0000805393

Leichter, A. (December 31, 1993) Rockin' All Nite Long: The Shirelles. Staunton, VA. *News Leader*, 23.

Macaulay, A. (February 8, 1970). *The Hackensack Record*. The Cool Hand at Scepter's Helm. 86.

Ramone, P. *Making Records: The Scenes Behind the Music*. Hyperion: New York, 2007.

Recording complex to open in county. (October 25, 1972). *White Plains Journal News*, 30.

Terras, L. (December 20, 1960). In Show Business. *Brooklyn King's County Chronicle*, 21 (51),1.

Weller, D. (August 9, 1992). The Scepter Story: Various. (Capricorn). *The Honolulu Advertiser*, 61.

Young, M. (June 16, 1962). The Grapevine. They're Talking About. *Pittsburgh Courier*, 17.

SHEPPTON DISASTER

Bever, L. (February 25, 2016). Cannibalism: Survivor of the 1972 Andes plane crash describes the 'terrible' decision he had to make to stay alive. Independent. Retrieved from https://www.independent.co.uk/news/world/americas/cannibalism-andes-plane-crash-1972-survivors-terrible-decision-stay-alive-a6895781.html

Furek, M.W. *Sheppton: The Myth, Miracle & Music*. Charleston, SC: Create Space, 2015.

McKerns, G.L. *The Black Rock That Built America: A Tribute to the Anthracite Coal Miners*. Xlibris Corporation: Bloomington, IN, 2007.

Ney, F. (2003). Sheppton Mine Disaster: 40 Years Later. *News Item*.

O'Boyle, B. (2007). Book salutes 1963 rescue. *Times Leader*.

Patton, B. (January 27, 2016). New book digs up dark secrets of Sheppton mine disaster, NEPA's 'greatest urban legend.' NEPA Scene. Retrieved from https://nepascene.com/2016/01/new-book-digs-up-dark-secrets-sheppton-mine-disaster-nepa-greatest-urban-legend/

Pennsylvania: Start of a Legend? (1963). Time. Retrieved at http://www.time.com/time/magazine/article/0,9171,870450,00.html

Sando, J.R. (2006). *The Famous Sheppton Mine Rescue: The Untold Story: The Blood and Sweat of the Rescue Team*. PublishAmerica: Frederick, MD.

Smiles, J. (January 31, 2016). Chapter in new book explores the Sheppton–Timothy connection. The Citizens Voice. Retrieved from https://www.citizensvoice.com/arts-living/chapter-in-new-book-explores-the-sheppton-timothy-connection-1.2000814

Smiles, J. (April 28, 2002). In 'Timothy's' Time: Area group's odd song about coal miners now a cult classic. *Times Leader Sunday Dispatch*, 21.

Waller, M. (1998) Sheppton Folks Recall Mine Disaster: Throne's death finds Sheppton folks recall mine disaster vividly. Rescue put patch in international spotlight. *Pottsville Evening Herald*.

SLY AND THE FAMILY STONE

Copeland: The Next Janis Joplin? (September 3, 1971). *Fort Lauderdale News*, 101.

Furek, M.W. (July 2020). Sylvester Stone's Fall from Grace. *The Sober World*, 9 (7), 10.

Hunlock Creek Rock Concert Ends in Late Traffic Tie-up. (July 12, 1971). *Scranton Times-Tribune*, 7.

Richard Prior's Tragic Accident Spotlight's a Dangerous Drug Craze: Freebasing. (June 30, 1980). People. Retrieved from https://people.com/archive/richard-pryors -tragic-accident-spotlights-a-dangerous-drug-craze-freebasing-vol-13-no-26/

Santos-Longhurst, A. (February 21, 2020). Everything You Need to Know About Free-basing. Healthline. Retrieved from https://www.healthline.com/health/freebasing

Shannon, L. (November 8, 1986). On & off the record: The sad tale of Sly Stone. La Crosse, *Wisconsin Tribune*, 39.

Sly and Family Stone Block Highway Traffic for 9 Miles. (July 12, 1971). *Times Leader*, 19.

Sly and Family Stone Concert Triggers Massive Traffic Jam. (July 13, 1971). *Berwick Enterprise*.

Sly Stone charged: Cocaine possession. (June 10, 2020). *San Francisco Examiner*, 14.

Sly, Family Stone Here. (December 29, 1971). Madison, *Wisconsin State Journal*, 41.

Smith, M.D. (November 17, 2011). Why did we let Sly Stone slip away? TheGrio. Re-trieved from https://thegrio.com/2011/11/17/why-did-we-let-sly-stone-slip-away/

Stone faces cocaine charge. (June 24, 1983). Kenosha, *Wisconsin News*, 16.

Toughill, K. (June 23, 1983). Lee officers hold Sly Stone on cocaine charge. *Fort Myers News-Press*, 1.

SYNCH AND JIMMY HARNEN

Biebel, M.T. (January 12, 1987). Synch has 'em dancing in the aisles. *Times Leader*.

Butkiewicz, J. (May 26, 1989). Jim Harnen is moving up fast. *Times Leader*, D1.

Butkiewicz, J. (December 26, 1986). Synch gets all decked out for the new year. *Times Leader*, D1.

Chisak, R. (June 25, 1989). Jimmy Harnen's Debut Album to Be Released by CBS Tues. *Citizens Voice*.

Choman, A. (October 24, 1991). Harnen and Company display Christmas spirit early. *Citizens Voice*.

Geist, V. (December 30, 1991). Rock band brings cheer to some local hospitals. *Times Leader*, 3A.

Graham, J. (January 27, 1989). An Overnight hit- 7 years later. *USA Today*, 3.

Robert Gryziac Jr. (November 16, 2020). RE: Jimmy Harnen. Personal phone interview.

Hudak, J. (November 6, 2011). Jimmy Harnen: To Nashville by way of Wilkes-Barre. *Times Leader*, 57.

Kernan, P. (July 20, 2019). Plymouth native Jimmy Harnen celebrates promotion to president of Nashville record label. Times-Leader. Retrieved from https:// www.timesleader.com/news/750383/plymouth-native-jimmy-harnen-celebrates -promotion-to-president-of-nashville-record-label

Snyder, S. (November 11, 1988). Six thousand turn out for local anti-drug rallies. *Times Leader*, 1A.

Urbanski, B. (October 31, 1993). Local artist's song chosen for theme of child-find agency. *Times Leader*.

Jumping Jeff Walker. (July 20, 2021.) RE: Synch. Personal interview.

Weeks, D. (May 1986). The New Payola Rocks Rock and Roll. Northeast, 39.

TIMOTHY

Beebe, J. (March 19, 1971). Record Review: 'Timothy' Probed. *Port Angeles Evening News*, 18.

Chisak, R. (February 13, 1998). Buoys "Timothy" shows up on another compilation CD. *Citizen's Voice*, 41.

Chisak, R. (May 9, 1994). Out of print for two decades, "Timothy" returns on CD. *Citizen's Voice*, 23.

Paul Costa, Psy.D. (August 5, 2020). RE: "Timothy" and "DOA." Personal e-mail correspondence.

Eder, B. (August 13, 2020). Buoys: Timothy. *AllMusic Review*. Retrieved from https://www.allmusic.com/album/timothy-mw0000114358

Fran Festa. (April 5, 2020). RE: Bob Gryziac. Personal interview.

From the folks who brought you 'Timothy.' (October 23, 1971). *The Allentown Morning Call*, 31.

Hazlett, T. (July 4, 1971). Disc Talk. *Canonsbury Daily Notes*, 2.

Ihnat, G. (May 2, 2017). Power Hour: "Timothy was delicious: 60 minutes of death-fueled '70s story songs. AV Club. Retrieved from https://music.avclub.com/timothy-was-delicious-60-minutes-of-death-fueled-70-1798261962

Jancik, W. (1997). Buoys "Timothy." The "Golden Hits of the '70s." Retrieved from http://www.onehitwondersthebook.com/?page_id=16548

Jerry Hludzik, of Jeddo, With Popular Rock Group. *Hazleton Standard-Speaker* 16.

Monitz, K. (August 15, 2013). The Truth About 'Timothy.' *Hazleton Standard-Speaker*, S24.

Nash, Bruce, and Allan Zullo. The Wacky Top 40: The Most Outrageous, Hilarious, and Unforgettable Songs in Pop History. Holbrook, Massachusetts: Bob Adams, Inc., 1993.

Reynolds, T. *I Hate Myself and Want to Die*. New York: Hyperion, 2005.

Texter, C. (April 10, 1985). DJ swaps spinning 45s for preaching liturgy. *Pottsville Republican*, 2.

The Buoys – "Timothy." (February 20, 2020). Mental Itch. Retrieved from https://mentalitch.com/the-buoys-timothy/

'Timothy' 16-Mos. Old. (May 1, 1971). *Cash Box*. Vol. XXXII-Number 45, 9.

"Timothy" by The Buoys. (2005). Songfacts. Retrieved from http://www.songfacts.com/detail.php?id=2005

Whitburn, J. *Top Pop Singles 1955-1986*. Record Research Inc: Menomonee Falls, WS, 1987.

WHAZOOS/ GREAT BEAR

Mike Boback. (April 30, 2020). RE: Whazoos. Personal interview.

Eder, B. (May 17, 2020). Procol Harum Biography. AllMusic. Retrieved at https://www.allmusic.com/artist/procol-harum-mn0000304401/biography

John Gonska. (April 24, 2020). RE: Inside of You. Personal interview.

Kishbaugh, J. (October 25, 1991). The Whazoos will celebrate 25 years of making music tomorrow night at the Hex. *Citizen's Voice*, 31.

McNamee, D. (January 4, 2010). Hey, what's that sound: Harpsichord. *The Guardian*. Retrieved from https://www.theguardian.com/music/2009/dec/14/whats-that-sound-harpsichord

Procol Harum. (May 17, 2020). Beyond the Pale. Retrieved from https://procolharum.com

Paul Metzger. (July 19, 2021). RE: Great Bear. Personal phone interview.

Barry Rogers. (April 28, 2020). RE: Whazoos. Personal interview.

Smiles, J. (December 1, 1996). Write on 11: How I Rocked My Life Away. *Sunday Dispatch*, 18.

WVIA

Krawczeniuk, B. (November 26, 1999). Documentary on Buoys sounds a local chord. *Scranton Tribune*, 3.

O'Boyle, B. (October 1, 2019). Harry West: WARM thoughts of a radio legend. *Times Leader*, 5.

Rochelle, L.D. *Blast From Your Past! Rock & Roll Radio DJ's: Book 2. The Swinging Sixties 1960-1969*. San Diego: Penchant for Penning, 2018.

ABOUT THE AUTHOR

MAXIM FUREK is among the first wave of regional Rock Journalists. He is founder of *Timothy: Northeastern Pennsylvania's First Music Publication*, created "to promote Northeastern Pennsylvania's musical talent," and named after The Buoy's "Timothy" (1971), at the time, the region's most successful rock song. Curiously, through a strange sequence of events, *Timothy Magazine* evolved into the highly successful *Pennsylvania Musician* and *Maryland Musician*.

The cultishly popular Jordan Brothers from Frackville became the focus of Furek's first book, *The Jordan Brothers, a Musical Biography of Rock's Fortunate Sons* (1986). The Jordan's were the first group to release "Gimme Some Lovin'"—written by England's Spencer Davis Group. On November 12, 2011, Furek inducted the Jordan Brothers into the Schuylkill County Council of the Arts Hall of Fame.

In 2008 he published *The Death Proclamation of Generation X: A Self-fulfilling Prophesy of Goth, Grunge and Heroin*, investigating the connection between

Twenty-two-year-old Vietnam Veteran Maxim W. Furek, attending the legendary 1969 Woodstock festival, along with 400,000 other hippies.

grunge music and heroin, and the origins of the opioid crisis and has been utilized as course material at Penn State University and College Misericordia.

Furek's latest book, *Sheppton: The Myth, Miracle and Music* (2015), explores the supernatural mythology surrounding the 1963 Sheppton mining disaster and has been popular within paranormal circles.

The author is a regular contributor to *The Sober World* and his column, "Cultural Trends," appeared in *Counselor, the Magazine for Addiction and Behavioral Professionals.* He has written for numerous music publications and has crafted LP liner notes for rock groups Hybrid Ice and the Glass Prism.

www.maximfurek.com

Made in USA - North Chelmsford, MA
1315841_9781620065686
05.25.2022 0855